FOLK LITERATURE OF THE YAMANA INDIANS

Martin Gusinde's Collection of Yamana Narratives

Published for the
UCLA Latin American Center
in cooperation with
Anthropos-Institut
St. Augustin/Siegburg, West Germany
as Volume 40 in the
UCLA Latin American Studies Series
Series editor: Johannes Wilbert

BOOKS PUBLISHED BY THE UNIVERSITY OF CALIFORNIA PRESS IN
COOPERATION WITH THE UCLA LATIN AMERICAN CENTER

1. Kenneth Karst and Keith S. Rosenn, *Law and Development in Latin America: A Case Book*. Latin American Studies Series Volume 28, UCLA Latin American Center. 1975.

2. James W. Wilkie, Michael C. Meyer, and Edna Monzón de Wilkie, eds., *Contemporary Mexico: Papers of the IV International Congress of Mexican History*. Latin American Studies Series Volume 29, UCLA Latin American Center. 1976.

3. Arthur J. O. Anderson, Frances Berdan, and James Lockhart, *Beyond the Codices: The Nahua View of Colonial Mexico*. Latin American Studies Series Volume 27, UCLA Latin American Center. 1976.

4. Johannes Wilbert, ed., *Folk Literature of the Yamana Indians: Martin Gusinde's Collection of Yamana Narratives*. Latin American Studies Series Volume 40, A Book on Lore, UCLA Latin American Center. 1976.

(Except for the volumes listed above, which are published and distributed by the University of California Press, Berkeley, California 94720, all other volumes in the Latin American Studies Series are published and distributed by the UCLA Latin American Center, Los Angeles, California 90024.)

Martin Gusinde

(Courtesy Foto-Promitzer, Mödling.)

FOLK LITERATURE
of the YAMANA INDIANS

Martin Gusinde's Collection of Yamana Narratives

JOHANNES WILBERT
Editor

University of California Press

Berkeley Los Angeles London

University of California Press
Berkeley and Los Angeles, California
University of California Press, Ltd.
London, England
Copyright © 1977 by The Regents of the University of California
ISBN: 0-520-03299-3
Library of Congress Catalog Card Number: 76-20026
Printed in the United States of America

Preface

Folk Literature of the Yamana Indians is the third volume in a series of lore books dealing with the folk literature of South American Indians. The first volume, *Folk Literature of the Warao Indians* (Wilbert 1970), presented two hundred and nine narratives of the Warao Indians of the Orinoco Delta in Venezuela; the second volume, *Folk Literature of the Selknam Indians*, is a collection of ninety-five narratives of the Selknam Indians of Tierra del Fuego of southern Argentina and Chile (Wilbert 1975). As pointed out by Lévi-Strauss in his endorsement of the series: "South American mythology belongs to the spiritual inheritance of mankind on a par with the great master-pieces of Greek and Roman antiquity and the Near East." Yet the appreciation of this verbal art by scholars and laymen has so far been seriously handicapped. Hidden in a multitude of publications some of which are difficult to locate and rendered in a variety of different European and Indian languages, this treasure of lore needs to be mined first through field research and archival toil.

Lore books on folk literature of South American Indians are intended to assist in this task in two distinct ways: first, by assembling the narratives in a single language namely English; second, by indexing the motifs to each corpus as an initial step toward organizing and systematizing the narrative content. It is hoped that both these services will bring the folk literature of South American Indians to the attention of the general reader and facilitate its future analysis and comparison by the specialists.

As with the previous volumes, I owe a great debt of gratitude to my assistant Karin Simoneau who furnished the first draft of the translation and who assisted in all the other tasks of preparing the volume for publication especially in the motif analysis and proofreading of the motif dictionaries. The translation was further checked by myself and my son Werner Wilbert, while Charlotte Treuenfels, Peter T. Furst, and Teresa Joseph edited the manuscript for style and consistency. Nelly Williams, Sofía Speth, and Colleen Trujillo rendered most efficient secretarial services.

The Anthropos-Institut, St. Augustin near Bonn, Germany, generously conceded the translation rights to the texts and permission to use the photograph of Julia taken from Gusinde 1939. The photograph of Martin Gusinde is courtesy Foto-Promitzer, Mödling, Austria. To all, my heartfelt thanks.

Contents

THE NARRATIVES
How the World Came To Be

Myths and Legends

Contents

THE MOTIF INDICES

Introduction

In the years between 1918 and 1924 Martin Gusinde undertook four expeditions to Tierra del Fuego where he studied the indigenous populations of this southernmost inhabited part of the world. His fieldwork resulted in the publication of a monumental three-volume work entitled *Die Feuerland-Indianer* (1931-1974) of which the first volume (1931) is dedicated to the Selknam (Ona), the second (1937) to the Yamana (Yahgan),[1] and part one of the third volume (1974) to the Halakwulup (Alakaluf) Indians (map 1). (Volume three, part two, published in 1939, contains data on the physical anthropology of the three tribes.)

In the introduction to *Folk Literature of the Selknam Indians: Martin Gusinde's Collection of Selknam Narratives* (Wilbert 1975:1-6), I recounted the events that had led to Gusinde's research and that placed him, in 1913, in a most favorable and strategic position to conduct the study of these Indians shortly before they became culturally extinct. Thanks to these fortunate circumstances the sketchy information contained in the literature (Cooper 1917; Valory 1967) was comprehensively augmented and the cultural heritage of one of America's most remarkable cultures saved from oblivion.

Gusinde's collections of Selknam and Yamana narratives form an especially valuable part of his study. Unfortunately, when the explorer finally reached the Halakwulup, in 1923, the tribe had been reduced to a small group of approximately eighty individuals who had forgotten their oral tradition and were capable of recalling only disconnected fragments of their lost verbal art (Gusinde 1970:335). It is, therefore, with utmost satisfaction that I present in English the rare corpus of Yamana folk literature which was placed in our hands by the last members of this tribe in testimony of their ancient ways of life and thought.

INFORMANTS AND SOCIAL CONTEXT

Gusinde recorded the texts from the lips of some of those Yamana whom he had encountered for the first time at Punta Remolino on his

---

[1]See also Gusinde 1961.

1

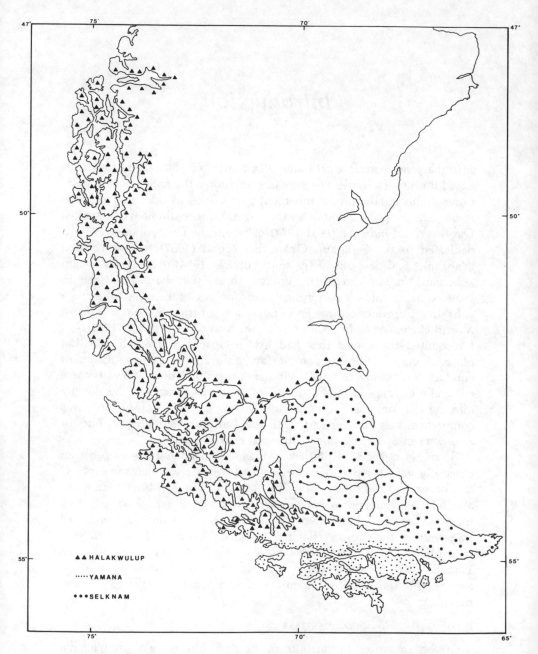

MAP 1.   Geographical Distribution of Indian Tribes of Tierra del Fuego.
Adapted from M. Gusinde, *Die Feuerland-Indianer*. (Courtesy Anthropos-
Institut.)

return trip from Selknam country, in 1919. Punta Remolino, a sheep farm, had become a gathering point for the Yamana where they found work and protection during shearing time. Here the explorer met a Yamana woman, Nelly Lawrence, wife of Fred Lawrence, an influential white man. The couple had established an excellent rapport with the surviving Yamana and Nelly, once she understood Gusinde's research goals, took great pride and personal interest in transmitting, for posterity, as much of Yamana culture as stood in her power. On two subsequent expeditions, in 1919-20 and 1921-22, Gusinde made Punta Remolino his headquarters. Most of the narratives contained in this volume were collected in 1919–20 with the assistance of the Indian residents of this remote outpost (map 2).

Gusinde gives little personal information about his Yamana informants beyond an occasional brief observation in passing. In contrast with his Selknam material where the name of the informant is recorded after almost every narrative, the informant is seldom identified here. Gusinde explains that frequently a narrative was told him more than once by different people, so that it would have been incorrect to ascribe it to a particular informant. He does give the names of Alfredo, Calderón, Charlin, Mary, Mašemikens, Nelly Lawrence, Richard, Whaits, and William and credits them with a little over a dozen narratives. But particular mention is made of a fifty-five-year-old woman by the name of Julia (plate 1). She was an especially valuable informant because of her narrating skills and her extensive knowledge of Yamana mythology, a knowledge she meticulously communicated to Gusinde in long interviewing sessions over several days and with the aid of four interpreters. Elaborates the author:

> What can be found in the following pages may well represent the entire treasure of myths our Indians from Tierra del Fuego have called their own since ancient times. Favorable circumstances led me to obtain it in the course of my second expedition. Although it is not customary among our Indians for a woman to be sitting in a mixed group and tell, at length, episodes of her personal experience or passages of a myth, some women, nevertheless, preserve much narrative material in their faithful minds and offer it quite willingly to their female friends and neighbors at occasional gatherings. It is my impression that since they are less anxious than the men to display themselves by recounting their deeds and startling accomplishments, women find it easier to unravel the basic theme of a myth with fewer distractions and greater logical consequence. Thus, most of the narratives current

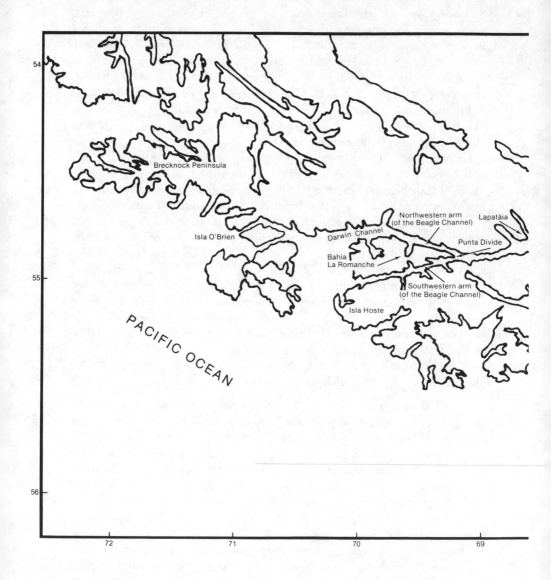

Map 2. The Homeland of the Yamana. Adapted from Karl Streit, "Magallangebiet und Feuerland." In M. Gusinde, *Die Feuerland-Indianer*, vol. II. Mödling, 1937. (Courtesy Anthropos-Institut.)

ATLANTIC OCEAN

54

Punta Remolino

Ušuáia   Bahía Ušuáia
                            Isla Gable   Bahía Brown
Beagle Channel   Puerto Harberton   Bahía Thetis

Angostura
Murray   Puerto Mejillones
Estero Ponsonby
Río Douglas
                            Isla
                            Navarino   55

Hardy Peninsula   Bahía Packsaddle

                    Wollaston Islands

                            Cape Horn   56

ANTARTIC OCEAN

68   67   66   65

among the Yamana I owe indeed to the intelligent Julia, wife of
old Alfredo. She is unanimously considered by her fellowmen to
be the most knowledgeable person of them all. I studied with her
for several days. What I collected in addition during my third and
fourth expeditions were supplementary commentaries and details
of no consequence. Several myths were also repeated by other
people, so that I believe I have recorded the entire corpus of
myths as it has been treasured by the Yamana from the distant
past to the present day (Gusinde 1937:1142).

In accordance with Gusinde's own explanation we must assume,
therefore, that the narratives ascribed to Julia personally as well as
the anonymous ones were obtained through the authorship of this
Indian woman.[2]

Storytelling formed an integral part of Yamana daily life. Men rather
than women would entertain their audiences during the long evenings
around the campfire. But by the time of Gusinde's sojourn among them
much of the traditional social fiber had been torn; the individual
families no longer banded together for any length of time, and on the
rare occasions when they did the elders refused to tell the stories which
they felt had become outmoded relics of the past. The younger generation had turned away from tribal lore and had occupied themselves
with European styles of life. Quite apart from this modernistic trend
among the younger set, however, it had traditionally been considered
bad taste and disrespectful for a young man to tell a story or even to
ask an older person to do so. Thus, in Gusinde's time, storytelling had
become a rarity among the surviving Yamana, and the ethnologist had
no recourse but to prevail upon a woman who under normal
circumstances and on account of her sex alone would have been the
least likely informant for such ends.

Emphasizing this detail of provenience of Gusinde's collection of
Yamana narratives has a purpose beyond the obvious one of keeping
straight the record of data collecting. The fact is that most of the larger
corpuses of South American folk literature were recorded with the help
of male informants. While we assume that the lore of a tribe is
essentially shared by members of both sexes, we do not actually know
to what extent this really is true; there may very well be significant
differences in style, emphasis, selection, or other factors according to
the sex of the narrator. Besides, there is also the fact that in the past

---

[2]Page numbers following the identification of the informant at the end of each narrative
refer to those in Gusinde's (1937) Yamana volume.

PLATE 1. Julia. (Photograph by Martin Gusinde. Courtesy Anthropos-Institut.)

most fieldworkers were men. Moreover, women may not only be
reluctant to narrate to a male investigator but may also choose to
withhold certain narratives that are considered improper to tell cross-
sexually. Finally, as I found in my own fieldwork, young women are
severely inhibited when talking with male foreigners whereas older
women are not. For instance, the collection of *Yupa Folktales* published
earlier was given me in its entirety by a Yupa woman on the threshold
of old age (Wilbert 1974). Her narrations provoked no unusual
reactions in the audience of men and women during the recording
sessions. When I asked her much older sister to tell me the stories that
she knew, she repeated many of the narratives I had already recorded
but there was a marked preference for stories of sex considered both
normal and abnormal. My judge on this issue was the Yupa audience's
reaction of disapproval, embarrassment, and/or outright scandal. I was
reminded of this situation when reading the narratives Julia told
Gusinde because of the emphasis on sexual behavior in so many of
them. This may be idiosyncratic of the narrator; it may be related to
the sex of the personnel involved in the original data-collecting phase;
or it may simply reflect a general characteristic of Yamana oral lore.
What I suggest at this point is that we keep these various possibilities
in mind for eventual future reference. In primitive societies older
women are often permitted to disregard many of the social taboos they
had to observe during their younger years, and telling risqué stories
may represent a form of ventilating pent-up aggressions due to sexual
repression. In any case, the preoccupation with sex that permeates
Yamana folk literature has long been noticed by other investigators,
prompting one of them to write the first psychoanalytical treatise on a
South American Indian tribe (Coriat 1915). In an admittedly prelim-
inary fashion the author interprets, according to Freudian theory,
Yamana mourning rites, dreams, taboos, and myths with regard to
sexual repression and relates it to the nervous attacks during which
Selknam and Yamana men occasionally ran amuck. Again, whether or
not the sexual content of so many Yamana narratives is related to the
sex and age of Gusinde's informant is difficult to determine since,
unfortunately, we shall never come into possession of a Yamana
narrative collection obtained through a male informant. The Selknam
corpus of folk literature was collected primarily with male informants
and it may be worthwhile to point out that it does not reveal quite as
pronounced a concern with matters of sex; yet, Gusinde himself
considered the lore and folk literature of the two tribes quite closely
related.

FIELD CONDITIONS, STYLE, AND FUNCTION OF NARRATIVES

One peculiarity of Yamana storytelling that related to the sex of the informant was that women stuck to the red thread of the story and avoided mixing the narrative reality with actual life experiences. Not so the men, and this is an important difference. For while I am sure this characteristic female style of narration must have been appreciated by the European listener, the intertwining of personal experiences with thematic materials of folk literature was a most autochthonous feature of storytelling by a Yamana male (Gusinde 1937:1140). What was for a European audience digression in the typical disjointed male style of narration was for the Yamana audience precisely the desirable ingredient that made for superb entertainment. Through lifelong exposure to the narratives the native listener was already thoroughly familiar with the dramatis personae and their exploits. Relating the actors of the mythical past to the tribesmen of the present not only provided the narrator with an excellent opportunity to display himself and his artistry but also validated the dogmas of Yamana culture through reference to time-honored principles and tradition. In other words, Yamana storytelling as practiced by mature men in their peculiarly "disjointed" style brought the ancestors into the present and imbued the lives of the listeners with transcendental import. That the red thread of the narrative was severed by interjections of true-life episodes about the storyteller was of no concern to the native listener (Gusinde 1937:1140). And whether the unswerving rendition of a female narrator would have been quite as effective in this social context remains a moot question as far as Yamana tradition is concerned. What does emerge is an understanding of why the old men of the socially disintegrated Yamana survivors declined to tell stories to their acculturated tribesmen: the common cultural context had been dissolved as the traditional backdrop against which the narrator could project his personal experience. What had been lost was not the thread but the loom on which the tribal oral tradition, shared by the audience, provided the warp and the personal experience of the storyteller the weft. With the former gone, the latter refused to yield a meaningful pattern.

Similar conditions seem to have prevailed also among the Selknam. When recording their folk literature Gusinde found it equally impossible to transcribe neat stories with a beginning, a climax, and an end. Interfering with this were not so much the variations in style of the different informants but the storyteller's inclination to insert personal experiences that often ran longer than the actual narrative. Or, as

Gusinde puts it: "The form [of narratives] which I am able to present here, is the result of arranging the individual parts according to an implicit train of thought" (1931:569). The arrangements in that case were made by three separate informants, after discussing the sequences with other persons and the narrator himself.[3]

In sum, two factors are especially significant in connection with the method of assembling the myths: first, the collection of Yamana narratives was established by Gusinde primarily with the help of a female informant; second, there are considerable differences between the oral and the written forms of the narratives due to the differences in male and female styles of narration. The sex of the narrator and the form of rendition are both atypical of Yamana storytelling tradition. The former may be reflected in the content and the selection of the corpus; the latter is apt to veil an important aspect of the place of story telling in Yamana daily life, namely, that there existed but a fine line between the mythological past and the present and that mundane acts acquired meaning and validity through relating them to prominent mythological personages and events of the traditional past. How the young Yamana generation of Gusinde's time would have fared after turning their attention away from tribal lore to European traditions can only be surmised through comparison with acculturated youths of other tribes. The modern Yamana had no chance to prove the viability of their attitude; they became culturally extinct. We do know, however, that the traditional attitude of their elders had proved life-sustaining for millennia in Tierra del Fuego, a land basically hostile to human survival.

THE NARRATIVES

Gusinde pointed to several shortcomings of his collection (Gusinde 1937:1143) and was aware that particularly the first section of the corpus was somewhat limited in depth. The narratives about heaven and earth do not convey a comprehensive picture of Yamana cosmology but represent, instead, all the elderly individuals of the surviving group were able to recall.

As it turns out, the narratives about heaven and earth are mostly debacle myths, as such closely linked to the all-important *kína* myth (narrative 65) that tells of a protohuman gyneocratic era when women had supremacy over men. The primeval ancestors, among them Sun (senior and junior), Moon, and Rainbow, migrated to what became

---

[3]It will be interesting to see whether this form of recording does interfere with a structural analysis of the narratives according to the Propp method.

known as Yamana country from a distant place in the East. They came on foot, as anthropomorph or zoomorph beings, and, after their various earthly adventures, ascended to the sky or stayed on earth in animal form. More specifically, the place where these primeval beings ended their worldwide wanderings was known to the Yamana as Yáiaašága. It is mentioned repeatedly in the myths about heaven and earth and the *kína* myth as the place where the matriarchal social order was uprooted and changed to a patriarchate.

To assure their dominant position over the men, the women impersonated spirits and thereby hoodwinked the men into obedience. Leader of the women was Hánuxa, the moon-woman, wife of Rainbow. She was the oppressor of all men but particularly of her brother-in-law, the (younger) sun-man, who was a skillful hunter and whose special task it was to keep the ruling women supplied with plenty of game. The revolution of Yáiaašága was triggered by (younger) sun-man's discovery of the *kína* hoax. It resulted in the uprising of the men against their oppressors and the killing of all adult women in the process. Hánuxa survived the massacre and escaped to the sky where her face can still be seen covered with scars she carried away from the battle. The (younger) sun-man followed his sister-in-law to the sky where he is visible as the sun. He not only gives life and warmth to the people on this side but also to those on the underside of the earth, by alternating between the two worlds on a daily basis. He thus continues to be of the same benevolent disposition that he was prior to the revolution at Yáiaašága, quite the opposite of his father, the senior sun-man, who was a truculent old man and who caused the first world conflagration by making the ocean boil and by setting the world ablaze in a primordial fire. He afterward turned into a star (possibly Venus). Liberator Sun-man's brother was Rainbow.

The second cataclysm was caused by Moon-woman who, infuriated over her defeat at Yáiaašága, destroyed the world and its protohuman inhabitants by causing the deluge. This she accomplished, according to Cojazzi's (1914:31) version, by plunging into the sea. Bridges (1884:18) ascribes the flood to the sun who fell into the ocean. Yet a third version, this one Gusinde's, imputes the deluge, from which only a few people survived on five very high mountaintops, to the over-sensitive ibis-woman who provoked it in retribution for untoward behavior on behalf of earthlings. Universal glaciation and a subsequent deluge caused by the melting ice were the fateful results.

Among the primordial immigrants to Yáiaašága were the Yoálox brothers and their sister Yoálox-tárnuxipa, the actual culture heroes of the Yamana. Their exploits are narrated in the section of myths about culture heroes. The mother of these siblings as well as several of their sisters are also mentioned occasionally but they play only minor roles.

The Yoálox cycle of fourteen narratives is "perhaps the most important single phase of the mythology" (Cooper 1946:105). The era in which the Yoálox heroes exercised their mission as bringers of culture appears to come between the eras of Sun, Moon, and Rainbow on the one hand and that of the fully human Indian ancestors of the Yamana on the other. These ancestors became the pupils of the Yoálox brothers and their sister who taught them, among other things, the use of fire, the seasonality of berry-picking, the art of killing birds, hunting sea lion, getting fish oil, and making tools and specialized points for arrows and harpoons. The culture heroes also named objects and places, and introduced sexual intercourse, rules governing menstruation and child-birth, the use of body paint, as well as other customs. It is particularly remarkable that the older Yoálox is stupid and espouses a *Schlaraffen-land* philosophy, whereas his younger brother stands out as the actual culture hero, advocating a Spartan ethic. Unusual in the context of South American folk literature (Lowie 1938:502) but quite consistent with the primordial social order under which they lived, the Yoálox sister outdoes both of her brothers in intelligence. The descendants of the pupils of the Yoálox siblings, that is, of those people and their offspring who survived the deluge, are the human ancestors of the Yamana. Since the revolution at Yáiaašága the men have celebrated the *kína* ceremony to keep the women in submissiveness.

The relevant Yoálox narratives were withheld from prepuberty children as they formed an element of Yamana culture pertaining to the initiation rites and festivities of the *čiéxaus*-hut (Koppers 1968:115). This ceremony is more autochthonous with the Yamana than the complex surrounding the *kína* tradition. The former, in turn, is related to the Halakwulup *yinchihana* initiation complex while the latter is equivalent to the *klóketen* of the Selknam. Martial (1888:213) learned that the Yamana tradition dates the *kína* revolution to the time when the Selknam lived near Ušuáia, so that according to traditional Yamana and Selknam history the social system of both tribes was believed to have been changed at the same time (Lothrop 1928:177). Upon completion of their mission the Yoálox brothers and their sister transformed into stars but, like any of the other celestial bodies, did not receive any worship nor did they play the divine ambassadorial role of a Kenós among the Selknam.

The twenty-three explanatory narratives of the more general Myths and Legends section of *Folk Literature of the Yamana Indians* include etiologies of birds and land and sea animals. The origin of certain birds is explained in connection with the myth of a stone giant vulnerable only at the soles of his feet. This mythologem, although more recently also encountered among the Sanemá-Yanoama and the Warao (Wilbert 1963:244-45), appears to be rare among South American Indians but frequent and of wide geographical distribution in Mesoamerica and especially in North America (Lehmann-Nitsche 1938:267-273). Of similar comparative interest is the extraordinary narrative of the "Lecherous Father" who tricks his two daughters into incest. It is reminiscent not only of the same story among the Selknam but also of the North American tale "Coyote and his Daughters" (Lowie 1938:502).

As pointed out by Gusinde (1937:1187), explanatory myths figured prominently in Yamana folk literature; they were favorites and told frequently. Their implicit purpose, here as elsewhere, is to probe and explain the antecedents or causes of certain animal characteristics. In view of the special place of animal stories in Yamana folk literature it is doubly laudable that Gusinde expended so much effort on proper zoological identification of the featured species.

The few ethical myths included in the collection place little or no stress on etiological detail but comment instead upon certain laws and customs or emphasize that abnormal behavior and transgressions are swiftly dealt with and severely punished. Accordingly, these narratives formed part of the curriculum presented by their elders to adolescent candidates during the initiation ceremony.

Tales about Shamans, Spirits, and Ogres is the final section. Shamans enjoyed exalted status in Yamana society and the tales describe their powers as healers, defenders, and protectors of their people. They are depicted as proud and sometimes vain individuals who when offended demand complete satisfaction or play havoc among their enemies. Tales of cannibal beings, water spirits, and giants round off the collection.

THE TRANSLATION

In translating the texts we endeavored to adhere as closely as possible to Gusinde's German, because I considered it important to translate as literally as the English language would allow.[4] The titles of the narratives are mostly Gusinde's, others were changed. Some of the narratives that had at least a minor plot were taken out of the general context where they occurred without special headings, treated as separate narratives, and given an invented title.

[4]See also Gusinde 1961 containing translations into English by Frieda Schütze of about half the Yamana narrative collection.

The phonetic rendering of the native terms in Gusinde's original is according to the Anthropos-Alphabet, an early attempt by Wilhelm Schmidt (1907) at symbolization of sounds with specially defined phonetic values. I have simplified the spellings where uncommon diacritics occur. The reader interested in the phonetic system of the Yamana language may consult Gusinde's phonetic key (1931:xxxi-xxxii) or his special treatise on the subject (1926:1002-1010). Passages referring to sex and sexual behavior and rendered only in Latin by Gusinde were translated into English. In some cases in the text new paragraphs were introduced.

Some footnote material in italics (other than technical terms) was added by the editor and relates mainly to bibliographical references of Yamana narratives. In an attempt to establish the uniqueness of Gusinde's collection, I have compared his Yamana texts with Fuegian narratives published by other authors (Valory 1967:181-184). I found that Gusinde's versions were almost always more complete. Koppers (1924), who accompanied Gusinde on one of his expeditions and probably used the same informants, has much myth material. All his narratives follow Gusinde's closely but in forms slightly different from those in the present collection. One brief variant of the flood myth in Cojazzi (1914) cannot be found in Gusinde's collection. For the sake of comparative studies I have called attention in italicized footnotes to variants of particular Gusinde narratives recorded mainly by Bridges (1948), Cojazzi (1914) who obtained his data from on-the-spot observers and residents, Dabenne (1911), Koppers (1924), and Martial (1888).

THE MOTIFS

To facilitate future comparative research, I have appended a comprehensive motif listing after each narrative and a motif dictionary at the end of the book. Identification of the motifs follows Thompson's (1955-1958) *Motif-Index*. Thompson motifs that needed to be amplified to accommodate Yamana idiosyncrasies are marked by a plus (+) sign, and Thompson's original wording of the extended motif is inserted in parentheses for instant comparison. In the text itself insertions in parentheses are by Gusinde, insertions in brackets by the editor.

Eagle Mountain, California
April 1, 1976

THE NARRATIVES

How the World Came To Be

HEAVEN AND EARTH

1. The Older Sun-man

In those days there lived a man here among the first families who was of evil nature. He was not only unfriendly toward all, but quite openly hostile, always intent on hurting everybody else. Everyone despised him, which angered him the more, and made him try even harder to do everybody harm. He was extremely powerful and wielded great authority. Once, in a rage, he set fire to everything within reach, for he made the water of the ocean boil by bringing forth intense heat. Also all the forests burned down, and from that time to this very day the mountaintops have remained bald and bare. All this happened because at the height of his fury he produced tremendous heat.

Táruwalem had been repulsive to the people from the start but since that time they hated him altogether. They loathed and detested not only him but also his closest kin. His whole family was shunned and despised by all the people, because each member of that family was unkind, always bent on hurting others. Only Lem, the son of old Táruwalem, was remarkably different, showing great kindness toward the rest of the people. He was an excellent hunter and skilled in many things. He went around with love for everyone, always ready to help.

The women[1] conferred secretly for a long time, and then finally decided to kill evil Táruwalem. One day everybody attacked the old man and almost strangled him to death. But since he was very strong he managed to free himself. He fled to the sky where he became a bright

---

[1] Here one must realize that in this mythic time rule over the men was allocated to the women, who alone had a voice; therefore it was only they who gathered for discussions and made decisions that were binding on all, especially on the men.

star. Now he has lost his original strength; today he is visible no longer. Only after the great revolution in the women's *kína* did Lem also ascend into the sky to join his father Táruwalem.

Informant: Not known; pp. 1145-1146.

Summary

Primeval evil man (senior Sun) makes all forests burn down (that is why mountaintops today are bare). Of all his family only his son is loved by the people. The women, who at that time had authority over the men, attempt to kill him but he escapes to the sky. He is now a star.

Motif content

A220.2.	The sun-god and his family.
A225.	Son of the sun.
A227.	Two sun-gods.
A512.4.	Sun as father of culture hero.
A515.2.	Father and son as culture heroes.
A526.2.	Culture hero as mighty hunter.
A566.2.	Culture hero ascends to heaven.
A711.	Sun as man who left earth.
A720.2.	Formerly great heat of sun causes distress to mankind.
A727.	Raising the sun.
A727.1.	Sun originally so hot that it threatens all life.
A733.5.	Sun dries out earth with its heat.
A736.	Sun as human being.
A738.2.+.	Sun as evil tyrant hated by people. (A738.2. Mental powers and disposition of sun.)
A739.2.	War with the sun.
A761.	Ascent to stars. People or animals ascend to sky and become stars.
A900.+.	Why mountaintops are bare today: scorched by sun. (A900. Topograhy—general considerations.)
A1030.	World-fire.
D293.+.	Transformation: sun-man to star. (D293. Transformation: man to star.)
F565.1.	Amazons. Women warriors.
F565.3.	Parliament of women.
F932.7.+.	Ocean boils. (F932.7. River boils.)
F961.1.	Extraordinary behavior of sun.
N818.1.	Sun as helper.
P233.	Father and son.
R9.1.	Sun captured.

2. The Land of the Dead

A long time ago all the *késpix* of the (then so-called) human beings who died here in our country went far away to Šamaxáni.[2]. There these *késpix* formed a people of their own. All of them, big and small, took great joy in *kálaka*, a game of ball. Once, powerful Táruwalem appeared quite suddenly in the east and set fire to the entire region. Later, when he wanted to withdraw the intense heat, he was unsuccessful, so that the *késpix* had to leave the area. Only when Táruwalem himself left the region did it cool off. At that time the whole world burned up all at once, and later everything cooled off again.

Informant: Not known; p. 1146.

Motif content

A720.2.	Formerly great heat of sun causes distress to mankind.
A1030.	World-fire.
A1031.3.	Evil demons set world on fire.
A1036. +.	Earth restored after world-fire. (A1036. Earth re-created after world-fire.)
A1038. +.	Men hide from world-fire. (A1038. Men hide from world-fire and renew race.)
E481.	Land of the dead.
E494.	Ball game in lower world.
F30.	Inhabitant of upper world visits earth.
F961.1.	Extraordinary behavior of sun.

3. The Younger Sun-man

Lem was an excellent person who had a strong influence over all the men. They willingly submitted to him because he behaved in a friendly and benevolent manner toward everybody. He was so handsome and so beautifully built that every woman wished to stare at him all the time. But each kept from revealing her desire, refraining even from looking at him openly, for fear the others might make fun of her. Lem was delightful. The women were all in love with him; the men regarded him highly.

[2]The Yamana give this name to a very remote region which they neither know nor describe more precisely.

Lem's wife was also very beautiful. Nobody knows her name. Lem had several pretty daughters, like the seagull Tákaša *(Larus belcheri)*, the seagull Wémarkipa *(Larus glaucodes)*, the sea duck Wíyen *(Anas cristata)*, the seagull Kiwágu *(Larus dominicanus)*, the Magellanic goose, Kímoa *(Chloëphaga picta)*, the duck Wípatux *(Querquedula cyanoptera)*, the vixen Čilawáiakipa *(Canis magellanicus)*, and the rat Wesána. The latter two secretly carried off the meat their father brought home from the hunt, robbing him regularly. They carry on this (stealing) even today. Besides them, Lem had several other daughters. He also had a number of sons. One of them is Yéxalem, who constantly follows his father about.

Lem was diligent and hard-working, kind, always cheerful, and friendly toward everyone. He was on the best of terms with all the men, and a model of an active and congenial person. To this day nothing in this (that is to say, in his basic personality) has changed. At the time of the great uprising in Yáiaašága he helped the men decisively to seize the women's *kína*. After the upheaval was over he went up to the sky. There he is still good-natured and ready to help the people by giving much light and warmth to everybody. All the men are openly proud of him, for he uncovered the secret of the women's *kína* and in so doing freed them from female domination.

Actually there is yet another world. That is why Lem leaves the land of the Yamana every evening to go there. In that other world, too, he furnishes sufficient light and warmth. Then, the next morning he comes back to us again. In this way he helps the people there as well as here.

Informant: Not known; p. 1147.

Summary

Primeval good man (junior Sun) is loved by all women, admired by all men. He has several sons and daughters (all of them animals). He helped the men gain independence from the then dominant women. Today he is the sun, leaving during the night for another land but returning with warmth and light every day.

Motif content

A220.2.	The sun-god and his family.
A221.	Sun-father.
A225.	Son of the sun.
A515.4.	Culture hero has faithful attendant.
A566.2.	Culture hero ascends to heaven.
A711.	Sun as man who left earth.
A722.+.	Sun's night journey. Goes to otherworld. (A722. Sun's night journey. Around or under the earth.)

A736.	Sun as human being.
A738.1.	Physical attributes of sun.
A738.2.+.	Sun as benevolent leader. (A738.2. Mental powers and disposition of sun.)
A1372.9.	Why women are subservient to men.
A2455.	Animal's occupatoin: stealing.
F565.3.+.	Parliament of women overthrown. (F565.3. Parliament of women.)
F575.1.	Remarkably beautiful woman.
F575.2.	Handsome man.
N440.	Valuable secrets learned.
N818.1.	Sun as helper.
P236.	Undutiful children.
T148.	Matriarchy.

4. The Rainbow

Old Akáinix was a magnificent-looking man. He knew how to paint himself much more attractively than the rest of the men. He belonged to a privileged family; handsome Lem is his brother, Hanuxéakuxipa is his wife. She, too, is extraordinarily beautiful; after all, she is his wife. Akáinix also has several sisters, all of them very pretty, clever, and cunning. Once Akáinix proved before all the people that he was also a very capable *yékamuš* [shaman].

One day the sisters were again playing *kína* in Yáiaašága. Old Akáinix was allowed to go into the big *kína*-hut. He knew all about the women's secret doings so that they allowed him in. Here Akáinix's sisters were entertaining themselves by playing dead; they wanted to see how long they could remain still and without breathing, as it is with dead people. The women intended to thoroughly fool their relatives [at home] with this act and frighten them just for fun.

The sisters had been busy with these experiments for a long time. But despite trying their utmost, they had not succeeded at holding their breath very long. Some other time when the girls were once again experimenting with this old Akáinix approached the *kína*-hut. He was the oldest among all his brothers and sisters. When his youngest sister saw him coming, she right away informed the others, saying: "We had better stop our experiments and efforts at once; our brother is quite close and might discover what we are doing." But by then Akáinix was already standing in the *kína*-hut. He asked his sisters: "What are you doing here?" "Nothing in particular," they said. "As usual we are devoting ourselves to our songs and our work." Akáinix replied: "What you are saying is not true at all. I know perfectly well what you were just doing here: you were all trying to appear motionless, as though dead, and to go without breathing for a long period of time. But you did not succeed. I know that very well. Now then, I myself shall show you how to do it right!" Akáinix knew that the girls planned to fool their relatives who lived in the south, and that they wanted to amuse themselves by purposely frightening them. They were the only ones who had come from the south and were participating in the *kína* in order to hide their real intentions. Since Akáinix saw through all that he offered to help his sisters.

So Akáinix lay down on the ground and stretched out; he became very still, soon stopped breathing, and lay there motionless, exactly like a dead person. His sisters, watching it all, admitted: "Indeed, our brother is really good at this; he is lying there just like a corpse!" Akáinix was a capable *yékamuš*.

The *kína* festival came to an end and all the participants left the Big Hut. Each family headed toward its homeland. Akáinix and his sisters also got into their canoe and headed south where their relatives lived. They had to travel several days because it was far away. But before reaching the huts of their folks, the travelers made a brief stop. Akáinix remained there; he stretched out on the ground and feigned death. His wife Hanuxéakuxipa and all his sisters painted their bodies black all over as a sign of deep mourning. Thus (prepared) they entered the hut of their relatives. In great dismay the latter immediately asked: "What has become of Akáinix? Why do you come in mourning paint?" The girls replied sadly: "Our brother has died just now, a short distance away from here. We left him lying there, close by that hut. That's why we wear the paint of mourning!" Upon these words from the desolate girls several men promptly rose and went to where old Akáinix was lying. They soon brought him back and laid him down in their hut. All the time Akáinix was acting as though truly dead. In view of this the others prepared themselves for a *yamalašemóina*. All the relatives gathered, wept loudly, and sang for several days.

Meanwhile a few amorous men approached Akáinix's wife and sisters. They began flirting with them because these women were extremely beautiful. The men caressed them and slept with them. Although Akáinix was lying there completely motionless he watched closely everything that went on. Several days went by. Then finally the enamored men began pressuring the girls to become their wives. They had been playing around with them long enough. Akáinix's wife and sisters had yielded to everything, knowing that Akáinix was not dead and would take full revenge. The men behaved more frankly all the time as though the women already belonged to them as wives.

One day, because there was no meat left in the huts, the amorous men went hunting. They wanted to look for cormorants on the nearby rocks. Their (female) relatives, the *kímoa* and *lúrux*, the *šékuš* and *wípatux*, stayed behind with Akáinix's wife and sisters.

Once the men had gone far enough from the hut, Akáinix arose unnoticed and, taking a different way, ran after them. He was the first to reach the cliffs where the men were going to hunt cormorants. Here, Akáinix startled and scared all the birds. Large numbers of them flew up, circled in the air for some time, and then flew far out over the sea. Akáinix hid nearby. From far away the hunters noticed all the birds flying up from the cliffs. They said: "No doubt some man is running around there. The cormorants fly up, circle in the air, go up and down, and finally fly far out to sea. Who might the man be?" As the hunters got close to the place the cormorants were hovering far out over the waves.

Suddenly, Akáinix came out of his hidingplace and confronted the men. Coming face to face with Akáinix so abruptly they were very startled. Instantly they knew what would now happen to them. Akáinix said: "I suppose you've come to hunt cormorants? The birds have all flown away. Only over there, not far from here, you can still find many of them standing close together. Just step into the water without fear: it is not deep!" The men obeyed without delay as though they had lost all ability to think; they were so overcome by fear and horror that they no longer knew what they were doing. They pushed ahead into the water so as to get close to the cormorants. But no sooner had the men gone out to where they could move only with difficulty than Akáinix skillfully swung his powerful sling and killed them all. That is how he avenged himself, his wife, and his sisters.

Akáinix now hurried back to the hut, but he did not reveal that he had killed all those men. Some time later, though, their relatives asked: "Why are our men staying out so long? Did you perhaps see them over there near the cliffs?" Akáinix replied: "Of course I saw them. They went into the sea to reach the cormorants that were swimming far out there. Be patient, they'll soon be back!" Again the women waited for a long time but the men failed to return. After a while they became convinced that Akáinix had killed every one of them. They were overcome with rage; they began to accuse Akáinix openly and to attack him fiercely. He became indignant and began to defend himself. Soon a violent struggle was in full progress between Akáinix and the men present. Being outnumbered Akáinix was at a disadvantage. The men seized him firmly but were unable to kill him. For a long time they sought to strangle him and to break his neck. But they failed despite their great effort, because Akáinix was a powerful *yékamuš*. They succeeded only in bending his neck and his long back way down. So that since then he has been unable to stand up completely straight. In defense of his father, Yái, the son of Akáinix, also took part in the wrestling. The men, therefore, throttled him just as they did his father and they also bent his spine. From that day on Akáinix and his son Yái[3] have remained crooked and bent over.[4] The relatives of those amorous men whom Akáinix had killed also carried away something from the wrestling bout: they soiled themselves with *imi* while trying to choke Akáinix. Being a *yékamuš*, Akáinix had been painted red all over, as is customary for a *yékamuš* who has died. Even today these birds[5] carry spots of red color on their feathers.

Informant: Alfredo; pp. 1148-1151.

Summary

Shaman of prominent family helps his sisters trick relatives by playing dead upon return from journey. After mourning ceremony some men claim "dead" man's wife and sisters as their wives, but are killed by him in revenge while on a hunting expedition. In subsequent struggle with villagers the man (Rainbow) and his son acquire their present bent-over posture, while villagers (who are birds) even today have red spots from touching shaman's body paint.

Motif content

A220.2.+.	Rainbow is sun's brother. (A220.2. The sun-god and his family.)
A791.	Origin of the rainbow.
A2257.	Animal characteristics from duel.
A2411.2.	Origin of color of bird.
D1711.+.	Rainbow as magician. (D1711. Magician.)
F565.3.	Parliament of women.
F575.1.	Remarkably beautiful woman.
F575.2.	Handsome man.
F617.	Mighty wrestler.
F830.+.	Extraordinary sling. (F830. Extraordinary weapons.)
J53.+.	Ambush betrayed by movements of birds. (J53. Army saved from ambush by observation of birds' movements.)
K810.	Fatal deception into trickster's power.
K1600.	Deceiver falls into own trap.

[3]The second, pale rainbow that sometimes accompanies the bright one.
[4]The Selknam also know this unambiguous myth motif (Wilbert 1975:52n).
[5]They were neither specified by name nor designated in any other way. The story presupposes the general state of affairs after the great revolution.

K1860.	Deception by feigned death (sleep).
N360.	Man unwittingly commits crime.
N440.	Valuable secrets learned.
P233.	Father and son.
P681.	Mourning customs.
Q65.+.	Filial duty. (Q65. Filial duty rewarded.)
Q211.	Murder punished.
Q252.2.	Wife-stealing punished with death.
T230.	Faithlessness in marriage.

5. The Moon-woman

Hánuxa had only one son. Like his mother he was extremely handsome and well built. He died very early and out of grief over her great loss Hánuxa made many small cuts in her face so that much blood flowed. That is why one sees her alone today, still colored red all over, a sign of her mourning.[6] Her son became a star; nobody knows his name.

Informant: Mašemikens; p. 1152.

Motif content

A745.+.	Moon has son. (A745. Family of the moon.)
A750.+.	Why moon is red. (A750. Nature and condition of the moon.)
A751.5.5.+.	Moon spots as scarifications. (A751.5.5. Moon spots are tattoo marks.)
A751.8.	Woman in the moon.
D293.	Transformation: man to star.
F575.2.	Handsome man.
F1041.21.6.1.	Wounding self because of excessive grief.
P231.3.	Mother-love.

6. The Sensitive Ibis-woman

Once in the old days when spring was approaching a man looked out of his hut and saw a *bandurria*[7] fly overhead. He was so happy about

---

[6]Two known ways of expressing mourning are specified here, namely, painting and nicking the skin. The latter was more popular with earlier generations than with the Yamana of modern times.

[7]The sturdy, rusty brown, spectacled ibis, *Theristicus melanopis*, bears this name in Argentina and Chile. See also narrative 7 in this volume.

it that he called over to the other huts: "A *bandurria* is flying over my hut. Look!" Hearing this the others rushed out of their huts shouting loudly: "Spring is here again. The ibises are flying already!" They jumped for joy and talked loudly.

Léxuwa, however, is a very delicate and sensitive woman: she wants to be treated with special deference. She heard the noise of the screaming men, women, and children, and became very angry. Deeply offended she called forth a sudden heavy snowstorm, accompanied by strong frost and lots of ice. From then on snow kept falling and falling for months on end. Snow fell incessantly and as it was extremely cold, the whole earth became covered with ice. The water froze in all the waterways. Many, many people died because they could not get into their canoes to gather food. They were unable even to leave their huts in order to collect firewood, for there was deep snow everywhere. More and more people died.

At long last it ceased snowing, and soon the sun began shining brightly. It burned so fiercely that it melted the ice and snow that had covered the earth to the highest mountaintops. Then much water came flowing down into the channels and into the sea. The sun was so hot that the mountaintops were scorched. They have remained bare to this day. The ice covering the wide and narrow waterways also melted. At last the people were able to get to the beach again and into their canoes to look for food. Only on the vast mountain slopes and in the deep valleys has the thick ice remained until today. Here it was too thick even for that sun to melt it. One can still see this enormous mass of ice lying there; it even reaches down into the sea,[8] so thick was the mantle of ice that then enveloped the whole earth. At that time there was an extraordinarily severe frost, and a fearsome amount of snow had fallen. All this had been caused by Léxuwakipa; she is a very delicate, sensitive woman.

Since then the Yamana treat the *bandurria* with utmost respect. When she approaches their huts, the people remain silent and quiet; especially the little children are kept still and prevented from screaming.

Informant: Not known; pp. 1232-1233.

Summary

Upon seeing bird that signals arrival of spring, people give vent to their joy. Offended by the noise, bird covers earth with snow and ice, and many people die. Then part of snow melts, but many glaciers still remain. Ever since, people treat this bird with respect and silence.

[8]This obviously refers to the big glaciers that dot principally the northwestern arm of the Beagle Channel in considerable numbers (Gusinde 1937:12).

Motif content

A720.2.	Formerly great heat of sun causes distress to mankind.
A900.+.	Why mountaintops are bare today: scorched by sun. (A900. Topography—general considerations.)
A990.+.	Origin of glaciers. (A990. Other land features.)
A1018.3.	Flood brought as revenge for injury.
A1040.	Continuous winter destroys the race.
A2520.+.	Sensitive bird. (A2520. Disposition of animals.)
A2536.+.	Bird as sign of spring. (A2536. Animals of good omen.)
A2545.+.	Why people treat bird respectfully. (A2545. Animal given certain privilege.)
B172.	Magic bird.
B299.1.	Animal takes revenge on man.
D1812.5.0.2.	Omens from flight of birds
D2141.0.11.	Magic storm produced by animal.
D2143.6.3.	Snow produced by magic.
D2143.6.4.	Snow magically caused to melt (burn).
D2144.	Magic control of cold and heat.
D2144.5.1.	Ice produced by magic.
D2145.1.	Winter magically produced.
W185.	Violence of temper.

7. The Flood and the Sensitive Ibis-woman

Léxuwakipa,[9] who was very touchy, felt offended by the people. In revenge she let it snow so much that an enormous mass of ice came to cover the entire earth. When it eventually began to melt there was so much water that the earth became completely flooded. That woman intended to destroy the whole world and all the people in it. The glaciation occurred precisely at the time of the great upheaval of Yáiaašága, when the men battled against the women and seized the *kína*.

After the glaciation the whole earth became flooded. The immense mass of water rose steadily and rapidly. All the people hurried to their canoes and embarked to save themselves. The water rose higher and higher, up to and over the mountaintops, covering them one after the other. Finally only five peaks remained above water. The enormous flood came so quickly and with waves so high that the people were unable to provide themselves with food; many did not even reach their

[9]The strong rusty brown spectacled ibis, *Theristicus melanopis*. See also narrative 6 in this volume.

canoes, and nearly all of them perished in the immense floods of water. The misery everywhere was indescribable. For someone who failed to escape in his canoe early enough and hold on in a sheltered place there was no salvation.

Lucky were those who in their canoes reached one of the five mountaintops that towered above the waves. There they found safety. Those mountain peaks: (1) Ušláka, in what is today Bahía Packsaddle, by the Hardy Peninsula. High up there one can still see broad horizontal stripes that indicate the level reached by the great flood of that time. (2) Wémarwaia, across from Isla O'Brien. There one notices an indentation that encircles the rock in its entirety. It came about because initially people had tied up many canoes there, most of which were destroyed anyway. (3) Auwáratuléra, in a hidden corner of Estero Ponsonby. There even today stands a thick stake to which a few canoes were tied in those days. The massive stake has turned into stone, as it has been standing there for a very long time. (4) Welalánux, on Isla Gable. The peak there used to tower even higher but with the violent waves constantly pounding against it, it has become considerably lower. (5) Piatuléra, two steep hills on both sides of the mouth of the Río Douglas. Today they are no longer as high as when the great flood covered all the land.

After the enormous flood had reached its highest mark leaving only the five peaks barely uncovered, the water level remained steady for two full days. Then it subsided and rapidly lowered. Practically all the Yamana had drowned; only a few families had managed to save themselves. Once the great flood had subsided those few people began to rebuild their huts on the shore. Ever since that time the men have ruled the women.

Informants: Alfredo, Charlin, and Richard; pp. 1155-1156.

Summary

Offended woman takes revenge by covering the earth with snow which, after melting, causes a great flood. Only a few people manage to save themselves by tying their canoes to five mountaintops still above water. The water then subsides; survivors start a new life. Since then the men command the women.

Motif content

A900.+.	Indentations on mountaintop from primeval flood. (A900. Topography—general considerations.)
A1005.	Preservation of life during world calamity.
A1006.1.	New race from single pair (or several) after world calamity.

A1010.2.+.	Great flood lasts two days. (A1010.2. Great flood lasts eight months.)
A1016.3.	Flood caused by melting of ice after great spell of cold.
A1018.3.	Flood brought as revenge for injury.
A1021.	Deluge: escape in boat (ark).
A1022.	Escape from deluge on mountain.
A1029.6.	Survivors of flood establish homes.
A1372.9.	Why women are subservient to men.
A2520.+.	Sensitive bird. (A2520. Disposition of animals.)
B172.	Magic bird.
B299.1.	Animal takes revenge on man.
D471.6.+.	Transformation: wooden stake to stone. (D471.6. Transformation: tree to stone.)
D1654.3.1.	Indelible mark.
D2141.0.11.	Magic storm produced by animal.
D2143.6.3.	Snow produced by magic.
D2143.6.4.	Snow magically caused to melt (burn).
D2144.5.1.	Ice produced by magic.
D2145.1.	Winter magically produced.
F565.3.+.	Parliament of women overthrown. (F565.3. Parliament of women.)
W185.	Violence of temper.

8. The Flood[10]

The moon-woman Hánuxa caused the great flood. That was at the time of the great revolution in Yáiaašága. Hánuxa was full of hatred against the people, mostly against the men who had seized the women's *kína*. It was then that all the people drowned, except for a few who were able to save themselves on five mountaintops where the water did not reach. The great flood had barely subsided when those few survivors came down from the mountaintops to the shore of our channels, and our country became populated again.

Informant: Whaits; pp. 1154-1155.

Motif content

A240.1.	Moon-goddess.
A1005.	Preservation of life during world calamity.
A1006.1.	New race from single pair (or several) after world calamity.

[10]*See also Bridges 1948:165; Cojazzi 1914:31.*

A1015.+.	Moon-woman causes flood. (A1015. Flood caused by gods or other superior beings.)
A1018.	Flood as punishment.
A1018.3.	Flood brought as revenge for injury.
A1022.	Escape from deluge on mountain.
F565.3.+.	Parliament of women overthrown. (F565.3. Parliament of women.

THE CULTURE HEROES

9. The First People[11]

For a long time the Yoálox family wandered through the wide world until they finally came to where we Yamana live today. Here they began doing all kinds of work. When the (real) people, who were born right here came into being, the Yoálox taught them how to arrange their lives, how to act toward one another, and how they should interact. The Yoálox also showed the people all kinds of implements and utensils, weapons and tools, and taught them how to use these things successfully. They were, of course, very able men, and consequently invented the various weapons and tools that we use to this day in hunting and fishing, in collecting, and killing animals. They also showed us how to reach the animals in the water and on land—the big whales and sea lions, the otters and foxes, the many birds, the shellfish and crustaceans—and how to skin the animals and make the skin serviceable, how to utilize and prepare the meat. All this the Yoálox invented and taught the people. The cleverest of them was Yoálox-tárnuxipa; the younger of her brothers was, in turn, far superior to the elder. From them it can be seen that a younger brother is often smarter and more talented than his elder brother.

Informant: Not known; p. 1160.

Summary

Family of culture heroes arrives in primeval Yamana country. They teach the first people crafts and skills and give them tools and weapons.

[11]*See also Koppers 1924:202–208.*

Motif content

A513.	Coming of culture hero (demigod).
A515.1.+.	Culture heroes two brothers and a sister. (A515.1. Culture heroes brothers.)
A527.+.	Remarkably clever culture heroine. (A527. Special powers of culture hero.)
A530.	Culture hero establishes law and order.
A541.	Culture hero teaches arts and crafts.
A545.	Culture hero establishes customs.
A1404.	Gods teach people all they know.
A1446.	Acquisition of tools.
A1459.1.	Acquisition of weapons.
A1520.	Origin of hunting and fishing customs.
P251.5.4.	Two brothers as contrasts.
P253.0.2.	One sister and two brothers.

10. The Invention of Fire

Once the elder Yoálox had collected many small stones and was amusing himself by hitting them against one another. Among them there was also a good *šewáli*. When he struck this stone against another a small spark came out. Surprised at this he struck the stones together several times and each time sparks came out. Hurriedly, he took a handful of very dry down. These he put on the ground. Once more he began to draw a spark from the *šewáli*. He stood in such a way, striking in a certain direction, that the spark sprang into the down. The down began to glow, caught fire, and soon a small flame leaped up. Yoálox quickly went to fetch kindling and wood and put it on the flame. Thus a big fire flared up. It even warmed him pleasantly. Yoálox found it delightful to sit close to it during the day and to sleep beside it at night. The fire turned out to be useful for many other things too: it helped roast the meat, dry the hides, and bend or straighten sticks and pieces of bark.

Overjoyed, the elder Yoálox exclaimed: "Fire is really extremely pleasant and most useful. Let's keep it burning all the time so that it will never go out. Once lit, may it always keep burning by itself so that the people may use it without trouble. They should not have to make a special effort to light it anew every time (in every emergency) or constantly feed it wood!" Hearing this the younger Yoálox became very upset. He did not at all like what his elder brother was planning and quickly responded: "I disagree with your wish. It is much better that the people have to trouble themselves. Everyone should make an honest effort for the fire and guard it carefully. May everyone light the fire again when he has let it go out. People must work!" He immediately seized a long stick, poked around with it in the embers, and scattered the smoldering pieces of wood. Soon the fire went out altogether, and since then every fire will go out if it is not constantly and carefully tended. Thus everyone is obliged to work.

Yoálox taught the people how to light a fire with the *šewáli*, how to fan and maintain it. Since then, whoever lets his fire go out has to light it again with considerable effort. According to Yoálox's wish all people are forced to tend their fire with constant care; he who fails to do so has his fire go out and must painstakingly rekindle and maintain a new one.

Informant: Not known; pp. 1160-1161.

Summary

Culture hero accidentally discovers how to make fire with two stones. He wants to keep it burning constantly to save people the work, but his younger brother objects and puts out the fire. Since then everyone has to work.

Motif content

A515.1.	Culture heroes brothers.
A525.1.+.	Culture hero argues with his elder brother. (A525.1. Culture hero fights with his elder brother.)
A541.	Culture hero teaches arts and crafts.
A1414.3.+.	Origin of fire—culture hero strikes rocks together. (A1414.3. Origin of fire—children strike rocks together.)
J21.50.	"Idleness begets woe; work brings happiness."
J702.	Necessity of work.
J2079.	Absurd wishes—miscellaneous.
M416.	Curse given to negate good wish.
P251.5.4.	Two brothers as contrasts.

11. The Hunt for Birds

The two Yoálox went hunting as often as they needed meat. They always killed birds with their slings. All this was too troublesome for the elder Yoálox who found this most inconvenient. One day he said to his brother: "I would like it better if we killed birds by merely a glance; a bird we stare at ought to fall dead on the spot. So be it, then:

whoever needs the meat of birds shall fix his eyes sharply on a bird, and kill it in so doing. This way everybody can catch his quarry without effort and carry it home!" The elder Yoálox promptly gave it a try. Just then some birds were flying overhead. So he turned his sharp eyes on them, while simultaneously wishing them to fall dead to the ground. And that is precisely what happened; the birds instantly crashed down before him, dead. The elder Yoálox was overjoyed and said: "From now on it shall always be like this, and we shall also tell the people about it: he who stares at a bird to make it instantly fall dead shall always be successful. In this way we'll save ourselves much bother and trouble, lengthy journeys, and many dangers." These words reached the ears of the younger Yoálox. He was thoroughly displeased with his elder brother's plan and angrily opposed it. He said to his brother: "It is much better for the people to have them make weapons and tools for themselves and let them go hunting with them. They should make an effort and use cunning when they sneak up on the birds and surprise them in order to kill and seize them. This is how it shall be, everybody must work and trouble himself!"

These words of his younger brother put the elder Yoálox into an extremely bad mood; but he did not reply. On the following day he attempted once again to kill birds by merely glancing at them. A whole flock of them was just flying overhead. He quickly stared steadily at the animals, wishing them to fall dead. They kept on flying, however, unharmed. Disappointed and discontented the elder Yoálox followed them with his eyes. Since then every man, too, must use much cunning and effort when bird hunting. Quite frequently the quarry escapes the clumsy hunter.

Informant: Not known; pp. 1161-1162.

Summary

In order to save himself and all people work culture hero invents way of killing animals with a mere glance. His younger brother objects and makes it again necessary for people to work for their food.

Motif content

A515.1.	Culture heroes brothers.
A525.1.+.	Culture hero argues with his elder brother. (A525.1. Culture hero fights with his elder brother.)
A526.2.	Culture hero as mighty hunter.
A527.3.	Culture hero as magician.
A545.	Culture hero establishes customs.

A1346.   Man to earn bread by sweat of his brow.
A1520.   Origin of hunting and fishing customs.
D1741.   Magic powers lost.
D2061.2.1.   Death-giving glance.
J21.50.   "Idleness begets woe; work brings happiness."
J702.   Necessity of work.
J2079.   Absurd wishes—miscellaneous.
M416.   Curse given to negate good wish.
P251.5.4.   Two brothers as contrasts.

12. The Hunting of Sea Lions

The elder Yoálox had once received an exquisitely made harpoon
from his elder sister. It gave him good service. The weapon never
missed its mark. Its owner always hit his quarry and it always returned
to his hand.

One day the elder Yoálox came back from the hunt loaded down
with a huge sea lion. But although he had killed the animal at the first
throw, he had broken and lost his harpoon. Therefore the elder Yoálox
told his younger brother: "How convenient it would be if I had a
harpoon that would never break or get lost! That is actually how it
should be: a sea lion ought to fall dead at the first throw and the
weapon instantly return to the hand of the hunter. That way we'd save
ourselves and the people a great deal of toil and trouble, and we would
not have to work so painstakingly at making harpoons. Everyone could
obtain sea lion fat and meat safely and with ease, instead of having to
muster so much cunning and effort to kill a sea lion." The younger
Yoálox listened to all this. But he resolutely opposed his elder brother's
proposition answering angrily: "It must never be the way you suggest!
It is good for the people to work and exert themselves. It is very useful
that everybody makes weapons with his own hands; this (these bene-
fits) would be lost if we gave each and every man a harpoon of the kind
you propose. It is also good that a clumsy, careless hunter breaks and
loses his harpoon. May the animal escape if an awkward and unskilled
man throws the harpoon badly. Everyone should make an effort and
exert himself!"

The elder Yoálox could not object to these words and that is why, to
this day, a clumsy hunter breaks and loses his harpoon if he has not
learned how to hurl it properly and with good aim; or why, if the
hunter has not thrown it forcefully enough, the harpoon remains stuck

superficially in the sea lion's back and the animal swims off with it. He who has lost his harpoon this way must simply trouble himself to make another one.

Later, Yoálox-tárnuxipa gave the elder of the two Yoálox still other weapons and tools, namely, the firm leather thong made from the hide of a sea lion, *úkeša;* the sharp knife made of mussel shell; the strong bone wedge, *íla,* with a stone for hammerhead; the strong sling, *šáfina;* the long snare-rod, *akámuš,* for making snares; and the compound snare-line, *úfka,* to catch birds; and finally all the other implements. His pleasure over all these things was great, because whenever he employed them he was successful. Therefore he wished nothing more ardently than that all these tools should neither break nor wear out; that they should neither slip from their owner's hand nor become lost in any other way. It was his intention to save people the trouble of having to make tools again and again.

The brother objected quite vehemently to the elder Yoálox's fine plans. He wanted to make people work. Every clumsy and awkward hunter should ruin and lose his weapons so that he learn how to be skillful; tools should wear out so as to force everybody to make new ones. That way everybody would be kept busy. The younger Yoálox insisted on his plan, and to this day nobody is spared from toiling painstakingly and laboriously over his weapons and tools, constantly making new ones, and treating them with care. A man is and remains dependent upon them on the hunt and in his daily occupations; in no way can he do without them.

Informant: Not known; pp. 1162-1163.

Summary

Culture hero's sister makes him marvelous hunting tools which always catch the animals he wants. His younger brother objects to his plan to give all people these tools in order to save them work. Since then all people have to work for food and look after their tools well.

Motif content

A515.1.+.	Culture heroes two brothers and a sister. (A515.1. Culture heroes brothers.)
A524.2.	Extraordinary weapons of culture hero.
A525.1.+.	Culture hero argues with his elder brother. (A525.1. Culture hero fights with his elder brother.)
A545.	Culture hero establishes customs.
A1446.	Acquisition of tools.
A1520.	Origin of hunting and fishing customs.
D1080.+.	Magic harpoon. (D1080. Magic weapons.)

D1602.6. +.	Self-returning harpoon. (D1602.6. Self-returning spear.)
J21.50.	"Idleness begets woe; work brings happiness."
J702.	Necessity of work.
J2079.	Absurd wishes—miscellaneous.
M416.	Curse given to negate good wish.
P251.5.4.	Two brothers as contrasts.
P253.0.2.	One sister and two brothers.

13. The Invention of the Arrowhead

Both Yoálox were highly skilled craftsmen. After all, in the course of their long wanderings throughout the world they had come to know a lot. They had also been the first to reach Yamana land. Thus it was incumbent upon them to produce and design the first weapons and tools in such a way that the true Yamana were able to employ them with success. But still their sister, clever Yoálox-tárnuxipa, surpassed by far her two able brothers by her wise judgment and prudence. She exerted considerable influence on everybody. She gave instructions to the rest of the women, all of whom willingly complied. The women, in turn, ordered their husbands about and the men obliged them in every way. The sister of the two Yoálox was really extraordinarily clever; she surpassed all people in wise insight, shrewdness, and talent. Whenever it seemed appropriate she would help her two brothers and all the women with their work. Then everybody was very successful, always reaping rich returns in their enterprises.

One day the Yoálox brothers were making a *yékuš*. But although they were skillful craftsmen and worked hard all day, the arrowhead would not turn out quite right. They had provided it with good, sharp edges, but were unable to fasten the point securely to the shaft. To accomplish tying the point firmly to the shaft was obviously essential if the arrow was to be of any use at all. But the two Yoálox had rounded the lower edge of the arrowhead so that the threads for attaching it found no secure hold nor did the point find enough support in the narrow notch at the upper end of the shaft. An arrow like this was good for nothing. The brothers labored hard trying again and again, and in every way possible, to mount the arrowhead securely onto the shaft. They had already made and tested a good number of points but none of them turned out to their satisfaction. The points came off very easily precisely because this lower end was rounded. Discontented they gathered the many arrowheads into a small basket and hung it up in their hut.

One day the two Yoálox went out hunting for some meat. When they had gone a good distance away from their hut Yoálox-tárnuxipa took down the small basket with the arrowheads. It had not escaped her how utterly unsuccessful her two brothers had been. She emptied all the arrowheads on the ground in front of her. Then, picking them up one after another, she started working them over and perfecting them so that they would become usable. On the lower edge she fashioned a plug-shaped peg, providing it with a shallow notch on both sides so that the binding could not slip off. In this fashion she improved each of the arrowheads, put them all back into the little basket, and returned it to its place. In the evening the two brothers came home; but the woman did not reveal to them that she had perfected all the arrowheads herself.

The next day the two Yoálox wanted to resume their work on the arrowheads and see how they could be fastened firmly to the shaft and whether they were usable. Sulky and annoyed, they took down the basket andd emptied it on the ground. They were very surprised to see that the points had been worked over, for each now came with a well-defined and plug-shaped peg at the base. They marveled at this change. They began testing them at once; they placed an arrowhead into the notch at the upper end of the shaft and wound fine tendons around the peg. And indeed, the point stuck firmly to the shaft and no longer fell off. Finally the arrow was usable.

Now the elder Yoálox exclaimed: "Who could have reworked these arrowheads, who could have made them usable?" To this the younger Yoálox responded: "Only our sister could have accomplished this; is she not much more capable and skillful than we are? She can do anything. Nobody but she could have improved these arrowheads and made them usable!" The elder Yoálox agreed with his brother: "Certainly, that's the way it is," he said. "Our sister outdoes us both in cleverness and skill. From now on we shall give her all our tools so that she may help us (in making and perfecting them)!" For a long time the two Yoálox continued to be very happy over these useful arrow points.

Informant: Not known; pp. 1163-1165.

Summary

Clever sister of two culture heroes improves arrowheads the latter have been working on in vain and makes them usable.

Motif content

A513.	Coming of culture hero (demigod).
A515.1.+.	Culture heroes two brothers and a sister. (515.1. Culture heroes brothers.)

A520. + .	Culture heroine as leader of people. (A520. Nature of the culture hero [demigod].)
A527. + .	Remarkably clever culture heroine. (A527. Special powers of culture hero.)
A541.	Culture hero teaches arts and crafts.
A1446.	Acquisition of tools.
A1459.1.	Acquisition of weapons.
A1459.1.	Origin of arrowhead. (A1459.1. Acquisition of weapons.)
F565.3.	Parliament of women.
F660. + .	Skillful craftsmen. (F660. Remarkable skill.)
J910.	Humility of the great.
N828.	Wise woman as helper.
P253.0.2.	One sister and two brothers.
W27.	Gratitude.

14. The Invention of the Harpoon Point

A short time later the two Yoálox began manufacturing long harpoon points out of whalebone. The bones of the whale are longer and harder than those of other marine animals, thus penetrating the hunted animal better and deeper. The men attached such a point to a long shaft with thin leather straps. They immediately went hunting to test the weapon.

A sea lion approached and they hurled the harpoon at it. The animal was not killed, however, but only superficially wounded. It quickly escaped by diving, surfaced soon again, and swam far away from the shore; the light wound had not harmed it at all. The two Yoálox failed to kill even a single sea lion with their harpoon. They did go out several times to hunt, but the animals they hit with their harpoon were only superficially wounded and escaped without any trouble. Each time, the two Yoálox returned home disappointed and empty-handed. They had already lost several harpoons, for whenever a sea lion was hit the harpoon remained loosely stuck in its skin and the animal swam off with it. All their efforts on such hunts remained unsuccessful; the harpoons were useless.

Disgruntled because of their many unsuccessful efforts, the two Yoálox one day decided to consult their elder sister. They said to her: "Why is it that although our harpoon hits the sea lion and the point penetrates its body it only inflicts an insignificant wound? We never seem to be able to kill it and it therefore never falls into our hands. For many days now we have been returning home without any catch!"

Wise and understanding woman that she was, Yoálox-tárnuxipa replied: "Bring me one of your harpoon points; I'd like to take a good look at it." Immediately they fetched a bone point and showed it to her. She held and studied it closely. The piece was indeed very pointed and provided with a peg at the other end suitable for attachment, exactly as on the arrowhead that Yoálox-tárnuxipa had improved. There was no doubt that the harpoon point was securely fixed in the notch at the upper end of the shaft and firmly fastened. But both sides of the long bone point were smooth from top to bottom. So now Yoálox-tárnuxipa worked out a large, pointed barb on one side. After she had succeeded with this she looked at the bone point with great satisfaction. At once she loosened her loincloth (mašakána) and cut off a long leather strap. One end she tied to the lower peg of the bone point, then placed the next part of the leather strap alongside the shaft and fastened it below [the middle by winding it once around the shaft]; the long, free end she rolled up. Next she showed her brothers how to handle this harpoon: the right hand grasps the harpoon approximately at the middle of the shaft and the left hand loosely holds the long, [rolled-up] free end of the leather strap. Then she told them: "Now start testing it!"

Both Yoálox thanked their sister for improving their harpoon and showing them how to use it. Immediately they left the hut to try out the harpoon on sea lions. They had hardly reached the beach when a powerful animal came swimming by. The younger Yoálox clutched the harpoon exactly as his sister had shown him: when hurling it he held the free end of the thong in his left hand. And indeed, the bone harpoon point penetrated deeply into the sea lion's back. Instantly the animal disappeared below the surface of the water. But it did not get very far, for the long strap had soon been pulled very taut and the stronger the sea lion jerked, the deeper the barbed harpoon point tore the wound. The shaft had become detached from the point but since it was fastened by its lower end to the leather thong it was floating on the surface of the water. By this shaft Yoálox could tell where the sea lion was swimming. The latter ceased tugging so hard on the long line, for the deep wound hurt very much and each jerk was painful. Slowly, the younger Yoálox began pulling in the long line; the shorter it got, the closer the sea lion came to the shore.[12] When it was finally lying on land the elder Yoálox killed it with a cudgel. Thus with this harpoon they had easily and safely caught the first sea lion, and provided themselves with plenty of blubber.

---

[12]Here is described in detail the way and fashion in which this big harpoon works and makes for success (Gusinde 1937:474). The explanation underscores the amazing ability and skill of these Fuegian innovators.

The two Yoálox were nearly beside themselves with satisfaction at this success. They spent the whole day hunting sea lions and made an exceptionally large catch. Not until evening did they decide to return to the hut. This time they were panting loudly under the heavy load of meat. Overjoyed they told their sister about their great success and explained how quickly they had caught each animal and why this time none had gotten away.

From this day on the two Yoálox abandoned all their other crafts, for it made them unspeakably happy to hunt sea lions with this harpoon. Later they taught all the men how to use the large harpoon. Since then the Yamana utilize this harpoon with the long leather thong to hunt sea lions.

Informant: Not known; pp. 1165-1167.

Summary

Two culture heroes try in vain to make a good harpoon point. Finally their clever sister makes one for them with which they catch many sea lions. Since then all Yamana use this kind of harpoon.

Motif content

A515.1.+.	Culture heroes two brothers and a sister. (A515.1. Culture heroes brothers.)
A524.2.	Extraordinary weapons of culture hero.
A527.+.	Remarkably clever culture heroine. (A527. Special powers of culture hero.)
A541.	Culture hero teaches arts and crafts.
A1459.1.+.	Origin of harpoon point. (A1459.1. Acquisition of weapons.)
N828.	Wise woman as helper.
W27.	Gratitude.

15. The Acquisition of Whale Oil

The elder Yoálox was particularly fond of sea lion fat and whale oil; they tasted very good to him and he craved this food. He was very careful always to have a large supply of whale oil on hand. One day he considered a plan to turn into whale oil and sea lion fat the water in all the channels, streams, and lagoons. But this enormous mass was always to remain fresh, never to turn bad, never to lose its good flavor, and never to run out. He said to himself: "If it were arranged that way, the people would always have fresh whale oil on hand; they could save themselves dangerous journeys and strenuous hunts; they would never have to do without these delicacies, and life would be a good deal more pleasant!"

He then put this plan before his younger brother and tried to win him over. The latter, however, wanted nothing to do with it and put his brother down: "It must never be as you plan. People must be obliged to work always. Men have to go hunting. When they have killed sea lions or whales the women will prepare the blubber; then all may greatly enjoy the delicious whale oil which only tastes good after strenuous work. People must not be granted pleasure without work!"

Thus once again the elder Yoálox had to abandon his plan and yield to the decision of his younger brother. Soon afterward the elder Yoálox undertook a long journey on foot during which he became very tired and hungry. He sat down on a stone to rest a while. The earth was very swampy, however, and water soon oozed up around his feet. Since he was hungry, the thought occurred to him: "How good it would be if all the water that rises up wherever I or anyone else puts his foot should instantly turn into whale oil. Everybody would have more than enough with which to appease his hunger!" This wish, too, he soon put before his younger brother. Displeased, the latter said: "It must never come to that! May people go hungry if they don't work!" This made the elder Yoálox sad again, and his wish has not been realized. It is because of this that from that time on it has become an inescapable rule for men to go hunting and for all people to worry about getting food. On numerous occasions the attitude of the younger Yoálox quite clearly reveals how younger brothers or sisters are frequently wiser and more prudent, but also more stubborn, than their older siblings.

Informant: Not known; pp. 1167-1168.

Summary

On two occasions culture hero who likes sea lion fat and whale oil wants to turn all water into these substances to save people work. His younger and wiser brother objects. Since then all people have to work for food.

Motif content

A515.1.	Culture heroes brothers.
A515.1.1.2.	Twin culture heroes—one foolish, one clever.
A525.1.+.	Culture hero argues with his elder brother. (A525.1. Culture hero fights with his elder brother.)
A545.	Culture hero establishes customs.
A1346.	Man to earn bread by sweat of his brow.

J21.50.	"Idleness begets woe; work brings happiness."
J702.	Necessity of work.
J2079.	Absurd wishes—miscellaneous.
P251.5.4.	Two brothers as contrasts.
X1503.	Schlaraffenland.

16. The Beginning of Sexual Desire

One day, upon feeling great desire, the younger Yoálox tried in every way to satisfy himself. With this intention he fashioned a human body. In it he first opened eye sockets and inserted his large penis, but he was not satisfied. Then he opened two holes under the nose but he felt no enjoyment here, either. Then he made the ear openings on both sides, but also in these places he found no satisfaction. Now he opened a wide mouth; however, he felt no satisfaction here, either. He continued trying to satisfy his lust, namely in the armpits, at the breasts and the navel, but nowhere did he find pleasure. Finally he made an opening between the legs; here he finally found full satisfaction.

Later, he instructed the men in this. Since then they, too, know how to satisfy their desire.

Informant: Not known; p. 1168.

Motif content

A1275.	Creation of first man's (woman's) mate.
A1313.2.	Origin of female sex organs.
A1352.	Origin of sexual intercourse.
A1352.3	Former intercourse by navel.
T117.11.	Marriage to a statue.

17. The First Menstruation

In the beginning the two Yoálox lived just with their own sister; neither of them had a wife. But the time came when they no longer enjoyed being always alone during the day and sleeping alone at night. Finally they revealed their feelings to Yoálox-tárnuxipa: "As you can see, we are all alone here. We don't want to go on living like this any longer. Help us to get a woman soon!" Yoálox-tárnuxipa agreed and promised to help her brothers.

The two brothers and their sister discussed what to do. The men had excellent weapons and were very skillful. Consequently they always brought home a great catch from the hunt and reveled in abundance; there were large supplies of meat in their hut. Hulušénuwa,[13] on the other hand, was in a different situation; he perpetually lacked meat because he had many wives. All the wives asked insistently to visit the two Yoálox and to gaze at them for a long time. When Halušénuwa was once again out of meat he personally dressed up each wife extremely beautifully and ordered each to decorate and paint herself even more with colors. Then he sent one woman after the other to the two Yoálox to fetch some meat. Each woman had decorated and painted herself with colors and designs of her personal taste; each was different from the others; all were very pretty.

With this was introduced the custom of painting one's face and entire body. This way the people make themselves attractive and get enjoyment from it. Since the time when little Hulušénuwa ordered his many wives to decorate themselves with colorful designs all Yamana realize that they have to paint themselves on certain occasions.[14] This is now the rule. To this day Hulušénuwa's women have kept the beautiful paint they applied at that time. Whenever the men perform the *kína* they imitate the colors and patterns on the coats and feathers of animals by painting their bodies in various ways.[15]

Without delay little Hulušénuwa sent first Tákašakipa[16] to the Yoálox. She entered the hut of the two Yoálox and introduced herself. The brothers considered the woman long and thoroughly. Then they said to their sister: "Give her a lot of meat." Yoálox-tárnuxipa gave Tákašakipa plenty of meat and with that she was dismissed. The Yoálox brothers and the sister had agreed ahead of time: the two brothers would look over each woman carefully and consider whether she was beautiful and to their liking. Every woman they did not like would be given a lot of meat by their sister and dismissed.

After a while Lášixkipa made an appearance. The Yoálox looked her over, but did not like her. Then Yoálox-tárnuxipa gave her plenty of meat and she was dismissed. One after the other little Hulušénuwa

---

[13]The smaller of the two Fuegian wrens, *Troglodytes hornensis.*

[14]In the ensuing discussion these were mentioned as special occasions by way of explanation: visits, menstruation, mourning and funeral ceremonies, puberty rites, and the *kína*-ceremony.

[15]One must realize, and it was expressly brought to my attention at this point, that all those women are not considered real people any more than the two Yoálox. The former turned into birds, the latter went with Yoálox-tárnuxipa up to the sky where one still recognizes them as stars.

[16]The noisy seagull, *Larus belcheri.*

sent the rest of his wives: the *šékuš*, the *kímoa*, the *lúrux*, the *wasénim*, the *lékakuta*, the *wípatux*, the *malépa*, the *šáneš*, the *wémarkipa*, the *kiwágu*, the *detehúrux*, the *čokóa*, and several others, for he had many wives. But as pretty as all of them were, the two Yoálox did not like them.[17] Their sister gave much meat to each of the women, who then hurried back to their hut. Thus, one after the other, the long line of little Hulušénuwa's wives presented themselves to the two Yoálox. The latter looked at each woman carefully, but none suited them. More women kept coming. They entered the hut of the Yoálox alone, but were all given much meat soon and dismissed.

The last to appear was Mákuxipa, little Hulušénuwa's most beautiful wife. When she entered the hut the two Yoálox liked her immensely and could not take their eyes off her. They whispered to their sister: "Don't give any meat to this woman! We want to keep her in our hut and prevent her from returning to her husband. We like this beautiful woman very much!" Therefore Yoálox-tárnuxipa said to Mákuxipa: "Just sit down quietly here beside my brothers; they both like you very much!" Without embarrassment, Mákuxipa sat down as Yoálox-tárnuxipa had told her to, namely on the bed of the two Yoálox. They soon began caressing the beautiful woman. Later they persuaded Mákuxipa to remain with them in the hut; the Yoálox frankly admitted to her how deeply they were in love with her. This pleased her very much and she said: "All right, I'll stay with you!" The two Yoálox were overjoyed that this beautiful woman agreed to stay with them. They soon began to satisfy their desire. But they especially thanked their sister who had helped to retain the beautiful woman.

Little Hulušénuwa waited in his hut for Mákuxipa, but she failed to return. Finally, after a long time he found out that the two Yoálox were keeping his wife for their own pleasure. It made him unspeakably sad and he cried out plaintively: "Oh, poor me! Precisely the most beautiful of my wives they have persuaded to stay and taken away from me. All the other less beautiful ones they let come home after giving them meat. How grievously I miss my lovely Mákuxipa!" Little Hulušénuwa kept lamenting incessantly this way.

The two Yoálox again amused themselves with Mákuxipa. She, too, liked it very much in the hut of the two brothers. They took turns sleeping with her and were very happy not to have to do without this any longer.[18]

[17]Here, to avoid superfluous repetitions only a few names have been quoted in the abbreviated form without the gender designation "kipa" and without a closer zoological classification.

[18]What is meant is frequent and free intercourse for sexual satisfaction, for which previously they had had no opportunity. So their relationship with the woman is not to be interpreted as polyandry.

One day, very early in the morning, the elder Yoálox went into the forest to hunt and collect wood. But his brother remained stretched out on his bed; by his side lay beautiful Mákuxipa. Since the elder Yoálox was away they abandoned themselves to their boundless desire. They spent the entire day on the bed without thinking of getting up. They day had passed much too quickly for them, and the elder Yoálox returned just as it was getting dark. Cautiously and unnoticed he approached the hut. Then he became aware of the fact that those two were still fondling each other and rolling around on the bed. That made him curious. Now he listened intently; he wanted to hear what they were talking about. He heard Mákuxipa whisper to the younger Yoálox: "I like your penis a lot. It is large and fills my vagina. It is red like the *máku*.[19] Your brother has a small one which doesn't excite me in this way. Look, I like your large penis much more than I do your brother's. I would rather lie with you for a long time." At these words the younger Yoálox was delighted. His elder brother, who was standing outside leaning against the hut, listened attentively and understood clearly what the two were whispering to each other.

After a while he entered the hut. He threw down the heavy pieces of wood that he had brought back and sat down by the fire, heavy rain had drenched him through. Unobtrusively the younger Yoálox moved away a bit from Mákuxipa, but both still remained lying on the bed. For a long time the elder Yoálox warmed himself by the fire, then he addressed the woman in a very ill-humored tone: "How can you lie with my brother from morning to night!" Said she indifferently: "I simply enjoy it very much with him!" This made him even angrier, and he blew up at her: "I know very well why you like it so much with him that you lie together the whole day. What did you just whisper to him?" Mákuxipa replied, embarrassed: "What could I have whispered to him? We only talked about unimportant things." To this the elder Yoálox answered: "In any case you have had a lot of fun with my brother. I also heard distinctly how you told him: "I like your penis a lot. It's large and fills my vagina. It's red like the *máku*. Your brother has a small one which doesn't excite me in this way. Look, I like your large penis much more than I do your brother's. I would rather lie with you for a long time." He approached the bed where she was lying stretched out, and his brother moved away. He began fondling and hugging Mákuxipa. Then he lay down on top of the woman and inserted his penis into her vagina. His penis swelled so that it tore the woman's vagina. Instantly a rather large amount of blood flowed out. Yoálox asked her: "Do you want my member to grow larger still? Are you satisfied?" Mákuxipa did not answer a word.

[19]The scarlet flower of *Embothrium coccineum*.

Then the elder Yoálox rose from the bed and told her: "You are now *túri!* So now you may take my younger brother for your husband! But first I shall give you a few instructions so that the blood will not flow excessively and you don't weaken!" He gave her all kinds of advice which still holds true for her and for all women. Emphatically he insisted: "You must remain still and silent and avoid all chattering. If possible, spend the entire period in your hut. Stay away from men, and should you meet one, make a wide detour. Abstain from all food and eat only what I allow you to. Be content with little water. During this time (of your first menstruation) work particularly hard, help the other women eagerly, fetch a lot of drinking water and firewood for everybody. Observe all this advice faithfully!" Much more still did the elder Yoálox instruct Mákuxipa to do. She followed the instructions closely and her condition improved. She soon felt better, and the bleeding finally stopped. After a few days, she also did not have to renew the design that Yoálox had painted on her face.[20] All this time Yoálox-tárnuxipa sat beside Mákuxipa, guarding and instructing her attentively, and constantly helping her. She also gave her other advice, with which Mákuxipa faithfully complied. Finally Yoálox-tárnuxipa suggested to her two brothers: "Let's have a big celebration, now that this woman is *túri!*" Her brothers agreed; they brought large amounts of meat and ate their fill. That was the first *túrikipa tátu.*[21]

Informant: Not known; pp. 1168-1172.

Summary

Man with many wives is always short of meat; sends wives one by one to unmarried culture hero brothers to get meat. Before going, women paint their faces and bodies. (Origin of custom of ceremonial body paint.) Brothers give them meat but keep one woman; both have intercourse with her. She prefers younger brother. Jealous older brother rapes her; her vagina is torn, she bleeds. (First menstruation.) Older brother lays down rules for behavior during menses.

Motif content

A515.1.+.	Culture heroes two brothers and a sister. (A515.1. Culture heroes brothers.)
A524.2.	Extraordinary weapons of culture hero.
1545.+.	Culture hero establishes customs pertaining to menstruation. (A545. Culture hero establishes customs.)

[20]This refers to the particular face paint that is obligatory during menstruation (Gusinde 1937:757, fig. 79).
[21]The details of this festive event are mentioned in Gusinde 1937:757.

A1313.2.+.	Origin of shape of vagina. (A1313.2. Origin of female sex organs.)
A1355.	Origin of menstruation.
A1530.+.	Origin of girls' initiation ceremonial. (A1530. Origin of social ceremonials.)
A1595.+.	Origin of body paint: initiation of designs on animals and birds. (A1595. Origin of tattooing.)
A2411.2.	Origin of color of bird.
B652.	Marriage to bird in human form.
C114.	Tabu: incest.
C140.	Tabu connected with menses.
C141.	Tabu: going forth during menses.
D489.+.	Penis becomes longer. (D489. Objects made larger—miscellaneous.)
F547.3.+.	Red penis. (F547.3. Extraordinary penis.)
F547.3.1.	Long penis.
F575.1.	Remarkably beautiful woman.
F679.5.	Skillful hunter.
H1381.3.1.	Quest for bride.
K330.+.	Women induce owners to give up food. (K330. Means of hoodwinking the guardian or owner.)
N450.	Secrets overheard.
N828.	Wise woman as helper.
T52.	Bride purchased.
T57.	Declaration of love.
T75.	Man scorned by his beloved.
T75.2.1.	Rejected suitors' revenge.
T92.	Rivals in love.
T146.	Polyandry.
T292.	Wife sold unwillingly by husband.
T310.1.	Ceremonial continence.
W181.	Jealousy.

18. The First Childbirth

Since then the younger Yoálox lived alone with Mákuxipa, who had become his wife. He slept with her, and she became pregnant. Eventually she gave birth to a son.[22] Yoálox was immensely pleased. At once

[22]The particular aim of this story is to demonstrate that both conception and childbirth, as both processes occur since then, were introduced for the first time through Yoálox. According to this, children previously had not been actually "born," and nowhere is it explained in what manner they came into existence. All the people of the "first times" are simply presented as adults. But from now on starts the process of growing up in the way characteristic of human beings.

he informed his wife in detail about what to do in childbirth and how to behave during the time immediately following it. All Yamana women still follow these instructions.

Yoálox's first child was a boy. He cried incessantly, most loudly during the night. He never stopped screaming; his mother and father tried everything possible to make him stop but to no avail. Yoálox looked highly displeased; since the mother had to go about her work, it was impossible for her to stay constantly with the child.

Very annoyed, Yoálox finally ran out of his hut, leaving the boy alone. At some distance away he built himself another hut. He went hunting as regularly as before and continued working on his weapons. But whenever he approached the huts, be it from the forest or from the beach, he could hear his son's loud crying from afar. When he stepped into his hut nearby the boy yelled even louder. He continued to cry incessantly, even when Yoálox made noises to make him be quiet.

Sulkily one day he again entered the hut where his little son was lying. With both hands he grabbed him under his armpits, lifted him up, stared sharply into his face, and roared: "Will you stop screaming!" This very instant the little boy split right down the middle, so that Yoálox now had two sons. They did not cry, though. They were the first humans.[23]

After some time Mákuxipa died. Since the younger Yoálox was always occupied he could not be busy watching his two sons. He looked for a woman to take care of his two boys and chose Čilawáia-kipa (vixen). Right away she moved into Yoálox's hut and devoted herself to his two sons. Now Yoálox could even go on long journeys without worrying.

The vixen named the two boys Šamanáuye. She was very clever and cunning, and was soon scheming to roast and eat the boys. Yoálox was very far away at the time; before he came back she could be gone and hiding in the woods. So now she wanted to carry out her plan. She told the two boys: "Go into the forest and collect plenty of dry wood! Bring it quickly back here to the hut; we are going to start a big fire!" The two boys ran into the forest. But Čilawáiakipa had treated them badly from the start. She had made them work very hard, and the two were angry at her. At last they wanted to avenge themselves. Instead of collecting dry wood they gathered green and wet sticks and carried them to the hut. The vixen tried to light a big fire with it but was not able to do so. Angrily, she scolded the boys: "You've brought me green

[23]These words mean: those two children are the first who were brought into the world by actual birth. Strictly according to the wording, however, this applies to only one of them.

and wet wood; it's impossible to light a big fire with that!" The following day she again sent the two boys into the forest to collect dry wood. But this time, again, they gathered only green, wet wood and carried it to the hut. They had noticed that the vixen was planning something evil. Yet they did not know how to cope with the difficult situation, for their father was far away on the other side of the channel. They had long since tired of having to stay constantly with ill-humored, stingy Čilawáiakipa who, in addition to sending them into the forest for wood, burdened them daily with lots of work. Deliberately they now gathered only wet wood. This made the vixen furious each time and she took her ill humor out on them in every conceivable way. The two boys suffered much unpleasantness.

One day Čilawáiakipa was lying on her bed fast asleep. Quickly the two boys lit a big fire[24] to signal a canoe. And indeed, soon a man appeared on the beach. The boys stepped swiftly into his canoe and begged to be taken to the other shore. This the man did, and the two boys disembarked on the opposite side. They continued running in the direction where they supposed their father to be. Unexpectedly they came to a wide river; they did not know how to cross it since it was very wide. They feared now the vixen might come after them. But Yoálox, their father, had seen them come running from afar; he knew that they were right then standing at the wide river, not knowing what to do. So he quickly drained the water in the river, and his two sons reached the other shore without effort. Soon they came to the place where Yoálox was sitting. He asked them: "Why are you following me; what has brought you here?" Tearfully the two sons now told their father how badly they were treated by Čilawáiakipa, how hard they had to work, how they were sent into the forest every day to collect dry wood, and that they got very little to eat. To this they added: "We had hardly stepped into that man's canoe and reached the middle of the channel when we looked back to see Čilawáiakipa throw herself over Mákuxipa's dead body and eat of it! She was surely planning to eat us, too. That's why she sent us into the forest every day to collect piles of dry wood for a fire over which she intended to roast us!"

The younger Yoálox became very angry at this. Full of rage he quickly made a *yékuš*. This he hurled at Čilawáiakipa so that she fell dead on the spot. From then on the two boys stayed with their father; they had grown up in the meantime.[25]

[24]What is meant is an actual signal fire, customary among the Yamana (Gusinde 1937:1020).

[25]In this story are repeated several details of what the Selknam tell about Kwányip's two nephews (Gusinde 1931:595).

But since that time one can occasionally see the fox dig up human corpses and eat of them. It is a disgusting animal.

Informant: Not known; pp. 1174-1176.

Summary

Culture hero's wife gives birth to a boy who screams incessantly. When harshly admonished by his father he splits and becomes two boys. They are first "real people" (born from womb of a woman). After the wife dies, culture hero's second wife treats boys badly and plans to roast them. They run away to their father who kills the woman in his anger.

Motif content

A545.+.	Culture hero establishes customs pertaining to childbirth. (A545. Culture hero establishes customs.)
A592.2.1.+.	Wife of culture hero gives birth to a boy. (A592.2.1. Daughter of culture hero gives birth to boy.)
A1200.	Creation of man.
A1351.	Origin of childbirth.
A2435.3.+.	Why fox sometimes eats human corpses. (A2435.3. Food of various animals—mammals.)
B651.1.	Marriage to fox in human form.
B652.	Marriage to bird in human form.
D670.	Magic flight.
D1813.0.3.	Father feels that son is in danger.
D2151.2.3.	Rivers magically made dry.
E257.+.	Ogre seeks firewood to roast boys. (E257. Ghosts seek firewood to roast man.)
G31.+.	Children flee from stepmother who turns cannibal. (G31. Children flee from father who turns cannibal.)
G72.1.	Woman plans to eat her children.
G81.	Unwitting marriage to cannibal.
J641.	Escaping before enemy can strike.
K500.	Escape from death or danger by deception.
N800.+.	Stranger as helper. (N800. Helpers.)
Q215.	Cannibalism punished.
Q285.	Cruelty punished.
Q411.	Death as punishment.
S31.	Cruel stepmother.
S139.2.2.	Other indignities to corpse.
T589.2.	Boy cut in two: each half becomes a boy.
T685.	Twins.
W182.	The crying child.

19. The Sister of the Yoálox Brothers Falls in Love[26]

The two Yoálox brothers had two other sisters but nobody can remember their names. These girls took particular pleasure in bathing and playing in the waves. Almost every day they spent happily in the water.

One day a big sea lion approached the girls. He did not frighten them in the least; rather, from the first he acted clearly amorous and offered to play with them. The two sisters found this quite all right; they amused themselves for some time, until eventually the elder one became strongly taken with the sea lion. Surreptitiously they went farther and farther away so that the younger sister could not see what they were doing. Then they fondled each other and played together for a long time below the surface of the water.

The two sisters always bathed in the same place. Every time they went into the water the big sea lion appeared, too. He came swimming under the surface and approached the elder sister. This was just what she wanted, for she had fallen very much in love with the sea lion. Unobtrusively the two left the other girl; she was not to notice how they gave in to their desire.

For a long time now they had been meeting for their love play. Then one day the younger sister asked her elder sister: "What is that big black thing that you hide so anxiously with your body? I saw it between your legs. What actually is it?" The elder sister answered evasively: "But what are you thinking of! You can only mean the shadow of my body. There can't be anything else!" The younger sister was not satisfied with this answer and asked again: "It seems strange to me that this black thing is supposed to be your shadow. A shadow is never that solid black. It must be something else!" Upset, the elder sister replied: "I can't understand what you are imagining! When I assure you that it is my shadow, why don't you believe me!" But the younger sister was not to be convinced and answered: "That black thing cannot possibly be your shadow! It would be much too strange to see your shadow only appear in the water and only below your body." Now the elder sister repeated insistently: "Please trust my words. There is nothing here but my shadow." The younger sister realized that further discussion would lead nowhere, so she merely added: "I cannot

[26]See also *Bridges 1948:161–163; Cojazzi 1914:32–33.*

believe that the black thing is the shadow of your body, even if you assure me again and again!" Nevertheless the two girls continued to go bathing almost every day, and every time the elder sister met the male sea lion.

The elder sister had now been pregnant for a long time. When her condition was far advanced she finally discussed with the sea lion how to prepare herself. At once he took the pregnant woman on his back and swam to his cave. There he prepared a soft bed and also brought a lot of food. Soon she gave birth to a baby boy.

The sea lion was tremendously happy over his son. But several days later he was seized with great fear. He said to the girl: "If the Yoálox, your brothers, find out about our forbidden relations, if it becomes known to them that you have given birth to a boy and are staying in my cave, they are going to get into a terrible rage and blame me alone. Then they'll ambush and kill me. I think it best for you to return to your brothers. Tell them how very fond we are of each other; then tell them how amicably we live together and how lively our little son is; ask them if I may live with them." Replied the girl: "Very well, I'll go back to my brothers' hut and tell them everything; I'll ask them if you may live with them." At once she prepared herself to leave. The sea lion took her again on his back and they made headway quickly.

The two Yoálox had long had a rather good idea of all that had happened and what was going on with their sister. When the sea lion was close enough to the hut of the Yoálox he sent his wife on alone. As for himself he stayed behind with the little boy. Quickly, the woman reached her two brothers' hut just when they were home. She entered and said unabashedly: "How are you, my brothers! My husband, the big sea lion, asks whether he may come to live with you. He would like to be near you, and I would like that, too. But he will only come if you promise not to kill him! He is more than ready to help you in hunting and in all the work, and he'll also be a good brother-in-law to you!" The two Yoálox consented: "You say the sea lion is your husband. All right, he may come; we'll take him into our hut. We promise not to do him any harm; if he behaves well we won't kill him."

The woman was happy to receive her brothers' consent. Without delay she hurried back to where she had left her husband with the little boy. When she reached the sea lion she told him happily: "I talked to my brothers. They asked me to tell you: since you are now my husband you may come and live with them. They won't do you any harm or kill you as long as you behave well." These words reassured the sea lion; accompanied by his wife and child he set out at once to the hut of the Yoálox. The woman entered first, carrying her child on her back. Just behind her the sea lion, too, tried to enter. But he was too powerful and too bulky to get through the narrow entrance. The two Yoálox had to remove a few stakes first from the doorway; then the sea lion finally forced himself through and came inside. He was extraordinarily large. The two Yoálox showed him and his wife the place opposite the entrance as their sleeping place; they now settled down there as though in their own hut.

Early next morning the sea lion got up from his bed and hurried out to fish at sea. And sure enough, he soon brought big fish, mussels, and crabs in large quantities. That was a considerable amount of food for his wife and his two brothers-in-law. Now the latter no longer wanted for anything. On his own initiative and always willingly the sea lion went out to sea again and again and carried back large amounts of meat.

One day the Yoálox brothers sent the two women who were living in their hut, Mákuxipa and the sea lion's wife, far away.[27] Only the two Yoálox and the sea lion stayed behind. Before the two women left the hut the sea lion's wife said goodbye particularly warmly. During this the sea lion whispered to her secretly: "If you hear me roar loudly and painfully, come back quickly. It may be that your brothers intend to kill me. Then I will need your help. So come back quickly if I roar loudly!" She assured her husband: "I'll pay close attention! But I'm sure my brothers won't do you any harm."

The two Yoálox, for their part, had secretly told Mákuxipa: "Once you have gone far away from here with our sister and you then hear the sea lion roar loudly and painfully, calm her down and tell her: 'It seems the three men are amusing themselves in our hut with games and jokes; they must be very cheerful and contented, that's why the sea lion is roaring so loudly, from sheer exuberance!' In any case, you must hold our sister back by all means. Do not allow her to come running back here to the hut. We are planning to kill the sea lion as soon as possible. That's why we're sending you two far away." Mákuxipa understood all that very well. The two women left the hut and started on the long way to where they were to carry out their task.

Soon afterward the two Yoálox resumed their daily work. They sat down in front of the hut and prepared the big harpoons. The sea lion also left the hut to go fishing again. He hurried down to the beach. It was a beautiful day and the sun was shining hotly. Soon the sea lion became weak and sleepy; he stretched out on a large rock on the beach and fell asleep. Now he began to snore, and gradually his snoring

[27]This event would have to be inserted before the preceding story if chronology were to be observed.

became so loud that the two Yoálox could hear it; they were sitting in
front of their hut. One brother now encouraged the other: "This is the
time to kill the sea lion. Surely he's fast asleep for he's snoring terribly.
Let's start in on him right now! Besides, we need oil to grease our big
harpoons. So far we've been using fat from snails for that, but sea lion
oil is much better. That sea lion is unusually big and fat; he'll give a lot
of oil and meat. Killing that one will certainly pay!" The other brother
agreed completely with this plan. Quickly they went back into the hut;
both wanted to consult their mother as to whether or not they should
kill the sea lion. They said to her: "Mother, we are tired of greasing our
harpoons only with snail fat. We think it is much better to kill that fat
sea lion there and take all his oil; we could grease our harpoons with
that from now on!" The mother did not like the idea at all and
complained loudly: "Oh, but I don't like your plan. The sea lion has
always brought me many big fish, precisely the kinds I like best. If you
kill him there'll be nobody here to provide me with so many tasty fish.
Besides, this sea lion is really kind and anxious to be of help." The two
Yoálox became annoyed at their mother's words and replied: "Certainly, it's true what you're saying, this sea lion is really kind and eager
to help, but after all he's only an animal and not a human being like us.
If we kill him we get all his fat and meat. What an enormous amount
that would be! You, too, shall eat much, for his meat is tastier and
juicier than that of fish and mussels. You are certain to like it. We'll let
you have a lot so that you'll have provisions for a long time." Finally
the mother gave in, saying: "All right! Do what you want; kill the sea
lion; I won't hold you back any longer."

Quickly the two Yoálox arranged their harpoon shafts and attached
to these the sharp bone points with the long line. Cautiously and
silently they sneaked up to the sea lion who was still fast asleep and
snoring mightily. Bringing their arms far back they raised their harpoons and thrust them with all their strength. So well did they hit their
target that the weapons entered deeply into the large body of the sea
lion, wounding him close to the heart. The sea lion woke up in pain; he
felt seriously wounded and near death. Then, with all his remaining
strength, he roared loudly and painfully, as he roars today when he
collapses from a mortal wound. So long and so loudly did he roar that
those two women far away in the distance could hear it distinctly.
"Alas," the sea lion's wife lamented to Mákuxipa, "do you hear how
loudly and miserably my husband is roaring? I'm sure he's calling me to
help him, for the two Yoálox are now killing him. I'll run as quickly as
I can to the hut and see if he needs me!" Mákuxipa tried hard to hold
her back and said persuasively: "How can you even think such a thing?

I'm sure the Yoálox are playing with the sea lion; undoubtedly all three are cheerful and merry, that's why the sea lion is laughing so hard. Don't worry and stay quietly here with me; later we'll go back to the hut together." But the sea lion's wife refused to take another step forward; instead, she hurried home as fast as she could, and the other woman realized that she was unable to detain her. They both changed direction and headed for their hut. On the way Mákuxipa continued her efforts to hold the other woman back.

While the two women were walking along their way the sea lion died on the rock where the two Yoálox had mortally wounded him with their big harpoons. They forthwith began to dismember the large animal and placed several pieces of meat on the fire to roast. Later they sat down to eat these pieces, enjoying them thoroughly. Then they carried other big pieces to the hut and put them on the fire to roast. Soon they wanted to eat again for they thoroughly enjoyed the roasted meat.

The two Yoálox had left the sea lion's small son alone in the hut when they had gone to kill the powerful animal. As soon as the boy realized that he was alone in the hut he sneaked out, sat down in the sand by the hut, and played. Now the two Yoálox caught sight of him. One of them went quickly over to give him some meat. The child ate with pleasure, for this roast was made from perfectly fresh meat. No sooner had he eaten the big piece than he demanded a second one. The Yoálox gave him a piece of roasted blubber, and he relished this too.

At this point the two women arrived. They met the boy sitting in the sand near the hut, enjoying a piece of totally fresh meat. When his mother saw the fresh meat in his hands she shuddered with frightful suspicion: she suddenly realized that the boy was eating his own father's flesh! Full of grief she sank to the ground. She became terribly infuriated, seized a large sea urchin from her hand-basket, and threw it at the boy's head as hard as she could. He instantly turned into a fish. The barbs from the sea urchin are still sticking in his head. That is the *súna*.[28]

Filled with grief and sorrow the sea lion's wife entered the hut. She became terribly frightened when she saw all the pieces of meat roasting on short sticks near the fire. Around the fire there were still other parts of the dismembered sea lion lying on the ground, already cut up to be roasted: head, flippers, stomach parts, flanks, back. She looked with horror at her husband's dismembered body. Boundless grief overwhelmed her and in her despair she sat down and cried bitterly.

[28] A thornfish, common in those waters. The Yamana do not eat it "because it used to be a boy."

Nobody exchanged a word with her. Her two brothers, the Yoálox, remained outwardly very calm and unobtrusive; they gave no sign to show that anything unusual had happened. They continued to cut up the meat and watched the pieces near the fire. Mákuxipa, too, behaved very quietly.

Finally, after a long time, the two Yoálox asked their sister: "Where is your little son? He was sitting outside in front of the door. Why doesn't he come in?" Upset and sad at the same time the woman answered: "When I came back I found the little boy sitting outside in front of the hut. To my horror I saw him eat of his own father's flesh. I became furious and lost control of myself. I grabbed a sea urchin from my little basket and threw it at the boy's head; he went into the water."

When the two Yoálox learned what had happened to the boy they became very angry at their sister. Furiously, they seized the pieces of sea lion meat which were lying around the fire by the hearth. First they took the front part of the head with the mouth and threw it at their sister's feet, all the while shouting at her sneeringly: "Here you have the mouth which has spoken to you of love and covered you with kisses!" Then they seized the flippers, hurled them over to their sister, and said insolently: "Take these flippers which have embraced you and touched you with lust." Soon afterward they threw the back part before her feet and shouted angrily: "There you have the back, too, on which you have sat and on which the sea lion has carried you to his cave."

Finally the two Yoálox seized the large stomach part of the sea lion, tossed it to the ground in front of their sister, and cried scornfully: "Now you shall also have the part with which the sea lion excited and satisfied your desire!" The woman remained speechless and so horrified that she knew not what to do. She dared not even look at the pieces of meat, much less touch them.

A long time has passed since then. Every day this woman witnessed her brothers and Mákuxipa enjoy the fresh meat from the sea lion. Then finally she, too, once timidly took a small piece and tasted it. She liked the meat very much, and soon took bigger pieces. Gradually she calmed down over her loss and eventually forgot her husband, the big sea lion. From then on she ate the blubber and meat of the sea lion with as much pleasure as did her brothers.

Informant: Not known; pp. 1176-1182.

Summary

Sister of two culture heroes secretly falls in love with sea lion and eventually has a son by him. They go to live with brothers on condition that sea lion will not be harmed. Latter turns out to be a skillful hunter and a willing worker.

One day brothers treacherously kill sea lion after ordering their wife to take sea lion's wife on journey. Upon return, seeing her son unwittingly partaking with the others of sea lion father's meat, wife angrily transforms son into fish and is subsequently harassed by brothers. Eventually she forgets her dead husband and eats of his flesh.

Motif content

A2320.	Origin of animal characteristics: head.
B211.2.7.+.	Speaking sea lion. (B211.2.7. Speaking sea-beast.)
B314.	Helpful animal brothers-in-law.
B551.+.	Sea lion carries girl across water. (B551. Animal carries man across water.)
B600.+.	Marriage of woman to sea lion. (B600. Marriage of person to animal.)
B610.	Animal paramour.
B610.1.	Girl's animal lover slain by spying relatives.
B621.+.	Sea lion as suitor. (B621. Beast as suitor.)
B631.	Human offspring from marriage to animal.
B871.2.+.	Giant sea lion. (B871.2. Giant wild beasts.)
D170.	Transformation: man to fish.
D1812.4.	Future revealed by presentiment: "knowledge within."
D1827.2.	Person hears call for help from great distance.
G61.	Relative's flesh eaten unwittingly.
K800.	Killing or maiming by deception.
K959.2.1.	Woman's father and brothers kill her husband in sleep for having married against their wishes.
K2010.	Hypocrite pretends friendship but attacks.
K2211.1.	Treacherous brother-in-law.
K2212.	Treacherous sister.
K2212.2.	Treacherous sister-in-law.
P214.+.	Wife eats flesh of slain husband. (P214. Wife drinks blood of slain husband.)
Q253.1.	Bestiality punished.
Q450.	Cruel punishments.
R315.	Cave as refuge.
S70.+.	Cruel brothers. (S70. Other cruel relatives.)
S73.1.2.+.	Brothers kill and eat animal brother-in-law. (S73.1.2. Brother kills and eats brother.)
S139.2.+.	Slain sea lion brother-in-law dismembered. (S139.2. Slain person dismembered.)
S183.	Frightful meal.
T35.+.	Deception in order to meet lover. (T35. Lovers' rendezvous.)
T41.3.	Lovers' signal.
T231.	The faithless widow.

20*a*. Death is Introduced

The mother of the two Yoálox had finally grown old and fragile; her strength dwindled more and more from one day to the next. Weak and tired, she lay there until she was finally unable to move. When all strength had left her the two Yoálox carried her outside the hut and placed her in a good spot on the grass where the warm sun could shine on her.

The elder Yoálox sat down beside his mother without ever taking his eyes off her. Though he kept his eyes constantly turned on her she did not utter a sound. It made him unspeakably sad that his mother was lying there completely motionless, but he did not disturb her profound sleep, firmly hoping that she would soon get up again.

Because the elder Yoálox kept his eyes for a long time on his sleeping mother, and because he kept looking at her intensely and unswervingly, she finally began to move again. She opened her eyes and moved a little; sleep gradually left her. Slowly she regained consciousness from her deep sleep. At first she hardly stirred at all, for her totally exhausted state improved so gradually that it was barely noticeable. But for the elder Yoálox that was enough of a sign. He was beside himself with joy. Quickly he ran into the hut to inform his younger brother "Listen and rejoice," he said. "Our mother has awakened from her profound sleep. Very slowly she has begun to move. I am confident she will soon rise again!" These words put the younger Yoálox into a very bad mood and he sharply disagreed with his brother: "It must not come to that! Our mother is asleep because she is very old and totally decrepit. She must sleep now forever!" This is what actually happened: the mother soon stopped stirring and did not get up. The elder Yoálox left the hut and went to the place where his mother lay; he looked at her closely. And indeed, she lay there totally stiff. Again, as he had done before, he turned his fixed stare on her for a long time, but this time she did not move. She remained motionless: she was truly dead.

That was the first death. Since then all people must die.[29] The younger Yoálox wanted it that way.[30]

---

[29]Noteworthy are several agreements on this point between the Yamana and Selknam. Among the latter it is the elder brother who was prevented by his younger brother from arising again from the sleep of old age; through this, actual death was introduced (Gusinde 1931:588).

In Gusinde 1931:589, note 28, I pointed out that the Selknam prefer to use the phrase "elder Kwányip" instead of the name. The Yamana do not have a name at all for the "elder Yoálox."

[30]Toward the end of the story much bitterness and sadness were evident on the faces of the many people present at the thought that everyone sooner or later inevitably will die. Without saying a word all went away and silently slipped into their own huts. Sometimes the thought of dying very much depresses every Yamana.

Informant: Not known; pp. 1182-1183.

Summary

When old mother of two culture heroes falls into a very profound sleep (the sleep of death), elder son restores her to life by staring at her fixedly. Younger son, however, rules that all people must die, and the mother subsequently dies. That is how death was introduced among people.

Motif content

A515.1.	Culture heroes brothers.
A525.1.+.	Culture hero argues with his elder brother. (A525.1. Culture hero fights with his elder brother.)
A1335.	Origin of death.
D993.	Magic eye.
D1822.	Loss of magic sight.
D1960.4.	Deathlike sleep.
E1.	Person comes to life.
E50.	Resuscitation by magic.
E121.	Resuscitation by supernatural person.
L13.+.	Compassionate elder son. (L13. Compassionate youngest son.)
P231.	Mother and son.
P251.5.4.	Two brothers as contrasts.
Q2.	Kind and unkind.
R154.1.	Son rescues mother.

20*b*. Death Is Introduced

The two Yoálox were extremely intelligent men. When their mother had reached a very advanced age she finally lost all her strength. Thus she lay there and a profound sleep came over her. Then she no longer moved. The two Yoálox cried bitterly for they had lost their mother and were alone now. They took her outside and buried her. But the younger Yoálox loved his mother less; he did not cry nearly as loud nor as much as his elder brother.

Their mother had been buried for some time when one day they heard her voice outside, near the hut. Suddenly the elder Yoálox stopped crying and declared: "I shall cry no longer for I hear my mother's voice!" He hurried out of the hut, hoping to see her there. The younger Yoálox remained in the hut and shouted furiously at his mother: "Why are you coming back here? Leave us at once and stay away forever!" Then the mother retreated very slowly never to return again. The younger Yoálox only said, as though displeased with himself: "Why didn't we tell our mother right away not to return any more!"[31] And indeed, after that she stayed away forever.

Informant: Mašemikens; p. 1183.

Summary

   Mother of two culture heroes dies. One day they hear her voice again outside hut, but the younger brother tells her to go away. After that she never returns.

Motif content

A515.1.	Culture heroes brothers.
A1335.	Origin of death.
E1.	Person comes to life.
E58.	Resuscitation by weeping (tears).
E323.	Dead mother's friendly return.
E361.	Return from the dead to stop weeping.
E381.	Ghost summoned by weeping.
E440.	Walking ghost "laid."
L13.+.	Compassionate elder son. (L13. Compassionate youngest son.)
P231.	Mother and son.
P251.5.4.	Two brothers as contrasts.
Q2.	Kind and unkind.
S21.	Cruel son.
W155.3.	Man unable to weep for hardness of heart.

21. The Yoálox Brothers Go Away

   The two Yoálox brothers gave names to all objects and places, all plants and animals. They remained here on the earth for a long time. After they had grown old they finally went up to the sky with Yoálox-tárnuxipa and their other sisters. There they still stand today as stars.

Informant: Not known; p. 1183.

Motif content

A515.1.+.	Culture heroes two brothers and several sisters. (A515.1. Culture heroes brothers.)

---

[31]These words mean: why did we not early enough, and at the right moment, prevent our mother from arising from the sleep of death.

A560.   Culture hero's (demigod's) departure.
A566.2.   Culture hero ascends to heaven.
A761.   Ascent to stars. People or animals ascend to sky and become stars.
A1191.   All things receive names.
A2571.   How animals received their names.
D293.   Transformation: man to star.

Myths and Legends

EXPLANATORY MYTHS

22. The Selfish Cormorant[1]

The *éetex*[2] was always very selfish. One day he found a small spring that contained some water. It had not rained for a long time, so that all the people were terribly thirsty. But the *éetex* kept the small hole hidden and only went there in secret, unwilling to share the water with the others.

The *wasénim*[3] suffered immensely from thirst. He searched everywhere for water but could not find any. The *éetex* appeared very happy and contented; after all, he did not have to go thirsty. The *wasénim*, however, seemed sad and depressed. Despite anxious searching he had failed to find any water and was extremely thirsty. One day he asked the *éetex:* "How can you be so cheerful? It seems to me you don't feel any thirst at all!" The *éetex* answered: "I just open my mouth when it rains; then several raindrops fall in and that's enough for me." But the *wasénim* was cunning enough not to trust the *éetex* completely. He suspected that he had a spring somewhere from which he alone was drinking. Therefore he said to himself with great determination: "Some time I'm going to follow that *éetex!*"

He promptly summoned several other *wasénim* and together they waited for the *éetex* in a hiding place. Soon the latter and five other *éetex* came passing by. Slowly and carefully the *éetex* led the way for his companions, looking back anxiously with every step they took. The *wasénim* followed them with utmost caution. Whenever the *éetex*

---

[1]*See also Koppers 1924:194-197.*
[2]The Magellanic cormorant, *Phalacrocorax magellanicus* (Gusinde 1937:1189, fig. 91).
[3]The well-known tufted cormorant, *Phalacrocorax gaimardi.*

turned around and looked back, the *wasénim* quickly crouched down. In this way all of them slowly advanced, until finally the *éetex* reached the place where the little spring was. Once more they looked around and then quickly bent down to drink with great satisfaction. This, too, the *wasénim* were able to see. Swiftly but silently they proceeded. Coming from behind they threw themselves over the *éetex* who were standing far below at the edge of the small hole. They gave them such a hard push that they slid even farther down. Then the *wasénim* themselves began to drink. They drank for a long time, finishing all the water. At last they felt their great thirst quenched and were very content.

Therefore even nowadays the *éetex* calls "e, e, e" in a loud voice, just as he did in ancient times. His throat has always remained moist, for he had found a well to drink from and that way he did not have to go thirsty. But the *wasénim* still calls "eh, eh, eh" from a hoarse and empty throat, just as he used to do. At that time he could not find any water, and therefore his throat dried up completely. And on all cliffs one can see the two types of bird distributed in such a way that the *éetex* inhabit the lower surfaces and projections while the *wasénim* have the holes located farther up. On that occasion the *wasénim* had given the *éetex* such a strong push that the latter slid down forever. To this day the *éetex* looks back all the time, exactly as when he clandestinely went to his little well. He is still afraid of being watched and secretly followed.

Informant: Not known; pp. 1187-1188.

Summary

During a bad drought the Magellanic cormorant finds a well but keeps it for himself and his kind. Tufted cormorants suffering from thirst discover this, follow the others, push them down into well, and drink all the water. Since then Magellanic cormorants live in habitat below the other birds, and their voices are not as hoarse as the others', since they always had water during the drought.

Motif content

A2210.	Animal characteristics: change in ancient animal.
A2423.1.+.	Why voice of tufted cormorant is hoarse. (A2423.1. Animal's ugly voice.)
A2426.2.+.	Call of Magellanic cormorant. (A2426.2. Cries of birds.)
A2431.+.	Why tufted cormorant nests on high ground. (A2431. Birds' nests.)
A2431.+.	Why Magellanic cormorant nests on lower ground. (A2431. Birds's nests.)

A2471.9.+.	Why cormorants always look back. (A2471.9. Why animals always look down.)
B263.5.	War between groups of birds.
B266.1.+.	Thirsty cormorants fight over well. (B266.1. Thirsty cattle fight over well.)
C429.1.	Tabu: mentioning secret water spring.
N452.1.+.	Remedy for lack of water in certain place found by spying on birds. (N452.1. Remedy for lack of water in certain place overheard in conversation of animals [demons].)
Q276.	Stinginess punished.
W152.	Stinginess.
W155.5.	Permission refused to drink from water tank.

23. The Revenge of the Tufted Cormorants

Once there was a man sitting on the beach while his wife was gathering mussels. She saw smoke rising nearby and asked her husband: "Who can that be who is coming here?" The man answered: "That has to be the *wasénim*, for they are very clumsy, deformed paunch-bellies!" Meanwhile these people[4] had gotten close enough to overhear quite clearly that man's contemptuous remark.

The *wasénim* got out of their canoes and right away started to build a hut. In the course of this they tried to strike up a conversation with the man asking him for fire. Their behavior was decidely peculiar. Then the man realized that the *wasénim* must have overheard his contemptuous comment. So he invited them in a friendly manner: "Come into my hut and make yourselves at home; there is room enough!" But the *wasénim* replied in a waspish tone: "We can't possibly accept your invitation. After all, we're deformed paunch-bellies and incapable of walking through the entrance!" Now the man was certain, and very courteously gave them the desired fire. The *wasénim* settled down in their own hut. They began discussing how they could make a fool of that man and take revenge on him who had insulted them gravely and behaved so contemptuously toward them.

Soon night fell. Now the *wasénim* asked the man: "Do you feel like accompanying us to fish and hunt? The weather is very favorable!" They intended to play a good practical joke on him. The man found himself more or less compelled to agree; his wife, the *éetexkípa*,[5]

---

[4] The tufted cormorant, *Phalacrocorax gaimardi*, common species in this area.
[5] The other species of native cormorant, *Phalacrocorax magellanicus*.

belonged to the family of the *wasénim,* and for this reason alone he was not free to refuse the invitation. So all of them got into the canoe of the *wasénim.* In the stern sat the *éetexkípa;* she paddled and steered the boat. They went far out. Finally they reached an island where they disembarked and killed many sea lions and collected large amounts of fish. They loaded the catch into their canoe.

The *éetexkípa* was very shrewd and cunning; besides, the *wasénim* had secretly given her some advance instructions.[6] She was still sitting in the stern of the canoe, paddling and steering it such that the current could not pull it out from shore. When the bulk of the catch had been loaded on board she continued to move her paddle as though to keep the canoe near shore. But that was deliberately deceitful. She actually let the canoe slowly drift farther and farther away from the beach. All the while the *wusénim* were bringing the last part of their catch from the island to the canoe. The latter was now floating far away from the island but the *wasénim* were flying back and forth, bringing meat and leaving again. The *éetexkípa* was still sitting in the stern paddling with preplanned deceitfulness.

The husband had remained on the island. He could not fly. When the last *wasénim* was about to leave the island to get into the canoe he asked the man: "Well, aren't you thinking of coming with us? All the men have already gotten in. Take a long jump and you'll be in the canoe!" Not until then did the man realize that the canoe had gone far out. Disappointedly he said: "I can't jump all the way there; it's too far for me." The *wasénim* encouraged him: "Don't you see how your wife is paddling all the time? She can't possibly bring the canoe closer to you! All right, then you have to stay here!" With a long jump the last *wasénim* sprang into the canoe. The man was unable to follow, because the canoe had gone too far out. All the *wasénim* laughed very loudly and maliciously shouted over to the man on the island: "Well, are you convinced now that we are no clumsy paunch-bellies? Just look at us: all of us have reached the canoe with one jump! But you may indeed have to stay behind over there." Then they paddled away and did not even look back.

Thus the man sat all alone on the island and found himself in a great dilemma. Yet he knew how to get out of it. The next morning he looked for a thick cudgel and with it killed a big male sea lion. He made a little cut in the stomach, and through this small opening he took out all the meat and fat. The skin he placed in such a way that it quickly dried.

[6]Here it is made clear that a woman unhesitatingly sticks by her family, even against her husband if he has offended her honor.

Then he sewed up all the openings and inflated the entire skin very tightly. He pushed it into the water where it stayed afloat. So he mounted it and finally, after a good while, reached the place where his hut stood. Those *wasénim* had surely taken revenge on the man who had ridiculed them so.

Informant: Not known; pp. 1188-1190.

Summary

A man ridicules some tufted cormorants. In conspiracy with his wife, a Magellanic cormorant, the cormorants abandon the man on an island during a fishing expedition. He escapes to the mainland on a blown-up sea lion skin.

Motif content

B211.3.	Speaking bird.
B299.1.	Animal takes revenge on man.
B652.	Marriage to bird in human form.
C94.3.	Tabu: mocking animal.
C871.+.	Tabu: refusing a request from wife's relatives. (C871. Tabu: refusing a request.)
F841.	Extraordinary boat (ship).
H1223.1.	Quest to recover one's honor through feats.
K700.	Capture by deception.
K778.	Capture through the wiles of a woman.
K1616.	Marooned man reaches home and outwits marooner.
K2010.	Hypocrite pretends friendship but attacks.
K2213.	Treacherous wife.
P211.	Wife chooses father's side in feud. Must choose between husband and father.
Q288.	Punishment for mockery.
R210.	Escapes.
S145.	Abandonment on an island.
X137.	Humor of ugliness.

24. The Revenge of the Eagle Owl

There once lived a widow. She had a son by her deceased husband. They were both living in his uncle's hut. But the uncle treated his nephew very badly and gave him little to eat. So the nephew grew thinner from one day to the next. Instead of good food all he ever got from his uncle was a *kéti*.[7] Although the casing was made from the intestines of guanaco, the blood inside was collected from the noses of several people. They poked around in their noses with a small stick until blood flowed.[8] It was this strange *kéti* that the uncle gave his nephew to eat. Precisely for that reason the little boy was getting very thin. Neither did any of the other people treat the little boy with kindness; nobody gave him anything to eat.

Finally the boy was unable to stand this mistreatment any longer. He had often complained to his mother: "My uncle gives me only a little bit to eat, and even what he gives me is bad. I'm so miserable from this that I can't stand it any longer!" Finally the mother advised him: "Then go hunting yourself and try to kill a guanaco." He answered: "How can I go hunting when I have no *kíli* (sandals)?" The mother then cut a piece of leather from her *mašakána* (loincloth) and made her son a pair of sandals. He put them on and hurried out to go hunting.

He promptly headed for a high mountain ridge. But his uncle had always said: "That mountain ridge over there is very high; nobody can cross it! It's a pity, for on the other side there are always many guanacos." Then the little boy said to himself: "I'll try to cross that ridge anyway. Maybe I can hunt a guanaco on the other side!" Thus he got close to the hill and began to climb. He crept forward and killed several large animals. Afterward he looked around and saw that the mountain ridge had completely disappeared. He was tremendously happy over this and said: "How wonderful! Now I can get back to my hut quite easily and quickly." He rested a little while. Then he loaded a guanaco on his shoulders. More he really could not carry, for he was still a child, and after all, not very strong. He left the other guanacos he had killed behind. Planning to return for them the following day, he had put them all together in a pile.

The boy did not return to his mother until late at night. She was very happy when she saw him arriving with a large guanaco. He immediately cut off several big pieces, and the two began to eat. Their neighbors in the adjacent huts soon heard how those two were crushing big bones with a stone and sucking marrow. They marveled among themselves: "Who could have given them the meat? One can clearly hear the old woman smashing big bones to get at the marrow." Finally several women went over to that hut and saw the large guanaco lying

[7]A kind of blood sausage which the Yamana find tasty (Gusinde 1937:584).

[8]The Selknam amuse themselves with this unusual play during the men's secret festival, pretending before their wives to mistreat certain spirits. The Yamana do the same thing during the *kína* (Gusinde 1931:914).

there. The old woman immediately invited her visitors to help themselves and eat with them. "My little son has just brought in this large
guanaco," she explained. "He killed it himself!" The women laughed
and shook their heads in disbelief. They said: "How could a child this
small have killed such a guanaco and carried it here? Besides, how is he
supposed to have carried it here from the other side of the mountain
ridge, which is not accessible even to a strong man." After they had
eaten well they went back to their huts. Everywhere they related what
the old woman had told them. Then the others, too, called the old
woman and questioned her. She confirmed everything and even gave
everybody a good piece of meat from the guanaco. Still nobody
believed what she said. Finally she replied: "Why don't you go tomorrow to the other side of the mountain ridge. Then you can see for
yourselves the many guanacos my little son has killed and left behind
because he couldn't carry them all!"

The old woman went back to her hut where she told her son: "The
people didn't believe what I said. So I finally suggested that tomorrow
they go there themselves and fetch the many guanacos you have killed
and left behind." The small boy, however, did not like that; after all,
he had been treated badly by these people and so was unwilling now to
share his catch with them. Nevertheless, many men went out with the
boy the following day. They easily passed the place that his uncle had
always said nobody was able to cross and then, a short distance on the
other side, he showed the men the guanacos he had killed the day
before. Indeed the animals were still completely fresh; not even the
intestines had been taken out. Therefore the men could no longer doubt
that this little boy had really killed all those guanacos.

Now the boy loaded a big guanaco on his shoulders and started on
the way back. Each of the men also picked up a guanaco. With this
they set off. But soon they noticed that their guanacos were getting
very heavy. They had to rest all the time and progress was slow. Only
the boy seemed not to notice the burden at all and soon left the rest of
the men far behind him! It vexed them that the little boy was advancing
so rapidly while they themselves had to rest every instant, exhausted.
They hardly took a few steps when they had to sit down and rest
again. Again and again they got up; but just as quickly did they tire
again. They worked so hard and grew so exhausted that all of them
turned into *kuhúrux*.[9]

Actually only the little boy made it back to his hut within a short
time. When the other people in the camp saw him arrive with a big

[9]The big eagle owl, *Bubo magellanicus* (Gusinde 1937:42).

guanaco they begged him for meat. But he told them: "I can't give you any of my guanaco. Wait a while until the other men, your relatives, who left with me this morning, get back. After all, you never gave me anything to eat either. So just wait for your relatives!" And they waited for a long time. But the eagle owls did not arrive until late at night. They brought nothing at all. They approached the huts where they and their relatives lived but did not enter. They also came to the hut where the little boy and his mother were sitting. They could see how the two were eating, but they did not receive anything nor did they enter. They only called: "Kuhúrux, kuhúrux." Then they went away and stayed in the forest forever. Even today they still come to the huts at night. But they do not come in and nobody gives them anything. They only call: "Kuhúrux, kuhúrux," then leave the huts and return to the forest.

Informant: Not known; pp. 1190-1193.

Summary

A fatherless boy is mistreated by his uncle and others. Finally, in order to get food he crosses a supposedly inaccessible mountain ridge and kills many large guanacos. Although he brings one back with him nobody believes his story. To convince them he leads several men to the place. On the way back the guanacos carried by each one grow so heavy that the exhausted men turn into owls. Only the boy reaches the village. Since that time eagle owls sit outside men's huts at night, calling "Kuhúrux, kuhúrux."

Motif content

A2238.	Animal characteristics: punishment for greed.
A2426.2.	Cries of birds.
D153.2.	Transformation: man to owl.
D932.	Magic mountain.
D1687.	Object magically becomes heavy.
D1691.	Magic suspension of weight.
D1717.	Magic power of children.
D1830.	Magic strength.
D2121.	Magic journey.
D2152.1.	Magic leveling of mountain.
D2188.	Magic disappearance.
F611.3.2.	Hero's precocious strength. Has full strength when very young.
F679.5.	Skillful hunter.
F701.	Land of plenty.
F851.	Extraordinary food.
J1341.	Retort from underfed servant (child).
N827.	Child as helper.

P231.   Mother and son.
W285.   Cruelty punished.
Q580.   Punishment fitted to crime.
S71.   Cruel uncle.
S183.   Frightful meal.
W11.   Generosity.

25. The Otter and His Five Brothers-in-law

The *áiapux*[10] lived in the same hut with his five brothers-in-law. But
the five brothers-in-law did not get along with him too well; they
constantly mocked and played nasty tricks on him. In the beginning the
áiapux did not realize this at all. But when his five brothers-in-law
continued to ridicule him, he finally became aware that they were
making him the object of their horseplay. He became really furious and
said to himself: "Something is wrong between me and my brothers-in-
law! They're making fun of me in a rude way!" Then he considered
what to do to them.

Furiously one day he left his hut; he wanted to run away and take a
full measure of revenge on his brothers-in-law. He went south, walking
far and long, until he came to a projecting rocky point against which
the surf beats strongly and the waves build up to mountains. From this
point one could clearly see the hut that he had just left, and where his
five brothers-in-law were still sitting. In this place he now quickly built
a hut for himself. Then he made a signal fire as though a whale were
beached there. His five brothers-in-law noticed the signal at once and
said to themselves: "The *áiapux* went south. It must be he who made
the fire. That will stand us in good stead, there must be a whale over
there!" Then they said to the youngest brother: "You're the youngest:
go and see what's there." So the youngest put on his fur coat and left.

Meanwhile the *áiapux* had cleaned all the ground around his hut.
Then he carried off a lot of sand so that the path to the entrance of his
hut rose steeply; finally he poured water on the path to make it very
slippery. When the youngest of the brothers got close he looked around
everywhere but failed to see any trace of a whale. From some distance
he also looked into the hut but no whale blubber or meat was to be
seen there either. Then he said to himself: "How is it that I can't find
anything? I see no trace here of a whale!" Now the *áiapux* called him

[10]The large otter, *Lutra felina* (Gusinde 1937:536; cf. ibid., p. 1277, fig. 94).

from his hut: "Come in here, my brother-in-law!" When the latter began to walk up the short path it was so slick that he slipped and fell. As he was lying flat on the ground the *áiapux* raised his harpoon and killed him on the spot. Then he dragged the body up to the hut and threw it to the side where it could not be seen.

Soon afterward there was another fire signal to fool the other brothers into believing that the two of them were having a feast. The brothers noticed the fire immediately and said to themselves: "Our youngest brother has not come back yet and the two are again making a fire. It would be best if the second youngest of us went to see what's really going on there!" This brother got up without delay and went to the hut of the *áiapux*. As he got closer he looked around but did not notice any sign of a whale. He approached the hut and looked inside, but there were no signs of a fresh whale there, either. The *áiapux* called to him from inside: "Just come in, we'll talk here. I notice you're looking for a whale! But first join me in here!" Then this brother-in-law, too, walked up the steep, slick path. Just as he was about to bend down in front of the entrance he slipped and fell. In this instant the *áiapux* threw his harpoon at him from inside the hut so that he fell dead on the spot. Again the *áiapux* was very pleased. This body, too, he threw to the side, saying to himself: "That's the way I'm going to take revenge on all of those who ridiculed me!"

Not long after that he again lit a fire and quickly smothered it so that a thick cloud of smoke rose into the air. The other three brothers noticed it and said: "How can it be that neither of our brothers comes back? They must be calling us!" They told the third youngest brother: "Now it's your turn; go there and see what's really going on!" He left at once. He, too, looked around on that cliff without noticing any sign of a whale. Finally the *áiapux* called him from his hut: "You, my brother-in-law, come into my hut!" And the brother-in-law went closer. But as he bent down to enter, he slipped on the treacherous ground and fell. At once the *áiapux* killed him, too, with his harpoon and threw the body to the side.

Again the *áiapux* made a big fire and quickly put it out so that a thick cloud of smoke went up. The eldest brother said to the other: "I can't explain to myself what's really going on there: Three of our brothers have already gone over, and none of them has come back! Maybe they're having a big feast over there? You go now and come back soon with our brothers." Thus the fourth brother went to the hut of the *áiapux*. The latter called him forward. As he went to enter the hut he likewise slipped and was killed. The *áiapux* threw the body to the side. Full of satisfaction he said to himself: "Four of my brothers-in-law have already paid with their lives for having ridiculed me; so now there's only one of them left!"

He made another signal fire. The eldest of the brothers noticed that and said to himself: "Again a fire, yet none of my brothers has come back? Now I'll take my weapons and see for myself what's really going on!" He suspected something bad for he remembered how rudely all five had earlier made fun of their brother-in-law. He reached the place and looked around but found no trace of a whale. So he said to himself: "There was no whale beached here, hence something evil must have happened to my brothers!" He approached the hut of the *áiapux*. The latter called to him: "Well, my brother-in-law, have you finally come? Just enter my hut!" The brother-in-law thought: "He must have lured my brothers into his hut and killed them in there!" Therefore he answered the *áiapux*: "Oh, I like it better out here; you come out for a while and tell me about my brothers, who have kept me waiting so long!" To this the *áiapux* replied from within: "I don't like it out there; you come inside!" Finally the eldest brother said: "All right then, I'll come." He rushed toward the hut but from the rear, and quickly pulled out a few stakes to let himself in. Then to his horror he saw the bodies of his brothers lying one on top of the other. In a rage he shouted: "Now I'll take revenge on you!" He immediately forced his way in with a cudgel and cut off the *áiapux*'s hands and feet; then he killed him.

Therefore even today the *áiapux* lives in holes under the ground. He comes out but rarely and then only when nobody can see him; otherwise he keeps himself hidden. He is after other animals, especially dogs, and is also an enemy of people. He behaves badly toward everybody. All his limbs have remained short since then.

Informant: Not known; pp. 1193-1195.

Summary

Otter is constantly ridiculed by his five brothers-in-law. In revenge he lures four of them into a trap one by one, then kills them. The eldest brother finally sees through the ruse and in his turn kills the otter after cutting off his hands and feet. This is why otter now has short limbs.

Motif content

A2230.	Animal characteristics as punishment.
A2371.+.	Why otter has short legs. (A2371. Origin and nature of animal's legs.)
A2433.3.+.	Why otter keeps hidden in holes underground. (A2433.3. Haunts of various animals—mammals.)

A2494.4.+.	Enmity between dog and otter. (A2494.4. The dog's enemies.)
A2585.	Why there is enmity between certain animals and man.
H1223.1.	Quest to recover one's honor through feats.
H1242.+.	Oldest brother alone succeeds on quest. (H1242. Youngest brother alone succeeds on quest.)
K810.	Fatal deception into trickster's power.
K815.	Victim lured by kind words approaches trickster and is killed.
K839.2.	Victim lured into approach by false token.
K912.2.+.	Men lured into trap one by one and killed. (K912.2. Men lured into serpent pit one by one and killed.)
K1641.	Ambushed trickster killed by intended victim.
K2211.1.	Treacherous brother-in-law.
P251.3.1.	Brothers strive to avenge each other.
Q288.	Punishment for mockery.
Q411.6.	Death as punishment for murder.
Q451.0.1.	Hands and feet cut off as punishment.
S50.+.	Cruel brothers-in-law. (S50. Cruel relatives-in-law.)
S115.	Murder by stabbing.

26. The Wild Goose Couple

In the old days, to cover their bodies women wore only their *mašakána*[11] and a short cover hanging down the back. They always took off the back cover when inside the hut. There once lived a woman who had a little son. One day her husband went out to hunt for several days. As usual, the woman devoted herself to her work in the hut. She did not pay too much attention to herself whenever she bent down, but her little son was watching her attentively and could see her private parts from behind. He took great pleasure in this and thought about it constantly. From then on he cried over and over: "I like that thing there! I like that thing there!" Since he was constantly crying the same words his mother wanted to let him have his wish. She brought edible mussels and snails, sea urchins and crabs, fish and berries, showed him one after the other, and offered it to him kindly. But discontentedly he rejected every single thing, turned away his head, and only repeated: "I like that thing there!" At the same time he pointed to his mother's private parts, but she did not understand what he wanted. She brought

---

[11]The loincloth is described in Gusinde 1937:406; cf. ibid., p. 408, fig. 16. For the women's back cover see Gusinde 1937:405.

little baskets and necklaces, feather ornaments and beautiful stones, weapons and tools, even small birds and a small dog. But the boy angrily rejected all this and turned away from it, saying again and again: "I like that thing there!" Finally the mother was completely at a loss and embarrassed; she no longer knew what to do. She was unable to discover what her small son really wanted and could not understand why he was always screaming: "I like that thing there!" She had shown and offered him everything within her reach, but nothing had calmed him down.

Finally the mother pretended to be very tired. She lay down and acted as if she were going to sleep, for she expected her little son soon to fall asleep, too. He did indeed remain still, likewise pretending that he was going to sleep. The mother got up after some time and looked for her baskets, talking quietly to herself as she went: "I'll go to the beach now to collect mussels." She took her basket and left the hut. Just a few steps from the hut she came across some big mussels. She bent down and gathered them in her basket. Meanwhile her little son had half sat up on his bed and turned his eyes on his mother. When she was thus gathering mussels in a bent-over position he again saw her private parts from behind and was delighted. He quickly got up and painted his head, his face, and the upper part of his body all black with charcoal dust, but his legs he covered with *imi* [red soil for painting]. He left the hut and hurried down to the beach where his mother was. He went by some women who were also gathering mussels. Unobtrusively he looked at their private parts from behind but did not touch any of these women. When he was standing close by his mother he put his hand on her genitals and began to play with them. He liked this play very much and it increased his pleasure. His mother liked it, too, and she gave in to him. But so that the other women would not notice what the two were doing to each other they hurried to their canoe, got in, and went over to an island nearby. Here they were all alone. They lay down and had intercourse. They stayed together for a long time in this way. During this they were eventually transformed into birds.

The following day both left the desert island and flew back to the shore where the huts of the people were. Here they sat on a stone exactly in front of the hut where they had lived until the day before. In the meantime the man had come back from the hunt, and when he could not find his wife and his son in the hut, he anxiously inquired among the other people: "Where are my wife and my little son? I see them neither in the hut nor elsewhere." The people answered him: "Just look at that stone: two birds are sitting there that were not there before.

Those two *šékus*[12] are your wife and your little son. They fell head over heels in love and were turned into birds." Since that time the two accompany each other constantly and, to this day, live together exclusively by themselves.[13]

Informant: Julia; pp. 1195-1197.

Summary

Little boy secretly enjoys looking at his mother's sexual organs. One day during husband's absence they have intercourse on desert island and subsequently turn into birds. Since then these birds always live together.

Motif content

A2411.2.	Origin of color of bird.
A2497.+.	Why bird is monogamous. (A2497. Monogamy among animals.)
C114.	Tabu: incest.
D150.	Transformation: man to bird.
D565.5.1.	Transformation by sexual intercourse.
J1820.	Inappropriate action from misunderstanding.
K1868.	Deception by pretending sleep.
P231.	Mother and son.
P231.3.	Mother-love.
T410.+.	Lecherous son. (T410. Incest.)
T412.	Mother-son incest.

27. The Little Woodpecker

Although little *detehúrux* was still very young[14] he had already fallen in love, and with his own mother, at that. She was always carrying her

---

[12]The powerful, heavy wild goose, *Chloëphaga hybrida* (Gusinde 1937:43).

[13]This story signifies that sexual intercourse between mother and son is completely unnatural and impossible among people; indeed, it is only among animals that it occurs. The so-called explanatory element in this myth lies in the couple's strictly monogamous life.

During a short discussion I pointed out that the female of the species *Chloëphaga hybrida* has a black head and front whereas the male is completely white. Old Julia, whom I have to thank for this myth, replied: "We know very well that the *šékuš* male has all white feathers and that the female is colored mostly black. However, the old people have always told us the story the way in which I just repeated it."

[14]In the Cape Horn area there are two species of woodpecker. This myth is dedicated to the smaller of the two, *Dendrocopus lignarius* (Gusinde 1937:42).

little son around with her. For that purpose she had made a bag from pieces of hide; she put the little *detehúrux* into it and constantly carried him around on her back. She never took the little boy out of the bag, and whenever she left her hut she slung the bag on her back. That way the small boy was never without his mother.

This woman went frequently into the forest. She told the people: "I find the *ésef*[15] so delicious that I always have to go out into the forest to collect a lot of these mushrooms." But she always went alone, taking only her son along in the bag. As soon as she found a hidden place in the forest she stopped. Her little son became a full-grown man and quickly left the sack in which he had been sitting. Without delay he climbed up into the trees and picked *ésef*. Then he threw many of them down to the woman below who gathered them up. After some time he called to his mother from up there: "Lie down on the ground and part your legs as far as you can; I want to throw *ésef* into your vagina!" The woman immediately lay down on the ground with great pleasure, and with her legs stretched far apart she opened her vagina very wide. The son hit his mother's vagina with the *ésef* thrown from the tree, which was a very great pleasure for both of them. After playing like this for a rather long time the son climbed down from the tree. Then he lay down on his mother and she received him with great pleasure, for his penis was extremely large.

After they had spent a long time doing this they finally got up. The son got into the bag, became smaller and smaller, until he had become an infant again. The mother hurried back to the hut with him. Again they had returned with a large amount of *ésef*. These they distributed among the other women; all ate a lot and appeared very content. The mother and her son went often to the forest, but always alone, and every time they played around in this wicked manner.

The other women were mystified and asked the woman: "How do you manage to gather that many *ésef* in so short a time? You always bring a large amount to the camp." Calmly the woman replied: "I always go out alone into the forest and climb up into the trees to quickly pick a lot of *ésef*." From then on the other women did exactly as that mother had told them; but still they were unable to gather that many *ésef* in so short a time.

Finally one day several women followed the mother unnoticed as she again disappeared alone into the forest. As usual, she was carrying only

[15]Mushroom; this general term is used for all stages of growth of the species *Cyttaria darwinii* (Gusinde 1937:554).

her son in the bag. When the two had gone far into the forest the astonished women saw how the little son quickly left the bag and became a full-grown man. He promptly climbed up into the trees and rapidly broke off a large number of *ésef*. Below, the mother hastened to gather up the *ésef*. Then after a while the son again called to her from above: "Lie down on the ground and part your legs as far as you can, I want to throw *ésef* into your vagina!" The woman immediately lay down on the ground with great pleasure, and with her legs stretched far apart she opened her vagina very wide. The son hit his mother's vagina with the *ésef* thrown from the tree, which was a great pleasure for both of them. After playing like this for a rather long time the son climbed down from the tree. Then he lay down on his mother and she received him with great pleasure, for his penis was extremely large.

The women saw and heard all this from their hiding place and were horrified. Unnoticed, they rushed back to their huts and soon revealed to the husband of the woman that the two of them, the mother and the son, would go off together and yield to incestuous pleasure. He seemed very surprised, for until then he had believed his son to be very small still. Indeed his mother always carried him in the bag on her back without ever letting him out; the father had so far only seen his face. In fact, the mother had never allowed the little boy to leave the bag if another person was in the hut. She carried the bag firmly strapped to her back. For she said to herself: "If I let my son out of the bag his father will notice at once that his penis is very long. In view of this he will start to suspect that he has intercourse with a woman!" Thus she kept the son always tied up in the bag and carried him constantly around with her. She did not let him out at night either, because he had nothing with which to cover his body.

The husband now considered what those women had revealed to him. He took a knife and made it sharp enough to cut leather. The following day his wife hurried again into the forest and did not return until evening. As usual she was carrying her little son in the bag on her back. She brought very many *ésef*. Then he spoke to her in a friendly tone: "Why do you never put down the bag with the little boy? After all, that load must be very heavy if you carry it around with you all day." She replied curtly, fending him off: "Our little son is still very small, so that I have to protect him extra carefully! Actually I don't notice any burden at all; our boy is still very small, you know." But the husband quickly replied: "Do rest a little now and trust me with the bag!" In saying this he took his sharp knife and severed the leather straps by which the bag hung from his wife's back. At once the bag dropped down and tore apart. The little boy fell to the ground and on his back with his legs far apart. Then the father could see his son's large penis, as he was not dressed. Now he knew enough! Beside himself with horror he seized the knife he had sharpened, and cut off his son's large penis. Although much blood flowed, the furious man let him lie there. Finally the little boy became a bird. Since then he has stayed in the forest and never again returned to his parents' hut. That is the little *detehúrux* who even today has a powerful beak with a long, red tongue inside.[16]

Informant: Not known; pp. 1197-1199.

Summary

Mother always carries infant son in a bag on her back. Every day they go to gather mushrooms in forest, where baby son becomes full-grown man and they have intercourse. When other women discover this they notify husband who cuts off boy's penis. Boy becomes a woodpecker and goes to live in forest.

Motif content

A2343.3.2.+.	Why woodpecker has strong beak. (A2343.3.2. Why woodpecker has sharp beak.)
A2344.	Origin and nature of animal's tongue.
C114.	Tabu: incest.
D153.1.	Transformation: man to woodpecker.
D631.1.	Person changes size at will.
F547.3.1.	Long penis.
H79.+.	Recognition by long penis. (H79.Recognition by physical attributes—miscellaneous.)
K1500.	Deception connected with adultery.
K1521.	Paramour successfully hidden from husband.
K1550.1.	Husband discovers wife's adultery.
K1558.1.	Husband castrates paramour.
N440.+.	Secret learned. (N440. Valuable secrets learned.)
Q242.	Incest punished.
Q451.10.1.	Punishment: castration.
Q584.2.	Transformation of man to animal as fitting punishment.
T412.	Mother-son incest.
T475.	Unknown (clandestine) paramour.
T615.	Supernatural growth.

[16]Although the myth is in itself obvious, its meaning is made even more explicit with these words.

28. The Woodpecker Brother and Sister

The two *lána*[17] were brother and sister. From their earliest youth they lived with their parents and grew up together. When they had grown a bit older they began to meet in a hiding place. Here they caressed each other and yielded to their desire. For a long time they secretly carried on their evil pleasure in this way.

The other people finally noticed that the two were meeting secretly. They became very upset over this, loudly criticized the evil doings of the brother and sister, and threatened them with severe punishment because of their disgusting behavior. But neither the boy nor the girl listened to people's scolding; they met secretly and carried on with each other as before. After a long time all the people were extremely angry and would no longer stand for the improper behavior of the brother and sister. They explained everything in detail to their parents. When the father heard this he became furious; he was beside himself with anger over what his degenerate children were doing. He summoned both of them, took some *ími* and painted his daughter's head with it. At the same time he said furiously: "Since you are doing such bad things you shall henceforth remain together always! Now get out of my hut!"

Then the two left their parent's hut and fled into the forest where they had been meeting for their evil doings. Since then those two, brother and sister, have stayed together and to this day live all by themselves as husband and wife.[18]

Informant: Julia; pp. 1199-1200.

Summary

As punishment for sexual relations between woodpecker brother and sister their father paints girl's head red and then banishes them. Since then they live together in forest.

[17]The large woodpecker of the Tierra del Fuego region, *Ipocrantor magellanicus.* It has coal black feathers, and the male has a bright scarlet tuft. Couples live strictly monogamously.

[18]After old Julia had finished this story I asked for some explanation. As is well known, *Ipocrantor magellanicus* shows a striking difference between the sexes in that only the male has bright scarlet feathers on his head. I pointed to this and asked whether she might not have made a mistake in speaking. She only replied: "The south-people tell this story as I have told it." Obviously this confusion of sex is of no importance. A year later I heard the following variant of this myth from Calderón, who belongs to the western group. In this, the animal with the head painted red appears as the brother, in closer agreement with the sex of this species of bird.

Motif content

A2412.2.+.	Why woodpecker has red head. (A2412.2. Markings on birds.)
A2497.+.	Why woodpecker is monogamous. (12497. Monogamy among animals.)
C114.	Tabu: incest.
C987.	Curse as punishment for breaking tabu.
D525.	Transformation through curse.
J652.	Inattention to warnings.
M411.1.	Curse by parent.
N440.+.	Secret learned. (N440. Valuable secrets learned.)
Q242.	Incest punished.
T35.	Lover's rendezvous.
T415.	Brother-sister incest.
T415.5.	Brother-sister marriage.

29. The Woodpecker Couple

A brother had fallen in love with his own sister.[19] He therefore tried in every way possible to meet and sleep with her. His sister had long noticed his intention. She avoided him every time for she did not want to have forbidden intercourse with him. Yet she was of two minds, half willing, half unwilling. The brother considered what pretext to use to lure her out of the hut.

One day he discovered big berries[20] in a clearing in the forest. A sly thought occurred to him. He said to himself: "I shall tell my sister now that I have found big berries here. After that I'm sure she'll come here." He promptly ran back to the hut and told his sister: "I have found big berries in a certain place in the forest; you should go there and get them!" The girl took her basket and hurried into the woods.

Without anybody noticing it the brother quickly sneaked after her. He hid in a place where his sister had to pass. Once she had gotten close enough he embraced her. Then both lay down and yielded to their desire. But when they wanted to get up after the wicked thing they had done, they found themselves turned into birds. Both were all black. In addition, the brother has since had a bright red head;[21] it was those big,

[19]Here, too, males and females of the large woodpecker species *Ipocrantor magellanicus* are meant.
[20]The well-liked fruits of *Pernettya mucronata* (Gusinde 1937:121, fig. 12).
[21]This clearly refers to the dimorphism between male and female, already alluded to on p. 79 n. 18.

red berries that he pointed out to his sister in order to do bad things with her.[22]

Informant: Calderón; p. 1201.

Summary

Brother tricks his sister into sexual intercourse. As punishment they turn into birds and assume present-day physical characteristics of woodpecker.

Motif content

A2412.2.+.	Why woodpecker has red head. (A2412.2. Markings on birds.)
C114.	Tabu: incest.
D153.1.	Transformation: man to woodpecker.
K1330.	Girl tricked into man's room (or power).
Q242.	Incest punished.
Q584.2.	Transformation of man to animal as fitting punishment.
T415.	Brother-sister incest.
T415.1.	Lecherous brother. Wants to seduce (marry) his sister.

30. The Revenge of the Gerfalcon

There were once two brothers who lived together. The elder brother had a wife; the younger one was still a bachelor. They both lived in the same hut and had been together in this way for a long time. Eventually it came about that the younger brother fell in love with his sister-in-law. The two met very often and caressed each other in every way.

After some time the elder brother became aware of their love play. He watched the two until he was finally convinced that they loved each other. He did not reveal anything to his younger brother. But one day when the latter had gone far away the elder brother called his wife and said to her: "I have often watched you caressing your brother-in-law, because you are very much in love with him. If you don't stay away from my brother I'll punish you severely and much to your own great shame. Mark my words: if henceforth you don't stay away from my

---

[22]This tale is obviously a variant of the preceding one. Both set out to explain the strikingly close and enduring relationship of the monogamous woodpecker couple. The second version is a more substantive and perfect narrative, while the first lays greater stress on the moral gravity of incest.

brother I will no longer believe your love for me. Then I'll take thorough revenge; I'll turn myself into a powerful bird with claws strong enough to seize you and lift you up. So be careful! Otherwise I'll carry out my plan of revenge and you'll be disgraced and shamed." The woman listened in silence.

After a while the two renewed their love play. The woman seemed to have totally forgotten her husband's threats of harsh punishment and humiliating shame. For a long time the two met secretly just as often as before and yielded to their desire. At last the elder brother left his hut for good and withdrew into the forest to carry out the threats against his faithless wife.

In the forest he built himself a hut and stayed there. He now began experimenting to see if he could turn himself into a bird. He often left his hut to watch the birds. Before long he noticed that every bird builds its nest high up in a tree. He, too, then left his hut and climbed up into a tree. He continued to watch all the birds very closely to see what they did. He discovered how every bird sits on a twig or at the edge of the nest when it defecates and lets the excrement fall down. Thus he, too, from then on sat on a twig when he defecated and let the excrement fall down. He continued to watch the birds and soon began to imitate their singing. He studied their movements too and began to move his arms exactly as birds move their wings, and to jump exactly as they do.

After a long time he visited the hut where his wife was living with his younger brother. The latter received him with mocking laughter and said scornfully: "Well, when are you finally going to transform yourself into a bird? From what I can see you still have a long way to go. You probably won't make it at all. Anyway, it's taking you pretty long!" The elder brother said nothing in reply to these mocking words. He saw that his wife was still playing around with his younger brother, even more intensely than before. That made him sad. Without saying a word he left his hut and hurried back into the forest. Again he watched very attentively what the birds were doing, and for a long time imitated them in every detail.

He stayed there. Every day he tried to transform himself into a bird. Then his brother and his wife would become convinced and he would take revenge on them.

After a long time he again visited the hut. As before his younger brother received him with scornful laughter and addressed him with jeers: "I see you still haven't turned into a bird! It's taking very long. I think you'll never make it." To these insulting words the elder brother answered nothing. Again he had to watch his wife embrace and caress her brother-in-law. She spoke quietly but her husband could clearly hear the scornful words: "This blockhead will try for a long time and

still won't get anywhere! The better for us!" Thereupon the elder
brother became very sad and despondent. He left his hut at once,
firmly determined never again to return. He hurried straight into the
forest and stayed there for good. Again he watched the birds and
imitated everything they did. And indeed: from day to day he
gradually lost his own speech and adopted the sounds of the birds. Also
his mouth changed its shape and slowly a real bird's beak was formed.
His arms, too, changed into wings and his legs and feet became the legs
and feet of a bird. Little feathers began to grow all over his body.

For a long time he did not come back to the hut. So one day the
younger brother went out into the forest to look for him and see how
he was doing. Soon he found his elder brother and saw that he now had
changed a little. Then the younger brother gave a loud, scornful laugh
and jeered: "Listen, my brother! How are you? I see you are still far
from being a real bird! The whole thing is taking you quite some time!
Well, I wish you lots of luck in your transformation!" Then he laughed
very mockingly and went back to the hut. He told his sister-in-law
everything and both fondled each other even more contentedly than
before.

After this the elder brother stayed in the forest without interruption.
In fact he was slowly changing, becoming more and more like a bird.
By now he was more bird than man. He continued to imitate the birds
very closely in everything they did. That is how from day to day he
turned increasingly more into a bird.

Some time later the younger brother returned once more to the
forest; he wanted to look at his elder brother. Indeed he found him in
the same place and realized that he had almost become a bird. Scornfully he burst out laughing and said jeeringly: "Listen, my brother, how
are you? I see you no longer have far to go to be a real bird. That is
very good for me, isn't it! Then you'll always stay in the forest and
never again come back to the hut." Very pleased the younger brother
hurried back to his sister-in-law; he told her everything and both
yielded to their desire more carefree even than before.

In time the elder brother became a bird altogether. He lived more in
the trees now where he had built himself a large nest, as all birds do.
Whenever he had to defecate he sat on a branch and let his excrement
fall down. His mouth had turned into a bent, sharp beak, his arms into
wings, and his legs and feet had become the legs and feet of a bird, with
sharp, powerful claws. A thick layer of feathers covered his entire
body.

One day the younger brother again came to the forest to see what
had become of his elder brother. This time he brought his sister-in-law.
He found his elder brother in the same place as always. He had now

become a bird altogether and was sitting in his nest with several other birds. The two laughed and jeered up to him; they were glad that finally he had changed completely, for now he would never again return to the hut. Full of joy over this they lay down on the moss, just under the treetop in which the elder brother was sitting; they yielded to their lust and copulated. When the falcon[23] saw this he became furious. He left his nest, spread his wide wings, and began to fly. Slowly he descended, and hovering a short distance above the ground he flew very close to the heads of those two. But they, totally overcome with passion, did not notice the big bird at all. He rose very high into the air and from up there thrust downward for the second time, flying swiftly. He drove his powerful, sharp claws into the bodies of the two who were still lying on the ground, lifted them up, and carried them to his nest. There he put them down. The many smaller birds at once fell upon the two, quickly and greedily hacked them to pieces, devoured the flesh, and threw the bones down over the edge of the nest. Only the penis and the vagina they left untouched. When they had eaten all the flesh only the genitals of those two were still left. These organs of the man and the woman were still united as in coitus. Kíxinteka [the transformed elder brother] seized them now with his claws, left his nest, and on his wide wings rose up into the air with them.

It was a beautiful day. Not far from Kíxinteka's nest stood several huts, and many people lived there. Since the weather was so inviting everybody was playing *kálaka* in a wide, open meadow. The powerful gerfalcon came flying toward them and hovered in the air exactly above the spot where the people were playing. All noticed him. Then Kíxinteka opened his claws and let these united private parts of the man and the woman fall down into the circle of the people. As the genitals fell to the ground they made an odd sound. The people became frightened when they hit the ground so strangely. They wondered anxiously: "What kind of a strange sound is that? It's strange that something should come falling from up there!" They looked around everywhere and high up in the air they again caught sight of the powerful gerfalcon. Then they went up close to those genitals which had just fallen into their midst. Greatly surprised they stared at these things and said to one another: "Those are the genitals of a man and a woman, united as in intercourse. How odd!" They now discussed and thought about this incident. Soon they guessed it and said: "Those are the sexual organs of that man and his brother's wife! Kíxinteka let both fall down

[23]Here the story finally makes the point that the elder brother changed himself into the grey gerfalcon. *Circus cinereus*, a considerably smaller species than the big gerfalcon, *Polyborus tharus*, cf. p. 86 n. 24.

from up there!" At last they recognized in him the elder brother. They cried out loudly: "So the elder brother took revenge because his wife had forbidden relations with his younger brother! Both got what they deserved!"

Informant: Not known; pp. 1201-1205.

Summary

Younger brother falls in love with sister-in-law. Unable to prevent the relationship the elder brother goes into forest, intent on revenge. By watching and imitating behavior of birds he gradually turns into bird. Younger brother occasionally visits him and mocks him. Finally the elder brother lets his former wife and her lover be eaten by birds and lets their united sexual organs fall to the ground.

Motif content

A2272.	Animal characteristics: imitation of other animal or object.
C114.	Tabu: incest.
C920.2.	Death to wife for breaking tabu.
D152.4.+.	Transformation: man to falcon. (D152.4. Transformation: girl to falcon.)
D599.+.	Transformation to animal by imitation. (D599. Transformation by various means—miscellaneous.)
D651.1.	Transformation to kill enemy.
D681.	Gradual transformation.
F547.	Remarkable sexual organs.
J652.	Inattention to warnings.
J2133.5.1.	Wife carried up tree to sky in bag in husband's teeth.
K1501.	Cuckold. Husband deceived by adulterous wife.
K1550.1.	Husband discovers wife's adultery.
K2211.0.2.	Treacherous younger brother.
P251.5.3.	Hostile brothers.
Q241.	Adultery punished.
Q242.	Incest punished.
Q242.3.	Punishment for man who makes advances to sister-in-law.
Q252.1.	Wife-stealing punished with death.
Q288.	Punishment for mockery.
Q415.	Punishment: being eaten by animals.
Q580.	Punishment fitted to crime.
S0.	Cruel relative.
S73.1.4.	Fratricide motivated by love-jealousy.
T230.	Faithlessness in marriage.
T257.	Jealous wife or husband.
T425.	Brother-in-law seduces (seeks to seduce) sister-in-law.

31. How the Gerfalcon Lost His Wife

One day the big gerfalcon[24] went out to the rocks in the open sea. He wanted to kill sea lions there. Many other men accompanied him. All were married but they left their wives at home and set off without them. They had a long way to go and the weather was very bad. After several days they finally reached the rocky islands where they killed many sea lions. They were very happy over this. Then they sat down to rest, for they were exhausted. Soon one after the other fell asleep, until eventually only two men who were talking to each other remained awake. The gerfalcon had already lain down. But he was only pretending to be asleep; he just couldn't fall asleep.

The two men were sitting very close to the gerfalcon. One of them said quietly to the other: "Listen: next to us here lies Ketéla. Do you know his pretty wife, Lúškipa? Well, I'll let you in on something: I have long been having relations with her secretly. She's really a beautiful woman." The other one at once admonished him: "But don't talk about it here. After all, Ketéla is lying next to us; he might easily hear us talking!" The first man replied: "Well, now, don't worry about that! So far as I can see Ketéla is already fast asleep; he can't hear what we're whispering about. This encouraged the other man and he admitted: "Now I want to reveal something to you, too. I have also been having secret relations with beautiful Lúškipa for quite some time. I have already met her secretly many times. She is most certainly a delightful woman!" In this way the two men were confiding in each other, the one telling the other about his secret doings with the gerfalcon's beautiful wife. The gerfalcon, however, was still acting as though fast asleep. Therefore he heard their words very well.

The next morning the men loaded all the sea lions they had killed into their canoes and returned to where their families were waiting. When they arrived, every man went to his own hut. Ketéla, however, did not go to his hut where his wife was waiting but rather into that of one of his relatives. He did send a piece of meat to his wife in the hut, but without any greeting. She found it very strange that her husband did not come to the hut himself and had given her nothing but one piece of meat. Finally she realized what was going on. She said to herself: "My husband has probably heard what I secretly do with other men and with whom I've been sleeping. Surely that's why he comes to the hut no longer and sends me nothing but a small piece of meat!"

---

[24]*Polyborus tharus.* This big bird of prey is common in southern Chile and Argentina where it is generally known as *traro* or *carancho.*

Lúškipa was completely at a loss and did not know what to do. She was very sad at having to sit there alone. After a while she left her hut and ran away. She ran down to the beach intending to run along the shore until she met her father, old Dášlux.[25]

Lúškipa ran along the beach for a long time until she finally saw a canoe on the water. She waved to it to come closer. She had to signal for a long time, but at last the canoe changed course and turned to where Lúškipa was waiting on the shore.

Indeed, it was her father who was sitting in the canoe. She was very happy that she had finally reached him. She immediately told her father everything and explained why she had run away looking for him.

Soon Ketéla noticed that his wife had disappeared from their hut. That made him very sad. But he composed himself and quickly ran after her; he wanted to find her and bring her home again. He set off in the same direction she had taken. Finally he came close to the place where she was still sitting with her father. But when those two saw Ketéla approaching they quickly got into their canoe and left. Ketéla had come on foot, so he could not follow them far running along the beach. Angry and sad, he had to watch Lúškipa go farther and farther away with her father. He followed them with his eyes for a long time.

In his anguish he looked for a bird's egg. He threw it on the ground, breaking it; he wanted to ensure himself good luck. Promptly he summoned all the winds, the wind from the east and the wind from the west, the wind from the south and the wind from the north. All four winds came at once and they blew powerfully, each one from its direction. The canoe in which Lúškipa and her father were sitting no longer moved from its spot, for the winds were blowing very strongly from all sides. Thus the canoe now sat in the middle of the wide waterway unable to continue. That was Ketéla's intention. Not until the following day was it completely calm again, and then the two paddled off in their canoe. They traveled quickly, for they were paddling with all their strength. At last they reached their hut. There the old man and his daughter got out. From then on beautiful Lúškipa remained with her father forever.

Sadly Ketéla went back to his people's camp. He went into his hut and sat down by the fire. But now he was all alone. He sat there sorrowfully for a long time; he cried long and loud. A woman came by his hut and heard his lament. She asked: "Why are you crying so much?" Ketéla answered: "Oh, the wind blew some dirt into my eyes and it hurts a lot. That's why I'm losing so many tears!" But actually

---

[25]*Diomedea melanophrys*, the large albatross (Gusinde 1937:43).

he was crying over the loss of his beautiful wife. So long and so much did he cry that even today his eyes are still very red[26] from the many, many tears he has shed over beautiful Lúškipa, and he still continues to cry over her.

Informant: Not known; pp. 1205-1207.

Summary

Gerfalcon accidentally discovers wife's unfaithfulness and in his grief refuses to return home. Seeing herself found out, wife escapes with her father. Gerfalcon tries to stop their canoe by making strong winds blow, but in vain. He cries over his lost wife. Since then the gerfalcon has red, runny eyes.

Motif content

A2332.5.+.	Why falcon has red eyes. (A2332.5. Color of animal's eyes.)
B211.3.	Speaking bird.
B670.+.	Marriage of falcon to albatross. (B670. Unusual mating between animals.)
B736.1.	Bird sheds tears.
B673.	Reversed obstacle flight. Magic obstacles raised in front of fugitive.
D2072.0.3.	Ship held back by magic.
D2142.	Winds controlled by magic.
F575.1.	Remarkably beautiful woman.
J652.	Inattention to warnings.
K1501.	Cuckold. Husband deceived by adulterous wife.
K1550.1.	Husband discovers wife's adultery.
K1868.	Deception by pretending sleep.
N131.+.	Good luck by breaking bird's egg. (N131. Acts performed for changing luck.)
N451.	Secrets overheard from animal (demon) conversation.
N455.6.+.	Husband learns of wife's infidelity through conversation overheard. (N455.6. Husband learns of wife's fidelity through conversation overheard.)
P234.	Father and daughter.
P665.	Custom: boasting of sexual prowess.
R153.2.	Father rescues children.
R227.	Wife flees from husband.
R236.4.	Fugitive has magic wind against him, pursuer with him (caused by goddess).
T230.	Faithlessness in marriage.

[26]This coloration of the eyes, which frequently appear to be weeping, is very striking in the large gerfalcon, *Polyborus tharus*.

T251.1.+.	Avoiding the unfaithful wife. (T251.1. Avoiding the shrewish wife.)
T481.	Adultery.
W10.	Kindness.
W11.+.	Generosity toward faithless wife. (W11. Generosity.)

32. The Selfish Fox

Once there was a shortage of water in a region here and all the people were suffering terrible thirst. Cunning Čilawáia[27] looked around carefully and found a lagoon some distance from the campsite which contained a little water. He told nobody about it and built a solid fence around the lagoon so that no one could enter. All the time he kept himself hidden inside to make certain that no one else came near to drink. He took lots of water only for himself; and one by one he also allowed his relatives to drink from the lagoon.

After some time the other people found out that the fox had discovered a lagoon with water which allowed him to quench his thirst. Since they had all been suffering dreadfully from thirst for a long time they went to the fox and asked him for some water. He did not even listen to their pleas, but drove them away with harsh words. The condition of the people grew worse and worse. When they were so thirsty that they could hardly stand up they again approached Čilawáia. They offered him nice, big pieces of meat which they wanted to exchange for water. But he remained hardhearted and did not agree to the exchange.

All the people were now really close to death. In their helplessness they sent for little Omóra who had saved them from great distress once before. Omóra indeed came soon, for he was always ready to help others. Although he is a tiny, insignificant-looking little man[28] he is much braver and more daring than many a giant. All the people complained loudly to him of their distress, saying: "We're dying of thirst here! The fox has water but he gives us none." Other people sighed: "The selfish fox has built a solid fence around the lagoon; only he himself and his closest relatives can drink from it. Soon we shall perish of thirst!" Then Omóra became very angry with selfish

[27]The large fox of Tierra del Fuego, *Canis seu Cerdocyon magellanicus* (Gusinde 1937:35).

[28]The hummingbird *Sephanoides sephaniodes*, which is only rarely seen in that area. It appears again in the following stories; cf. p. 90 n. 30, p. 93 n. 36, and p. 97 n. 41.

Čilawáia. He rose at once and hurried to where the fox was. He addressed him harshly: "Listen! Are things really the way the people have assured me? Here you have access to a lagoon with water, but you don't want to share it with the other people! Soon they will all die of thirst." The fox jeered: "Why should I worry about other people? This lagoon contains only a little water; it's barely enough for me and my closest kin. I can't give any to the other people or I should soon go thirsty myself." Omóra became furious; without answering the fox he hurried to the camp.

He reflected briefly. Soon he rose again, took his sling, and once more went to where the fox was. On the way he collected several sharp stones. When he got sufficiently close and caught sight of the fox, he cried threateningly to him: "Will you now at last give the people some water? Come on, don't be so selfish; after all, they'll soon die of thirst!" The fox replied contemptuously: "May they all die of thirst! What do I care! I can't give everyone water from here, or I, too, will die, along with my closest relatives!" Now Omóra was so enraged he could no longer control himself; furiously he swung his sling and killed the fox with his first throw.

The other people had been watching; happily they came running. They promptly broke the thick fence, approached the lagoon, and drank their fill of water. They drank so much that the whole lagoon was emptied. All were overjoyed at having been saved from death. But a few birds came too late. They found barely a few drops with which to moisten their throats a little. All the other people had drunk so much because the long thirst had dried them out completely. Then Síta[29] and the birds that had arrived too late took the mud from the bottom of the lagoon and threw small lumps high up on the mountains. These clumps of mud caused jets of water to spurt from the mountains; large and small streams formed and a lot of water flowed to the valley below. When the people saw this they became extremely happy; they drank great quantities of the fresh, clear water, which was better than that from the lagoon, and now they were safe against thirst.

Until the présent day all those little streams are still flowing down from the mountains; they give a lot of good water indeed. Since then nobody has to die of thirst any more.[30]

[29]The brightly colored horned owl, *Nyctalops accipitrinus* (Gusinde 1937:42).

[30]Exactly as in two other stories the little hummingbird here acts as savior of a large group. His determination and outstanding cleverness qualify him for this, regardless of the insignificant size of his body.

The Selknam story is called, "How Táiyin came to the aid of the people" (Gusinde 1931:616; Wilbert 1975:57). As I said at the time, the "helper" is certainly the humming-bird. Both stories relate, in much the same manner, that through his actions he produced

Informant: Not known; pp. 1207-1209.

Summary

During bad drought everybody is dying of thirst except fox who has found a lagoon. In their despair people send for hummingbird helper who kills fox. They drink all the water, but some birds that come too late to drink create new streams and rivers by throwing lumps of mud on mountain. Since then no one has to die of thirst.

Motif content

A522.2.	Bird as culture hero.
A526.7.	Culture hero performs remarkable feats of strength and skill.
A930.1.	Creator of rivers.
A934.9.	Stream unexpectedly bursts from side of mountain.
A1111.	Impounded water.
B266.1.+.	Thirsty animals fight over well. (B266.1. Thirsty cattle fight over well.)
B450.+.	Helpful hummingbird. (B450. Helpful birds.)
C429.1.	Tabu: mentioning secret water spring.
D1486.1.+.	Magic mud makes rivers. (D1486.1. Magic stone makes rivers and lakes.)
F661.	Skillful marksman.
J715.	Kindness unwise when it imperils one's food supply.
L112.2.	Very small hero.
L311.	Weak (small) hero overcomes large fighter.
N440.	Valuable secrets learned.
N838.	Hero (culture hero) as helper.
Q411.	Death as punishment.
W276.	Stinginess punished.
W152.	Stinginess.
W155.	Hardness of heart.
W155.5.+.	Permission refused to drink from lagoon. (W155.5. Permission refused to drink from water tank.)

33. The Stone Man[31]

One day on the beach a girl found a stone that in every way resembled a small child. The girl picked it up and began to play with it

---

the many water holes and lagoons, streams and lakes of that region. Both the Yamana and the Selknam praise the little hummingbird as an extraordinarily clever man who is ready to help anybody; both peoples esteem him greatly.

[31]*See also Dabbene 1902:66-67; Martial 1882-1883:214.*

just as girls play with dolls. She carried the stone in her arms, rocked and hugged it, fed it and adorned it as a mother does her infant.[32]

Once those people[33] went with their canoes to the eastern Beagle Channel. When they got to Sínuwaia[34] the girl saw her stone slowly stir and move like a baby. Although it was and remained all stone, its eyes, the palms of its hands, and the soles of its feet were exactly like those of a foreigner (i.e., a European). The girl was extremely happy over this. She started to nurse it so that it would not be hungry. But instead of drinking from it the stone child bit off her whole breast and the girl soon died.

Then a woman took care of the stone child. She nursed and tended it well. But again when the woman gave it her breast to nurse the stone child bit off the entire breast, and the woman died. Although all the women became frightened at this, they still felt pity for the stone child and finally another woman took care of it. She tended and warmed it well. But when she gave it her breast to nurse it the stone child bit off the whole breast again. Thereupon also this woman died.

The men finally became indignant and angry at all this. They took the stone child and hurled it into the wide channel. But the stone child came right back and chased their canoes. Again they seized it and threw it on the beach. But there it quickly got up and pursued the people along the length of the beach. They were no longer able to get away from it. At last the men seized clubs and started flailing the stone child; they threw heavy stones at it, brandished burning logs at it, and again hurled it into the water. But all their efforts were in vain. They were simply unable to kill the stone child or in any way get rid of it. It followed them always and everywhere.

In time the stone child grew into manhood. He was so big and heavy that the men could no longer hurl him into the water or throw him on the beach. As time went by this stone man proved himself to be evil and unmanageable, even dangerous for all people. He started killing individual men and taking their wives to his own hut by force. His hut was in a remote place; there he lived with all the women he had kidnapped over time. He also began to bother the people who lived

[32]As they explained it to me, in the old days, that is, before what this story describes happened, a doll was usually a small oblong stone which a girl would like and play with. The girl would watch over, care for, and fondle it, but hardly ever give it any actual clothes. Since the stone man developed from such a doll, girls were forbidden to use a stone for a doll out of fear that a stone man might once again arise from it (Gusinde 1937:765).

[33]I.e., the family group to which this girl belonged.

[34]Name for Bahía Poste west of Puerto Mejillones, on the northern edge of Isla Navarino. The structure of the name closely follows the rule governing this matter among the Yamana, according to which the name of the birthplace is used in personal names. The translation would be: ancient Sinulu.

farther away. Only those of Molinare (in the channel south of Angostura Murray) were spared. But if he saw any other canoe he followed it immediately, killed the men, and dragged their wives to his hut. By now he had brought together a large number of women, with whom he begot many children. But every newborn baby boy he killed; only girls were allowed to live. When they were old enough themselves he also begot children with them. But since he had many wives he had many worries and much work to obtain the necessary food. He did not allow his wives to get too far away from the hut to look for food. He himself was so strong that he easily pulled up a large beech tree, roots and all, if there were many of the small *ésef (auáčix* and *aším* mushrooms[35]) on its branches. He carried this entire tree to the hut and placed it upright before the entrance so that his wives could pick off the mushrooms and eat their fill. The whole big beech had no sooner been picked clean of the many mushrooms than he dragged another one there. In this way he had already cleared half a forest.

One day, while the stone man was pulling up a large beech, he got a thick thorn in his foot. Although he was made completely of stone the soles of his feet were those of a foreigner (European). His foot hurt so badly that he could not walk on it; he dragged himself to the hut in terrible pain. "I have a thick thorn in my foot," he called to his wives from afar, "try to take it out for me at once!" All the women helped him to lie down on his bed. Then they fetched a long, pointed awl, the kind used to make holes in a piece of hide. They poked around with it in the wound to try to loosen the thick thorn. They actually found it, but acted as though it were very far into the flesh, and deliberately bored more and more deeply so that the wound became very large. The stone man could hardly stand it, so terribly did his foot hurt. But all the women continued drilling violently. At the same time they comforted him, saying: "Soon we'll reach the big thorn. Just endure it a little longer!" They had already bored a wide and deep hole in his foot. So much had the man suffered that he passed out on his bed. Soon he was snoring loudly and deeply.

Swiftly the women discussed how they might be able to kill the powerful stone man. This to them seemed to be an opportune time. For some time they had hidden among them a little man, clever Omóra.[36] They were keeping him safely concealed in a hole in the ground which they covered loosely with twigs; nobody could notice him there. Unobserved, they regularly brought him something to eat. Whenever

[35]The two well-known mushroom species *Cyttaria darwinii* and *Cyttaria harioti* (Gusinde 1937:554).
[36]The hummingbird *Sephanoides sephaniodes*, a rare visitor in the Cape Horn archipelago.

the stone man went far away from the hut the women let the little man out of his hole to enjoy a bit of fresh air. This little man was very dear to all the women. Since the stone man was now fast asleep and snoring loudly the women hurried to little Omóra and told him: "The evil stone man is fast asleep. Please help us kill him now!" At once he declared himself ready for this, and all the women sighed with joy. Little Omóra was extraordinarily clever and knew how to make excellent weapons. Earlier he had given many good arrowheads to all the women which they had carefully preserved. For a long time the women had had it in mind to kill the stone man.

Near the bed at his feet they thrust into the ground a sturdy forked stick. They lifted his foot and placed it in the fork. Into the deep wound they pushed a long thick awl. The women had placed the stone man in such a way to begin with, that the soles of his feet faced toward the entrance of the hut. Now they all tiptoed out of the hut. On the outside they built a fire all around. The hut had been there for some time and the wood in the structure was very dry, so that the fire instantly flared up high. Meanwhile little Omóra quickly shot several arrows at the healthy foot of the stone man. Awakened by it, the stone man rose from his bed and jumped to his feet. When he planted both feet firmly on the ground he pushed the long thick awl deeper into the wound in one foot and felt the pain in the other foot now badly wounded by several arrowheads. On account of the pain he could no longer stand upright; he fell down and the flames enveloped him. But nimble Omóra had shot two arrows into his eyes, totally blinding him. The stone man was unable to move from the spot and defend himself. Soon the whole hut tumbled down on top of him and the burning poles completely covered his body. Although he tried repeatedly to get up he always collapsed. Then there was a terribly loud explosion that was heard over great distances: the stone man cracked all over and burst; the pieces flew in all directions. But strangely, each one of these fragments was alive, ready in turn to become a complete stone man. All the stones were leaping from the fire and jumping around outside the burning hut, and the women worked frantically to throw them right back into the fire so that they would die. The many stone fragments continued to jump and spurt from the fire, and the women continued to hurl the stones back into it. Omóra had ordered them to do that. And so, in spite of great weariness, they moved about very diligently. Finally the stone man's heart burst. Then there was a much stronger explosion, sounding like loud thunder. The stone man was completely dead. The last spurts of stone fell down at a great distance from his hut, moving no more.

Today one can still find such *téši*[37] in that region. But the many women that were with the stone man turned into birds. Those are the *tuwín*[38] which even today live together in great numbers. Little Omóra himself soon afterward went back to the north; since then he shows himself in our country only occasionally and very briefly.

All the people, even those far away, had been living in anxiety and fear for a long time; they hardly dared go any distance out to sea in their canoes. That meant they often had to go hungry. For a while now they noticed that the stone man was no longer harassing them. Several men breathed a deep sigh of relief and speculated out loud: "That dangerous stone man is probably dead!" For everybody had heard the terrible, crashing explosion when the stone man burst. At last a few courageous men said: "Let's go out to his hut in order to see whether he'll attack us! If he doesn't show up we'll know for certain that he's dead!" No sooner said than done; they went out and drew close to his hut. There was nothing to indicate that he was there and still alive. That made all the men very much calmer and they happily returned to the camp. Several days later other men went to where the stone man's hut used to be; they found no trace of him. Now everyone breathed a deep sigh of relief and cried: "The stone man is dead; we're free once more!"

Informant: Not known; pp. 1209-1213.

Summary

Girl's stone doll comes alive and kills women who try to nurse it. Men try in vain to kill stone child. It grows into stone man terrorizing country, killing men and abducting women. His wives conspire with hummingbird to kill him by wounding his feet and eyes, which are vulnerable, and setting fire to his hut. Stone man explodes into living stone fragments which finally die. All people rejoice to be rid of monster. His wives turn into birds.

Motif content

A522.2.	Bird as culture hero.
A526.7.	Culture hero performs remarkable feats of strength and skill.
A531.	Culture hero (demigod) overcomes monsters.
A560.	Culture hero's (demigod's) departure.
A977.1.	Giant responsible for certain stones.

[37]These are the round black stones (Gusinde 1937:1213, fig. 93), used for the first time by the night-heron woman (ibid., p. 1220) as sinkers for fishing tackle (ibid., p. 547). They are thus thought to be "stone spurts" scattered about when the stone man burst. Similar round stones, called "boleadoras" (Gusinde 1931:268) may also be found on the Isla Grande in Selknam territory.

[38]What is meant here is the so-called *jilgero*, a small meadow bird with yellowish-green feathers, which lives in the company of many of its own kind (Gusinde 1937:42).

A2492.+.	Why certain birds flock together. (A2492. Why certain animals go in herds.)
B450.+.	Helpful hummingbird. (B450. Helpful birds.)
D150.	Transformation: man to bird.
D432.1.	Transformation: stone to person.
D435.1.1.	Transformation: statue comes to life.
D1840.3.	Magic invulnerability of ogres.
E35.	Resuscitation from fragments of body.
F531.3.10.	Giants carry trees.
F621.2.	Trees pulled up by giant.
G304.2.5.+.	Monster bursts from heat. (G304.2.5. Troll bursts when sun shines on him.)
G332.	Sucking monster.
G334.	Ogre keeps human prisoners.
G346.	Devastating monster.
G371.	Stone giants.
G477.	Orgre kills men and rapes women.
G511.	Ogre blinded.
G512.0.1.	Hero kills trouble-making evil strong men.
G512.3.	Ogre burned to death.
G630.+.	Stone man's eyes, palms, and soles like foreigner's. (G630. Characteristics of ogre.)
K515.6.	Escape by hiding in the earth.
K812.	Victim burned in his own house (or hiding place).
K1000.	Deception into self-injury.
K1871.2.	Sham cure by pretending extracting of object from patient's body.
L112.2.	Very small hero.
L311.	Weak (small) hero overcomes large fighter.
N838.	Hero (culture hero) as helper.
R11.	Abduction by monster (ogre).
S100.+.	Murder by biting off breast. (S100. Revolting murders or mutilations.)
S302.1.	All new-born male children slaughtered.
S325.0.1.	Monstrous (deformed) child exposed.
T411.	Father-daughter incest.
W154.2.	Monster ungrateful for rescue.
Z311.	Achilles heel. Invulnerability except in one spot.

34. The Sea Lion Rock[39]

Near the Wéakuf-rock[40] there once lived a powerful sea lion, extremely wild and dangerous. Whenever a canoe came near, it would

---

[39]See also Dabbene 1902:66; Martial 1882-1883:213.
[40]Located on the west coast of Isla Navarino, near the mouth of the Río Douglas.

throw itself upon it and shatter it; it would kill all the people inside, carry them to shore, and eat them. Many canoes had been destroyed this way, and many people had perished. The relatives of all those who had been killed and eaten by the sea lion often wondered: "Where can our relatives be? They haven't come back for a long time!" But nobody knew that they had been attacked and killed by that powerful sea lion.

As time passed great grief had come over many people because they had lost their relatives. Then it became evident to clever little Omóra[41] that all those canoes must have been lost in the same manner, for not one had returned and not a single person had saved himself. He said to himself: "What can be going on over there since not even one canoe has come back? Many have gone to that region but no one has come back!" He climbed a hill and fixed his eyes on a canoe that had just set off for that place. As the canoe approached the Wéakuf-rock he saw to his horror a powerful sea lion rise up. It threw itself upon the canoe, broke it to pieces, and carried all its occupants ashore. Here the animal slowly devoured them all. Then Omóra said very sadly: "So it is this sea lion who has killed and eaten all our people!" Disconsolate, he returned to the camp and told the people exactly what he had just seen. And so they all put on mourning paint.

Little Omóra was very clever. He knew how to make excellent weapons; he made the most beautiful harpoons and the strongest slings. He began now to make some new weapons; he expended much effort on a sling. He could hardly wait to try it out; more than anything he wanted to know how efficient his new sling was. He gave it a try. The sling turned out to be so effective that every stone he threw split a whole tree trunk. That fully satisfied him.

He called four women. They pushed his canoe down from the beach into the water. Then he loaded his weapons into it, got in, and, taking the four women with him, quickly departed. All the women were to paddle strenuously so that they would advance quickly. He himself rested during the journey. As they approached the Wéakuf-rock the powerful sea lion got up and slowly swam toward the canoe. Omóra took his sling and threw a stone. It squeezed out one of the sea lion's eyes. He followed right away with a second stone, and this one blinded the sea lion's other eye. Now the animal was totally blind. The sea lion opened its large mouth and roared loudly. Omóra was soon ready with his sling; in violent haste he threw one stone after another. Then he picked up his bow and arrows. He shot off a strong arrow that penetrated the very center of the sea lion's heart. Bleeding and fatally wounded, the sea lion barely made it to shore. It dragged itself up on

[41]The Tierra del Fuego hummingbird, *Sephanoides sephaniodes.*

the beach and reached its rock only with difficulty. There the sea lion turned into stone,[42] which can still be seen today.[43]

Informant: Not known; pp. 1214-1215.

Summary

Dangerous sea lion intercepts all passing canoes and eats passengers. Helpful hummingbird finally kills sea lion which turns into stone.

Motif content

A522.2.	Bird as culture hero.
A524.2.	Extraordinary weapons of culture hero.
A531.4.	Culture hero conquers sea monster.
A977.5.	Origin of particular rock.
B450.+.	Helpful hummingbird. (B450. Helpful birds.)
D429.2.2.1.+.	Transformation: man-eating sea lion to stone. (D429.2.2.1. Transformation: man-eating giantess to stone.)
D1087.	Magic sling.
F660.	Remarkable skill.
F661.	Skillful marksman.
G312.	Cannibal ogre.
G352.+.	Sea lion as ogre. (G352. Wild beast as ogre.)
G475.	Ogre attacks intruders.
G510.4.	Hero overcomes devastating animal.
G511.	Ogre blinded.
G512.9.	Animal kills ogre.
L112.2.	Very small hero.
L311.	Weak (small) hero overcomes large fighter.
N440.+.	Secret learned. (N440. Valuable secrets learned.)
N820.	Human helpers.
P681.	Mourning customs.

35. The Lašawáia Rock

Old Kiwágu[44] was a widow who had a lovely daughter. Ketéla[45] fell in love with both women at the same time and soon took them into his hut. And so the three of them lived together (as married people).

---

[42]From a distance the rough outline of this rock looks like a sea lion lying down.

[43]The similarity of this story to the preceding one has been pointed out (Gusinde 1937:1214). In both the hero, i.e., the little hummingbird, is the actual liberator of a large group of people, for which his extraordinary skill qualified him.

[44]The very common large sea gull, *Larus dominicanus*.

[45]The large gerfalcon, *Polyborus tharus*.

Ketéla was very skillful, particularly at making beautiful harpoons. He usually sat on a mound near his hut and worked on his weapons. Whenever Kiwágu went out in her canoe after fish and crabs he accompanied her; his younger wife remained alone in the hut.

Two *wasénim*[46] who were brothers had fallen very much in love with Kiwágu's young daughter. One day when Ketéla had gone out with his older wife to catch crabs, the two *wasénim* came secretly to his hut. The young woman was sitting all by herself. From the outset they flattered her in every way, became more and more importunate, and finally demanded crudely that she sleep with them. She refused and staunchly fended them off. Later when Ketéla came back to the hut with his older wife the two *wasénim* slunk away unobserved. They considered a new plan and were determined to carry the beautiful woman off by force; should she not let them have their way, they would take revenge on her.

One day when the young woman was sitting in her hut all alone, the two *wasénim* stealthily sneaked up close. One of them addressed her harshly: "Will you sleep with us today or do you still refuse?" She replied resolutely: "I don't want to! You are very repulsive to me, you cross-eyed *wasénim!*" These words hurt him deeply. He sat down near the fire with his back to the beautiful woman. He now pushed a small stone into the embers to heat it. The other *wasénim* threatened the young woman: "All right, if you don't obey us and don't yield to our demands, we'll simply carry you off with us by force!" Upset, she answered: "I won't do it. I don't like you, either, you cross-eyed *wasénim*. Get out of this hut!" He, too, became furious. He seized the young woman, threw her to the ground, pulled her legs apart, and held her down that way. Meanwhile the other *wasénim*, using fire tongs, took hold of the small, oblong stone which had been heating up in the embers, and inserted it into her vagina as though it were a penis. And thus the two *wasénim* took their revenge. The young woman died instantly. They said scornfully: "Since you didn't want to yield to our desire you shall not be Ketéla's wife, either!" They covered the dead woman with several furs and left the hut.

On the way they met Kiwágu who was just returning from fishing. In her presence the two *wasénim* pretended to be very sad. "Why are you so serious and sad?" the old woman asked. They replied: "We come from your hut. We went there to look at your daughter. Well, just keep her to yourself, we say; we have no desire for her! We were planning to have some fun with her but she rejected us out of hand and would have

[46] The tufted cormorant, *Phalacrocorax gaimardi*.

nothing to do with us. All right: keep her to yourself! We'll never again go to your hut looking for your daughter!" Kiwágu got the terrible suspicion that the two might even have killed her daughter. She hurriedly pushed her canoe away from the beach and paddled hard until she reached her hut. From the canoe she called to her daughter to come down to the beach with baskets; she was to help unload the crabs and the fish and take them to the hut. But despite her long, loud calls her daughter did not come out of the hut. Finally Kiwágu left her canoe and ran to the hut. When she entered she saw her daughter lying on her bed, covered as though asleep. Kiwágu shouted at her: "Will you finally get up, you lazy bones! How long have you been sleeping here?" She pulled at the hides, but the daughter did not stir. Kiwágu pulled all the hides aside and saw her daughter lying there dead. Smoke was coming from her mouth, for the stone which she had in her vagina was still very hot. Then Kiwágu broke down and wept long and loudly.

The two *wasénim* had continued walking and soon had reached the hill where Ketéla was sitting, working on his harpoons. When they were close enough they addressed him in a scornful tone: "Listen, you: just now we wanted to look at your stepdaughter. She would not talk to us, but turned us coldly away. Well, now we don't really need her any more. Keep her for yourself and take good care of her for your sake; we're no longer interested in her!" Thereupon they hit Ketéla over the head with a club, so that to this day his head has remained flat. Ketéla hurried back to his hut. Old Kiwágu was crying loudly so that the women from the neighboring huts came over. She told them everything and the women became very sad.

Kiwágu had many relatives. The whole family eventually arrived and they prepared themselves for a big *yamalašemóina*. All their acquaintances and friends came, too, even the two *wasénim*-murderers. They remained standing at a distance, though, on the cliff of Lašawáia.[47] When the crowd that had gathered in the hut caught sight of the two *wasénim* they flew into a terrible rage. The men seized their slings and wanted to kill them. But they were too far away for the slingstones to reach them. By now all the people had gathered; only little Omóra[48] was missing. He was the man who was most skilled in the use of the sling; as we know he killed Sínuluwatauinéiwa,[49] even though he was only a little bit of a man and of insignificant appearance. Kuhúrux is closely related to him. Some men said: "Let's call little Omóra; he's

[47]Located on the west cost of Isla Hoste opposite Molinare.
[48]The hummingbird, *Sephanoides sephaniodes*, occasionally seen there.
[49]Cf. the story about the stone man.

excellent at using the sling and will certainly help us out of this awkward situation!" Others found the suggestion ridiculous and said: "How could that tiny man surpass us? None of us was able to fling a stone far enough to reach the two *wasénim*, so he won't be able to, either!" Other men replied: "Still, Omóra knows how to handle the sling in a very masterly manner. We were convinced of it when he killed the stone man. We should ask him to come at once!" After some discussion they finally sent a messenger to summon Omóra. For all the people were highly indignant that none of the men were able to reach the *wasénim* and kill them.

Soon little Omóra arrived. Even so, he was late, for on the way he had been practicing continually. With his sling he first shot a big stone toward the south. When it came down the Molinare Channel opened and Isla Navarino was separated from Isla Hoste. Then he hurled a stone toward the west and this opened the northwestern arm of the Beagle Channel. He shot another stone somewhat to the south of the last one and through this the southwestern arm was opened. Then as he again threw a big stone eastward the long eastern half of the Beagle Channel opened up. He threw still more stones from his sling in all directions and where these stones landed new waterways were formed. That is how the numerous waterways and channels originated, and the many islands. Throwing this way one stone after the other from his sling, he slowly walked on until finally he arrived at the place where all the people were gathered and waiting for him. When Omóra's tiny figure appeared most of those present began to laugh. But then all the people quickly told him why they were in mourning and that they were furious, because the two murderers, the *wasénim*, had escaped the missiles of any of the men. When Omóra had heard all this, he, too, became enraged. He had only three stones at hand. One of them he now placed in his sling and sent it off; it passed very close to the heads of the two *wasénim*. Hurriedly he put a second stone in his sling and threw it with great force. It hit one of the *wasénim* right on the chest so that he fell over and no longer moved. Quickly he also threw the third stone; it hit the other *wasénim*, so that he died on the spot. All the people marveled at his strength and skill. But they were especially happy that those two murderers had been killed and that they had received their just punishment. After this they all went back to their huts.

The two murderers, the *wasénim*, turned into stone and remain lying there in the same place at Lašawáia where little Omóra killed them. One can still see them today. They are the two *watauineiwábei*, "the two old men," and by that name everybody knows them.

Informant: Not known; pp. 1216-1219.

Summary

Two rejected cormorant suitors take revenge on woman, killing her by inserting hot stone in her vagina. They show up at mourning ceremony. After trying in vain to kill them the men finally send for hummingbird helper. On his way there the latter practices with sling, each stone creating a new channel or waterway as it falls down. He kills cormorants with three shots and they turn into stone.

Motif content

A522.2.	Bird as culture hero.
A524.2.	Extraordinary weapons of culture hero.
A526.7.	Culture hero performs remarkable feats of strength and skill.
A901.	Topographical features caused by experiences of primitive hero.
A920.2.	Origin of sea channels.
A930.1.	Creator of rivers.
A934.2.	Rivers formed where certain stones are placed.
A955.6.+.	Islands from stones cast by hero. (A955.6. Islands from stones cast by giantess.)
A955.11.	Islands originally form continent, later separated.
A977.5.	Origin of particular rock.
A2320.+.	Why gerfalcon's head is flat. (A2320. Origin of animal characteristics: head.)
B450.+.	Helpful hummingbird. (B450. Helpful birds.)
D423.+.	Transformation: cormorants to stone. (D423. Transformation: bird [fowl] to object.)
B1087.	Magic sling.
D1486.1.	Magic stone makes rivers and lakes.
F660.	Remarkable skill.
F661.	Skillful marksman.
L112.2.	Very small hero.
L311.	Weak (small) hero overcomes large fighter.
N838.	Hero (culture hero) as helper.
P232.	Mother and daughter.
Q411.6.	Death as punishment for murder.
S112.+.	Murder by introducing hot stone into vagina. (S112. Burning to death.)
S112.2.+.	Murder with hot stone. (S112.2. Murder with hot iron.)
T70.	The scorned lover.
T75.2.1.	Rejected suitors' revenge.
T145.0.1.+.	Man marries widow and her daughter. (T145.0.1. Polygyny.)
T210.1.	Faithful wife.
T320.1.	Oft-proved fidelity.

36. The Unfaithful Heron-woman[50]

Túwuxkipa[51] went out to sea every morning to fish. She always did this with deep pleasure and joy, never taking her husband or any of her relatives along. She was secretly having an affair with a lover, Šége-tex.[52] Her husband knew nothing about this, nor did the others suspect anything. Precisely because of this she went out very happily every morning and did not return to the huts on the shore until late afternoon. Each time she brought a good number of big fish. As she approached the shore she would call to her husband from the canoe. He would come immediately, help her pull the canoe up on the beach, and unload the fish. Eventually she would say: "Now carry all the fish to the hut and prepare them. You must draw, wash, and preserve them well. For I have a bad case of diarrhea and must quickly go aside; I'll soon be back. Take good care of everything I just told you!" She would quickly disappear and run to her lover, Šégetex. She wanted her husband to be occupied and unable to follow her, so she ordered him to do the jobs which she actually should have done herself. But this man was very good-natured and obediently did everything his wife demanded of her. She spent a long time with her lover, during which both yielded to their desire.

These two had been meeting secretly for many months. Watching very carefully, the other people saw Túwuxkipa go out alone every morning to fish, return in the afternoon with a large catch, and keep her husband occupied with the fish for a long period of time. But gradually the people also noticed that she was secretly having intercourse with Šégetex. Finally one day the husband's relatives came to him and said: "Why do you so eagerly help your wife pull the canoe up on the beach, remove the entrails of the fish, and preserve the meat? That is her work; after all! She promptly runs away, upon returning from the journey. Your wife is surely having an affair with the kingfisher. For she runs to him as soon as she comes back from fishing. She tricks you; 'I have a bad case of diarrhea and must go aside at once, indeed!' But that is a lie; she doesn't suffer from perpetual diarrhea at all. She has no other desire but to run to Šégetex and continue their love play. Do not believe those daily lies of hers any more."

When the man heard that his wife had been deceiving him for so long he became furious. From that day on he no longer helped her with what really was her job; he no longer undertook to unload, cut up, and

---

[50]See also Koppers 1924:197-200.
[51]The familiar dark-gray night heron, *Nycticorax obscurus.*
[52]The beautiful kingfisher, *Ceryle torquata* var. *stellata.*

preserve the fish. Túwuxkipa wondered about her husband's changed behavior but could not make him do that work. She continued running to her Šégetex anyway.

Finally, one day the man decided to follow his wife in secret. He watched her with Šégetex and it made him extremely angry. Silently he sneaked back to his hut. The following day he made a strong *sírsa* (a crab-fork with four prongs). After his wife had returned in the afternoon and unloaded all the fish she told her husband as usual: "I'm suffering from a bad case of diarrhea and must quickly go aside. I'll be back soon." And she left. Her husband followed her unnoticed. His wife gave herself again to Šégetex and they carried on their love play. When the man saw the two embracing he threw his *sírsa* with such force that both were pierced simultaneously. They lay impaled on the ground. He left them in this condition and quickly went away. Later those two turned into birds.

Informant: Not known; pp. 1219-1220.

Summary

Woman who supposedly goes fishing every day alone is actually meeting her lover. When neighbors discover this they inform her husband; he follows her and kills both. Wife and lover turn into birds.

Motif content

D150.	Transformation: man to bird.
J2431.	A man undertakes to do his wife's work.
K1501.	Cuckold. Husband deceived by adulterous wife.
K1514.	Adulteress gets rid of husband while she entertains lover.
K1514.18.	Adulteress makes excuse to go and attend to bodily needs; meets lover.
K1550.1.	Husband discovers wife's adultery.
K1551.+.	Husband spies on adulteress and lover. (K1551. Husband returns home secretly and spies on adulteress and lovers.)
K1568.2.	Husband surprises wife and paramour.
N440.+.	Secret revealed. (N440. Valuable secrets learned.)
Q241.	Adultery punished.
Q411.0.2.	Husband kills wife and paramour.
Q461.3.	Impaling as punishment for adultery.
S112.2.+.	Murder with hot stone. (S122.2. Murder with hot iron.)
T35.	Lover's rendezvous.
T261.	The ungrateful wife.
T481.	Adultery.

37. The Water Sow Bug

Once there lived a woman who very happily went out to sea every day to catch birds. Hidden in her canoe she had a young man with whom she was deeply in love. It was precisely because she wanted to be alone and unobserved with him that at the crack of dawn every day she went so gladly far out to the open sea. She never returned until late at night. But she always brought many birds to the hut and distributed them among all the people. The other women often asked her: "How do you manage to gather so many large birds every day?" She answered: "Well, where I go, I always find these birds, and recently killed, at that. I only have to load them into my canoe and bring them here!" The other women exclaimed in amazement: "How can that be? After all, we too go from one place to the other, looking around everywhere. Yet nowhere have we come across as many large and freshly killed birds as you bring back every day." She replied curtly: "Well, it's the truth, I just find all these big birds. One only has to look for them carefully!" Her lover was a skilled hunter; he knew how to handle the sling well. It was actually he who always killed the large number of big birds and who gave them to the woman. Every evening, therefore, she brought many birds to the camp.

One morning the woman went out again in her canoe to the open sea. When she was far enough away from shore another woman from the camp watched her, and she could clearly distinguish two people in the canoe. Immediately she called several other women and drew their attention to it: "Look closely over there! I can clearly make out two people in that canoe!" The other women confirmed: "Yes, indeed, we can also quite definitely discern two people in that canoe. Who knows whether some man isn't sitting there with her!" A shrewd woman added: "If there are really two people sitting in the canoe, one of them is likely to be a man. It must be he who kills all these big birds with his sling. He gives them to that woman and she brings the whole lot to the camp. Then she pretends to us: 'I found all these big birds out there; they were all still fresh and had recently been killed!' That's probably how it is." The other women nodded in agreement and wondered: "But who might that man be? For it's no delusion; we can clearly distinguish two figures in that canoe."

Thereupon all the women went to the woman's hut to see whether her husband had perhaps gone out to sea with her. But he had stayed home and was sitting by the fire warming himself. The women resumed their chatter among themselves and once again wondered: "Who might that other person be who is sitting out there in the canoe with the woman? It has to be a man!" Finally the women went back to their huts.

In the evening the woman returned to the campsite in her canoe. Again she brought many large birds from her journey and distributed the big catch among all the women. They questioned her insistently: "Where did you get so many big birds again?" She replied: "I found them far out on the open sea. They looked so fresh, they probably had just been killed. I picked them up and brought them home." Whereupon all the women informed her: "Yesterday, we ourselves were exactly where you just came from, but we didn't find anything there at all. How come you alone were able to find so many big birds there today?" She insisted calmly: "It may well be that none of you encountered any birds there yesterday, but I actually did find all these birds there today and picked them up."

While the women discussed the matter the woman's husband listened to their talk unobserved. Shortly afterward the woman went off to look after her canoe on the beach. Meanwhile the other women sat down with the man and hinted to him: "Your wife must be having an affair with a stranger; early today we distinguished very clearly two people in her canoe! How else could it be possible that she regularly brings home so many big birds, while we find nothing at all?" A particularly shrewd woman added: "Something very strange is going on there! Who might that man be who so regularly accompanies your wife out to the open sea in her canoe. None of us have ever seen him get in." This talk upset the woman's husband and he pondered everything he had heard.

As always, the next morning the woman happily hurried down to the beach, got into her canoe, and went out to sea. As she went farther and farther out her husband kept a close eye on her. Then he returned to his hut without telling the other women what he had observed and what he was planning. Late in the evening his wife returned; as usual she brought back many big birds. Her husband was waiting for her on the beach. She hardly had the canoe out of the water and firmly settled when her husband jumped in and searched it closely. To his wife he said: "I see you have again brought many big birds today." She answered: "That's right! I was lucky again. I found all these birds out there and they had just been killed." He replied: "I'm very glad!" After a brief pause he continued: "But look here, your canoe takes in a lot of water! It would be good to plug up these big chinks right away!" His wife hastened to say: "That's really quite unnecessary! As far as I can see only a little water has come in; it is hardly worth stopping up these few cracks." But he insisted: "Still, it's good to fix everything right away; later the chinks will grow larger and the canoe will be in danger!" Upset, now the woman resisted: "I don't see why I should give myself all this trouble tonight!" So the man said harshly: "Since you don't want to do it I'll start the work myself; I'll push aside and lift out the *lúka*,[53] then the *ílax*[54] beneath them, and caulk the small chinks in the sides of the canoe." Anxiously now his wife implored him: "Spare yourself the trouble!" But he said: "It's necessary to take care of such small but urgent jobs immediately." Then she gave in and said sulkily "All right then, I don't care! If you absolutely want to stop up those small chinks I'll show you where they are. Look, they are right here up front!" "But that's impossible," replied her husband, "I can clearly see that the water enters at the stern." Before his wife could stop him he had lifted up a few pieces of bark at the rear part of the canoe. Here he saw a man hiding with his face turned upward. After all, he had to breathe, and therefore he lay face up on the bottom of the canoe where, in fact, there was some water. The woman turned pale with fright and terror. Her husband became livid with rage, seized a harpoon, and drove it into the body of his wife's lover, killing him instantly. The furious husband threw the body into the sea.

Husband and wife stole silently into their hut. The wife was so overcome with pain and grief that she could not eat. She uttered not a word and lay down. The following morning the husband sent his wife out to sea to fetch birds. This time she did not feel like going at all but finally went. She did not return until late at night, yet this time without a single bird. As usual the other women were waiting for her canoe to draw closer to shore, in the hope of receiving a share of her big catch. But to their disappointment they discovered that this time the woman had not brought one single bird. They burst out laughing and jeered: "Now look at her, everybody! Isn't it obvious now that she was lying to us all the time. It was her lover who hunted all these big birds and who gave them to her! And us she fooled: 'I found all these big birds; they had just been killed!' She had a lover hidden in her canoe; when nobody could see her she occupied herself with him, and they were together every day." The woman was deeply ashamed, said not a word in reply, and hid in her hut. Her lover became the *watewémuva* (i.e., in the western dialect; in the eastern dialect it is *aporpánuwa*).[55] He still swims on his back just as he had lain in the woman's canoe.

---

[53]Pieces of bark, bent to a half-circle, in the middle of the canoe.
[54]Pieces of bark lying lengthwise directly on the bottom of the canoe (Gusinde 1937:447).
[55]A small, very common type of isopod.

Informant: Not known; pp. 1222-1225.

Summary

Woman who supposedly goes bird-hunting every day alone actually has her lover hidden in canoe. He catches birds for her, for which she gets credit in village. Husband finds out through neighboring women. Pretending to repair canoe he discovers hidden lover whom he kills. Woman is disgraced; lover turns into crustacean.

Motif content

A2444.+.	Why crustacean swims on its back. (A2444. Animal's method of swimming.)
D100.+.	Transformation: man to crustacean. (D100. Transformation: man to animal.)
F679.5.	Skillful hunter.
K1501.	Cuckold. Husband deceived by adulterous wife.
K1514.	Adulteress gets rid of husband while she entertains lover.
K1521.	Paramour successfully hidden from husband.
K1550.	Husband outwits adulteress and paramour.
K1550.1.	Husband discovers wife's adultery.
K1569.9.	Husband kills surprised paramour.
K2050.	Pretended virtue.
N455.	Overheard (human) conversation.
Q241.	Adultery punished.
Q411.0.1.2.	Man (fairy) kills wife's lover.
Q461.3.	Impaling as punishment for adultery.
Q470.	Humiliating punishments.
T35.	Lovers' rendezvous.
T481.	Adultery.
W11.	Generosity.

38. The Stingy Grandmother

Old Wekatánaxipa[56] was a diligent fisherwoman. On every journey she was lucky and brought back a considerable amount of fish. She always used a *téši* for fishing. Whenever she went out to sea she took her small grandson along. He sat up front in the bow and kept his face turned forward; she sat at the other end looking in the opposite direction. Thus the two sat with their backs to each other.

---

[56]The *"wekatána"* in the eastern dialect is the same as the *"túwux"* in the western dialect and denotes the dark-grey night heron, *Nycticorax obscurus*.

Old Wekatánaxipa was very stingy. Every time a fish bit she pulled in her tackle, grasping it in such a way that her body completely hid the fish from the little grandson sitting up front. She did not want him to see how big the fish was. She kept the big fish she caught hidden under the boards at the bottom of the canoe; only the few little fish she caught did she throw to her grandson. He did not at all like getting only small fish. Finally, one day he asked: "Tell me, dear grandmother: How is it that you always catch only small fish? You keep throwing me small fish. Why don't you let me have a big fish for once? For I can well see that there are many big fish swimming around our canoe right now; they sometimes even bump against it quite noisily. But you always assure me: 'Only the small fish bite on my tackle, none of the big ones!' How is that?" As always, the grandmother answered: "Well, actually I don't know either why this is so! Nothing but small fish bite on my tackle, not big ones. That's why I can't let you have any big fish."

But the little boy did not believe his grandmother; after all, he kept seeing many big fish swimming around the canoe. From then on he watched his grandmother very closely. Soon he noticed that she caught many more big fish than small ones and that she hurriedly hid them under the boards at the bottom of the canoe, giving him only the few little fish, just as before. He became furious with his stingy grandmother; he did not want to stay with her any longer nor have anything more to do with her. So he said to her: "Grandmother, my stomach hurts; I have to go aside; go in to shore quickly, I'm in a hurry!" She replied: "How come? Hold out a bit longer and wait a little; soon we'll turn around." To this he said anxiously: "I really can't stand it any longer, I'm in a great hurry. Go in to shore quickly, otherwise something bad will happen to me!" So the old woman quickly went toward shore. When the little boy stood up to disembark he angrily threw the small fish into the water and jumped out of the canoe. Downcast he hurried to the hut. He was very annoyed with his grandmother and wanted nothing more to do with her; she had treated him very badly.

The boy's grandfather was sitting in the hut. As soon as he saw his little grandson return alone he asked: "Why are you coming back here all alone, and on foot at that? What happened that made you come back alone? Where is my wife?" His grandson answered plaintively: "She is still out there in the canoe. I didn't want to stay with her any longer and simply ran away. She gave me nothing but small fish to eat, and that I won't put up with any more. I became very angry and ran away." The old man did not answer a word. The little boy asked for some *imi* (red soil for painting) because he wanted to paint himself. His grandfather let him have his way. He gave him *imi* and the grandson painted himself. No sooner had he finished doing so than he left the hut without saying a word. He ran deep into the forest and became a bird. He never ever returned to the hut again but has stayed since then in the forest. That is the little *tulératécix*, the nimble tree-creeper (*Aphrastura spinicauda*) which elsewhere is called *tečikášina*.[57]

Not until evening did the grandmother enter her hut, calling at once: "My little grandson, where are you? Come to me quickly, I bring you many big fish!" But she got no reply. The old man said to his wife: "Our grandson is no longer here." "But didn't he come back?" asked the grandmother. "Certainly he came back," the old man replied. "But he was very angry. He just painted himself with *imi* and ran out into the forest without saying a word. I don't know where he is now." The old woman became very sad at this. Soon the two old people began to cry bitterly, for they were very fond of their little grandson. A long time went by, but the little grandson never again returned from the forest. Finally the two old people put on mourning paint and went into the forest to look for him. Crying, they searched everywhere; they climbed the hills and shed many tears. The tears became small brooks which are still flowing today. They are the tears of those old people crying over their grandson, for whom they are still searching the forest in vain.

Old Wekatánaxipa was the first woman to use the *téši* as a sinker on the fishing line, that is, the black round stone of porphyry with a shallow groove. Since then several other women have also acquired the *téši* and use it for fishing.[58]

Informant: Not known; pp. 1220-1222.

Summary

Woman takes her grandson fishing but keeps all big fish, giving him only small ones. Angrily the boy leaves her and becomes a bird in the forest. Grandparents search for him, crying; their tears become brooks and streams.

Motif content

A911.	Bodies of water from tears.
A1457.1.+.	Origin of the sinker. (A1457.1. Origin of the fish hook.)
A2411.2.+.	Origin of color of tree-creeper. (A2411.2. Origin of color of bird.)

[57]This form refers to the round pebble (Gusinde 1937:1213, fig. 93) which the grandmother used; cf. p. 95 n. 37.

[58]In this story the explanatory elements are the night heron's predilection for big fish and the origin of the many small brooks on the hills.

D150.	Transformation: man to bird.
F634.	Mighty fisherman.
H1385.	Quest for lost persons.
J1341.	Retort from underfed servant (child).
K1700.	Deception through bluffing.
P681.	Mourning customs.
Q276.	Stinginess punished.
R228.+.	Child leaves home because grandmother is stingy with food. (R228. Children leave home because their parents refuse them food.)
S41.	Cruel grandmother.
W152.	Stinginess.

39. The Stingy Elephant Seal and His Two Grandsons

Old Hášaxuwa had two grandsons who lived with him in his hut. He[59] was very niggardly and stingy; he gave his two grandsons only very little to eat. In his hut hung the stomach of a big sea lion[60] filled with delicious oil, but he let his grandsons have only small amounts of this. And even this small amount he scrupulously measured out in the little shell of an *auwéra* mussel.[61] That was all they got every day. Although they demanded more he inexorably allowed them only this tiny amount. The two grandsons grew thinner from day to day and hungrily implored the old man: "Come now, give us a little more to eat!" Sullenly the old man would answer: "I don't have enough oil to give you more. I have only a little bit left and that we must use very sparingly!" Since the two grandsons would not stop begging him, stingy Hášaxuwa put them off with harsh words and said at last: "Now the sea lion oil is finished!"

Both boys had become terribly thin. They considered killing stingy Hášaxuwa, for they were convinced that he was keeping the oil hidden, intending not to give them any more of it. One day they tiptoed out of the hut and ran far away; they wanted to search the beach for something with which to appease their hunger. During their search they

[59]The male of the southern elephant seal, *Macrorhinus leoninus*; cf. Gusinde 1937:482, fig. 40.

[60]The stomach of a sea lion is blown up tightly and hung up to dry; then it serves as a container, primarily for whale oil. It can easily be carried around everywhere and does not leak.

[61]The patella, which is common there on the beaches.

came upon a big shell of the *auwéra* mussel. They ran back to their hut
to show their grandfather the big mussel shell, saying: "Look what a big
auwéra shell we've found! Couldn't you fill it up with oil for us? Until
now you've only filled a very small *auwéra* shell for us which barely
holds a few drops." Stingly Hášaxuwa immediately inquired: "Where
did you find this big mussel shell?" The two grandsons answered:
"Come with us! We'll show you the island where we found it. There are
very many of these big *auwéra!*" The three of them set out at once.
When they reached the island the two grandsons said to their grandfather: "This is where the big *auwéra* are!" When the old man bent over
to pick up the mussels the two grandsons suddenly sneaked up behind
him and gave him a hard push. Heavy Hášaxuwa rolled down the
beach into the water and drowned.

The two grandsons ran back to their hut at once. Here they looked
through everything and discovered a large amount of sea lion oil which
their stingy grandfather had kept hidden. They were beside themselves
with joy. But on the inside of the *auwéra* shell to this day one can still
clearly discern the mark[62] up to which stingy Hášaxuwa filled the
mussel shell with sea lion oil for his two grandsons.

Informant: Not known; pp. 1225-1226.

Summary

Stingy and cruel grandfather is lured down to beach by starving grandsons.
They push him into water where he drowns. Shell of certain mussel still has ring
marking grandsons' daily ration of sea lion oil.

Motif content

A2411.5.4.	Color of mussel.
J1341.	Retort from underfed servant (child).
K832.	Dupe induced to look about: seized and killed.
K926.	Victim pushed into water.
K958.	Murder by drowning.
K959.4.	Murder from behind.
Q276.	Stinginess punished.
Q467.	Punishment by drowning.
S20.2. +.	Grandfather hides food from starving grandsons. (S20.2. Child hides food from starving parents.)
S42.	Cruel grandfather.
W152.	Stinginess.

[62]Inside the mussel shell the lower part is dark-colored, contrasting sharply with a
lighter upper ring. One is justified to call this a dividing mark.

40. How Little Lášix Killed the Dolphin

A long time ago a powerful dolphin[63] came here from the open sea. It swam very close to the surface of the water and the people could see it easily. It stopped when it got close to a large camp where many people had built their huts. All loudly gave vent to their joy; they wanted to kill it on the spot and let it beach itself. It was extremely large and promised much blubber and oil. Instantly all the men grabbed their harpoons and the women pushed the canoes into the water; the individual families got in and quickly paddled toward the dolphin. From all sides the men threw their harpoons against the animal's large body. They put up a great effort, but then they grew tired and ran out of harpoons. The dolphin did not seem to notice the multitude of large and deep wounds at all; there was nothing to indicate that it was exhausted and might beach itself.

Disappointed, the people returned to camp. Some of them still had one or two harpoons left in their huts which they brought out. Others sat down and hastily assembled new ones. Anyone who had a few weapons at hand got back into his canoe and went out toward the dolphin, again throwing his harpoon against it. Once again many men spent all their weapons, but totally without success. The powerful animal continued to swim about and to ignore the wounds; there was nothing to suggest that it was tired and might beach itself. The men had exhausted themselves.

The people found it strange that the dolphin kept opening its mouth wide and then leisurely closing it again. One of the men had a cunning thought and hastened to say: "This powerful *wéoina* keeps opening its big mouth wide and then very slowly closes it again. What if an agile man jumped into its mouth, proceeded quickly into its stomach, and cut it up completely from inside?" It was little Lášix[64] to whom this idea occurred. Timidly the other men replied: "You yourself may try to jump into its mouth if you have the courage!" He answered bravely: "All right, I'll try."

So all the people returned once more to the beach where their camp was. The men had again deployed all their weapons, and promptly started manufacturing new ones. But Lášix made himself a big, sharp knife. The women improved their canoes and caulked them well, for the vessels had badly suffered from knocking repeatedly against the dolphin and from the many movements of the men hurling their

[63]The big dolphin, *Globicephala melas*.
[64]The black martin, *Iridoprocne (Tachycineta) Meyeni*.

harpoons. After the people had finished their particular tasks they returned to their canoes and paddled toward the animal.

Once again the men threw their heavy harpoons against the huge body of the dolphin, but although the harpoons remained stuck in it they showed no effect. Little Lášix said to his wife: "Steer the canoe exactly in front of its mouth." His wife paddled on, steered her canoe exactly in front of the mouth of the dolphin, and stopped. As usual little Lášix sat up front in the bow. When the dolphin once again slowly opened its big mouth, little Lášix made a vigorous leap and jumped inside. The dolphin swallowed little Lášix without any difficulty.

But now the dolphin slowly left the coast and swam far out to the open sea. Inside the stomach little Lášix began to cut up the animal's inner organs with his big sharp knife. He cut up its lungs, stomach, liver, and bowels, so that the dolphin had to vomit; it opened its big mouth again and again and threw up all these pieces. For the time being, however, little Lášix spared the dolphin's heart, so that the animal would continue to live for some time. Little Lášix realized that the dolphin had to be swimming out on the open sea: through the wall of the dolphin's stomach he could hear high waves beating constantly against it. He hoped that the sick and weak animal would eventually approach shore exhausted; not until then would he cut up the heart. But all he heard was high waves beating and breaking against the powerful body. He began to feel very uneasy and said to himself: "All this is lasting too long for me. I'd better cut up the heart right now and try to get out of here, however I can! How do I even know where I am; certainly still on the open sea." Then little Lášix unexpectedly heard the quacking of the *wíyen*.[65] To him it was a sign that he was near land, for these *wíyen* live near the coast. He quickly cut up the big dolphin's heart and at once much blood flowed. The dolphin lost all its strength. It became very sad, feeling that death was near. Soon it was unable to breathe and could neither swim nor move; it only kept itself on the surface by floating, and the waves alone propelled it. Finally all strength left it and it no longer moved; it was now really dead.

Soon the big *dášalux*[66] came in a flock to have themselves a good meal from the huge animal. Little Lášix noticed this from inside, for he heard the big birds hacking on the back of the dead dolphin. At once he made up his mind, saying: "I'll knock hard against the stomach wall. This will frighten the birds; they'll fly up and hover high in the air. The people will observe this from afar and say to themselves: 'It must be a dead dolphin floating around there!' Then they will quickly set out and

[65]The wild duck, *Anas cristata*, which travels in flocks.
[66]The big albatross, *Diomedea melanophrys*.

come here; I'll be able to save myself." So little Lášix knocked hard against the stomach wall of the dead dolphin; all the *dášalux* became very frightened and flew up. They flew high up in the air and hovered excitedly for a long time. Then they lowered themselves again and perched on the dead animal, which the waves were slowly pushing along. There were so many *dášalux* hovering over the carcass that they attracted the attention of the people in the camp. They called to one another: "There must be a dead dolphin drifting out there, for many *dášalux* keep flying up all the time!" Once little Lášix had cut up the heart of the *wéoina* the dolphin had turned toward the coast again. When it got close to the camp those people there discovered it.

After a while little Lášix once more knocked against the stomach wall of the dead dolphin. Again the flock of *dášalux* became frightened; they flew away and rose up high. For a long time they hovered in the air and then returned to perch on the back of the dead animal, which the waves were slowly propelling. Little Lášix told himself: "I hope my people have been observing the many *dášalux!* Then they'll soon come with their canoes and I'll be saved!" And, indeed, he was soon overjoyed to hear the beating of the paddles, for that meant that many canoes had come up close to the big dolphin. He heard the lamentations and cries of his people. They were mourning for brave little Lášix whom they considered lost and dead by then. The many people that had gathered around the big, dead dolphin pooled their strength and pulled it closer to the coast, where the current would assist in pushing it ashore. Everybody exerted himself and pulled vigorously. When at last the huge animal lay on the beach they said to one another in low voices and full of satisfaction: "It's really an unusually big and fat dolphin!" It was already late in the evening, so they hurried back to their huts. All were very happy; now there was blubber and meat in abundance.

In this place the people were just enacting *kína* and a large number of men were participating. When so mighty a dolphin was given them completely unexpectedly they were beside themselves with joy, for now they had lots of blubber and meat available and were able to extend their *kína* for a long time. At dawn the next day they promptly cut up and distributed much fat and meat from the dolphin; each got a big piece. They ate large amounts and were very contented. Several days passed. One night two boys from the *kína*-hut, who were to be initiated, were sent to the beach where the dolphin was lying. They were to cut out a few pieces of meat and bring them to the *kína*-hut, where the men wanted more to eat. The two boys ran to where the animal was lying. They brought a long knife. With this, one of them made a deep cut into the dolphin, so deep that he hit a rib; he wanted to cut out a big piece. Then he suddenly heard from inside: "Hi, hi, hi"; it sounded as though a man had been wounded. He also heard: "Don't stab me!" The boy became very frightened and said to himself: "What can that be? It sounds exactly as if a man were sitting in there calling to me: 'Don't stab me!' Who might that be?" Fear seized him but he did not want to show it. Instead he called the other boy, and told him with decided satisfaction: "Look what a nice piece of meat I cut out of this part of the body! You cut with the knife, but very deep!" That was all he said. Then the other boy took the long knife and cut deeply into the dolphin. Now he, too, heard the cry from inside: "Hi, hi, hi, don't cut me!" That frightened him very much. Only then did the other boy admit: "I also heard this voice before! What can that be?" He replied: "How strange all this is! What can it be?" The two boys knew nothing of what had occurred, namely, that all the people had been harpooning the dolphin unsuccessfully for a long time and that finally little Lášix had jumped into its mouth. As boys about to be initiated in the *kína* they had not been allowed to leave the Big Hut at the time when all the others had been struggling over the dolphin.

The two boys went back to the *kína*-hut, each carrying a big piece of meat. They put the pieces down before the one in charge of the ceremony and hurried silently to their places. All the men inspected the pieces of meat approvingly. The one in charge instructed the two boys: "Roast these pieces of meat and distribute them among the men!" The two novices sat down by the fire, roasted the big pieces of meat, cut them up, and gave some to each man. Only then did they reveal what they had heard when they sliced off the pieces of meat. That also surprised the men. After all, they had just spent all their weapons on that dolphin, seemingly in vain, and they remembered that little Lášix had earlier intended to kill him. He had since disappeared, however, and the dolphin had left the coast. They finally agreed, assuming correctly, "The animal out there on the beach must be the dolphin we harpooned; it was certainly this one into whose mouth little Lášix jumped. So he's still alive!"

It was barely getting light in the east when all the men from the *kína*-hut rushed straight down to the beach where the big dolphin was lying. They did this very early in the morning so that the women and children would not be able to see from the camp what was happening. Each of the men cautiously sliced into the meat with his knife along the entire length of the big animal and together they lifted off the whole layer of meat that covered the ribs. Then with even greater care they lifted off all the meat lying between the ribs and close to the inside of the rib cage. Thus they reached the belly. This too they now opened with their knives, but taking special care. And here sat little Lášix, all huddled up, pale and thin, bald, and near death! Pity swept through the crowd when they saw him in this miserable condition. They immediately took him from the belly of the big dolphin and carried him quickly to the *kína*-hut. None of the women and children could witness any of this from the camp; the men had carried everything out very unobtrusively. Here in the *kína*-hut the men placed little Lášix by the fire where he could warm himself. They gave him much to eat so that he might grow strong and regain his speech. They also rubbed oil all over his body to revive him. On his bald head they sprinkled pulverized charcoal to make the lost hair grow back. Thus they attended to him and cared for him in the best possible way. Under the care given him by all the men in the *kína*-hut little Lášix soon felt better and quickly recovered. Also his hair was growing again. With each day he felt better and better.

Lášix spent a long time in the *kína*-hut with the other men; neither women nor children in the camp knew any of this. Little Lášix had three wives in all. Since he had been gone for such a long time and since he was believed dead, two of the three women soon looked for another husband. But the third wife was determined to continue waiting just in case her husband might still come back. She remained faithful to him. She already had several children by him.

According to custom, the men left the *kína*-hut at certain intervals and went out into the open. Women and children were then allowed to leave the camp, approach the group of men, and look at them. One day the men were playing *kálaka* and the women drew near so they could watch each player closely. One of them soon attracted attention; he was extremely skillful and thrilled all the spectators. Among the latter there was also the woman who had remained faithful to little Lášix. When she saw this man's extraordinary cleverness she watched attentively for some time. Then she said, barely audibly: "That player there looks very much like my husband, who was extremely good at *kálaka*. But of course, it is utterly impossible that he be my husband, for everybody assumes him to be dead by now!" The men finished their game of *kálaka* and went back to the *kína*-hut; the women and children returned to the camp.

Little Lášix was now almost completely restored. He realized that his father believed him long dead and was profoundly mourning his death. On several occasions he had already sent for his father to come to the *kína*-hut, but in vain. The old man was feeling the most bitter grief; each day he painted himself anew and wept all day long. For this very reason he did not want to leave his hut and show himself to other people. Once again the men in the *kína*-hut urgently sent for the old man. At last he came. The men put his son, little Lášix, before him; the latter was still pale and thin and noticeably bald. When little Lášix saw his old father deeply bent from grief he could no longer control himself and out of pity for him burst into loud sobs. He cried so loudly and so hard that the people in the camp could hear him. His wife who had remained faithful to him paid particular attention, saying: "That crying sounds exactly as though it came from my husband! I wonder if it's really him crying so loudly? But how could it be—he's been dead for so long! Did he not jump into the mouth of that *wéoina* which then swam out to the open sea and hasn't shown up since. What a pity it is about my dear husband!"

The men took great delight in the *kína*-celebration, and did not think of ending it soon. One day they went out again, intending to hunt seals. For some time they had already been in possession of extremely well-made harpoon points so that their hunt was always successful. By chance the woman who had remained faithful to little Lášix saw one of these harpoon points in the hands of one of the men. Unobtrusively she examined it closely and said to herself: "How could this man have gotten this extremely well-made harpoon point? The men spent all their harpoon points some time ago when struggling with the big dolphin that passed by here. Since then I have not noticed even a single man making new harpoon points. Besides, not one of these men is capable of fashioning such perfect harpoon points as my husband used to. He was really incomparably more skilled in this work than anybody else; nobody could match him. How much I miss my dear husband: how much I've already wept over him!" And again she cried bitterly.

After a long, long time the men decided at last to end their *kína*-celebration. Meanwhile all of little Lášix's hair had grown back and he was now fully recovered. Together, as usual, all the men left the big *kína*-hut and returned to the camp. Here brave little Lášix now showed himself to his faithful wife, his relatives, and all the other people. Everyone was speechless with joy and surprise. Little Lášix proceeded to relate in detail all he had gone through and how he had saved himself. The people marveled at this brave little man; they were very happy and thanked him for giving them this enormous *wéoina*. Happiest of all was his faithful wife; she had had to wait for him for so long.

Informant: Not known; pp. 1226-1232.

Summary

Villagers try in vain to kill big dolphin. Finally man jumps into dolphin's mouth and stomach to cut it up from inside. Animal dies with man trapped inside. Villagers find stranded dolphin but the men, occupied with *kína*-celebration, realize only after several days that man is inside, and rescue him. He is secretly taken to men's *kína*-hut and kept there until he has recovered.

Meanwhile he is presumed dead by rest of village, and his father and wife mourn him. After *kína*-celebration is over he returns to family.

Motif content

A526.2.	Culture hero as mighty hunter.
A535.	Culture hero swallowed and recovered from animal.
A2433.4.+.	Haunts of ducks. (A2433.4. Haunts of birds.)
B874.	Giant fish.
D1812.5.0.2.	Omens from flight of birds.
D1841.5.2.	Magic animal proof against weapons.
D2161.3.4.	Baldness magically cured.
F660.	Remarkable skill.
F679.5.	Skillful hunter.
F911.4.	Jonah. Fish (or water monster) swallows a man.
F912.2	Victim kills swallower from within by cutting.
F913.	Victim rescued from swallower's belly.
F915.	Victim speaks from swallower's body.
F921.	Swallowed person becomes bald.
F950.	Marvelous cures.
F989.15.	Hunt for extraordinary (magic) animal.
H30.	Recognition through personal peculiarities.
H31.	Recognition by unique ability.
H32.	Recognition by extraordinary prowess.
K477.	Attention secured by trickery.
K910.	Murder by strategy.
K952.	Animal (monster) killed from within.
L112.2.	Very small hero.
N681.0.1.+.	Return home to witness one's own mourning rites. (N681.0.1. Return home to one's own funeral.)
P681.	Mourning customs.
Q83.1.	Reward for wife's fidelity.
R245.	Whale-boat.
T145.0.1.	Polygyny.
T211.	Faithfulness to marriage in death.
T231.	The faithless widow.
U243.	Courage conquers all and impossible is made possible.
Z293.	Return of the hero.

41. The Ibis-woman's Berries

There once lived a woman here who always gathered berries for herself in alien territory,[67] because in the region where her husband

---

[67]This expression means: outside the territory of the group to which her husband belonged. Her behavior was contrary to custom and common law.

lived there grew no *šanamáim*[68] at all. That was Léxuwakipa.[69]. She was in mourning at that time. One evening when many people had gathered once more for the mourning ceremony she started to speak and complained loudly: "How I'd like to be in the region where my own closest relatives[70] live! There are many *amáim;* we all like them very much." Then she continued to sing and speak but repeated these words several times.[71]

A number of men had also come to the hut for the mourning gathering. One of them began to speak and, referring to Léxuwakipa's words, said sympathetically: "If there are lots of berries in your home territory we'll send a few men there to bring back as many as they can carry!" Then he continued to sing and chant in his sorrow. After the people had ended their ceremony they extinguished the fire and each returned to his hut.

The following day Léxuwakipa herself set off all alone in the direction where her family lived. When she reached the hut of her relatives she entered and said: "How are you? The Hítokuwinišináala[72] have sent me here. I'm supposed to gather lots of berries and bring them back, for, you see, there are no berries at all there!" The relatives were happy that the woman had once more come to visit. Immediately they wanted to help her. Soon a few people left to collect many *amáim*. They filled a big bag with *púxel* (in the eastern dialect; *uškúlempi* in the western dialect; the Selknam say *páxal*),[73] for these animals are Léxuwakipa's *amáim*. At the same time she herself had gone out with other women to gather the real berries. With these she filled her little basket barely half full, much too little for all the people who had sent her there. But the other women gathered *púxel* and filled a bag to the brim with them. They gave it to Léxuwakipa and she started home with the bag and the basket.

---

[68]This noun applies primarily to the small light-red berries of the *Pernettya pumila,* a Myrtacea (Gusinde 1937:556, fig. 67), but is sometimes also used for the larger berries of the *Pernettya mucronata* (ibid., p. 121, fig. 12).

[69]The ibis, *Theristicus melanopis,* known as *"bandurria,"* which plays the main role also in narratives 6 and 7.

[70]Because of her marriage she had exchanged her own family's territory for that of her husband, as demanded by the current rule of exogamy (ibid., p. 653).

[71]An allusion to the free expression of opinions and unrestrained discussion that is allowed everybody participating in the mourning ceremony (ibid., p. 1131).

[72]The *bandurria* invented this name herself in order to deceive and mislead her relatives.

[73]The big brass-beetle, *Carabus auratus,* favorite food of the ibis. It is said that this beetle bores a hole in the shell of bird eggs, crawls in, and eats the entire contents. Its presence is quickly noticed through the very unpleasant odor which it gives off to keep its enemies away.

When she reached her husband's hut, where his relatives were waiting, she gave all the people *amáim* from the basket that was half full. But the bag with *púxel* she hid in the hut; these she wanted to eat secretly herself. The people said in disappointment: "But how stingy this woman is; she gave us only a few berries! Yet she was bragging and showing off to us before: 'Where my family lives there are lots of *amáim!*' What a selfish woman!" When the quiet night had fallen and Léxuwakipa thought that nobody was watching her, she brought the bag out from its hiding place and stuffed one *amáim* after the other into her mouth. They were her *amáim*, that is [they were actually] *púxel*. But every time she bit into a *púxel* the people in the neighboring huts heard the cracking of something between her teeth. They soon realized what was going on and called to one another: "What a miserable woman Léxuwakipa is. Just listen: all night long she eats *amáim* by herself! Indeed, one can clearly hear it crack all the time between her teeth."

Soon afterward the people again felt a strong desire for *šanamáim*. They discussed how they might lure Léxuwakipa out of her hut and take away her bag full of *amáim*, to distribute them among themselves. Her husband and a few other men turned to her and said: "The tide is all the way out. Why don't you go to the beach and quickly gather some big mussels for us!" She said: "I'll go at once." She got up, took her little basket, and hurried down to the beach which was far away.

When she had gone a good distance one of the men said: "Now it's time for us to take revenge on that selfish, stingy Léxuwakipa!" Without further ado he hurried into her hut and searched it thoroughly. Finally he discovered the big bag. As he was about to open it he saw a *púxel* sitting on top. At first he thought that the beetle had simply gotten there by chance. But when he opened the bag and looked inside he discovered a great number of these beetles busily moving around. Alarmed and disgusted by the repulsive odor from all the *púxel* he quickly closed the bag and pushed it back into its hiding place. He rushed out and set fire to the hut from the outside. Soon the flames were raging high. From the beach Léxuwakipa became aware of this, but she had to watch how the flames rapidly consumed her house.[74] Sadly she exclaimed: "Oh poor me, all my things are burning up now. What a pity that I also lose all the *amáim!*"

[74]This part essentially agrees with the Selknam story about the great albatross (Gusinde 1931:657; Wilbert 1975:118). The role of the selfish woman in the latter is played by the lapwing, *Belonopterus chilensis*, which is not far from *Theristicus melanopis* in the natural order. The Selknam regard both birds as sisters (Gusinde 1951:661).

Léxuwakipa came running from the beach, sighing all the way: "How sorry I am about all the *amáim!*" Another woman heard her and replied: "We don't eat such stinking things and don't offer them to anybody: we eat something better!" The one who thus exclaimed was Aiakélum, daughter of the *epáiači*.[75] Smartly she added: "My relatives eat only excellent and very tasty things, namely oil from whales and seals. But the kind of stinking little animals that are your favorite food we don't even touch. Besides, my family always has an abundance of oil. Where I live there is always much of this delicious stuff around!" Old Epáiači, Aiakélum's father, was standing close by and heard his daughter's words; he immediately added: "Well, we're all going to stay here for a while. I want you to go at once to your family's territory and fetch whatever is stored in your kinfolk's ample oil supply!" Aiakélum's husband (one also says Aiakélem)[76] was little Lefkóiya;[77] he agreed to his wife's journey. For these people had all gotten together here for a big mourning ceremony and with the intention of staying for several days. Meanwhile, the woman was to undertake the journey to her home.

Léxuwakipa's hut was still burning in the place where the people had gathered for their mourning songs. When they saw the flames they stopped singing, fetched a lot of water, and put out the fire. Then they all returned to their huts.

The following morning the weather was beautiful. Aiakélum quickly got into her caoe and left. With her went little Čámux,[78] her son. The territory of her family was far away and she had to travel long. Because there were always many whales there, the *lakúma*[79] also went there. But this woman was very clever and cunning. Every time a *lakúma* approached her canoe she addressed it in a friendly tone: "Are you all right, my dear grandfather?" The *lakúma* heard these friendly words and allowed her to proceed without hurting her in the least. Soon another *lakúma* came toward her, and to this one, too, she called in a friendly voice: "Are you all right, my dear grandfather?" Then it likewise let her continue unmolested. In this way she managed to get through the infested waters without harm. At last she reached her home. She brought her canoe up to the shore so that her little son could comfortably get ashore. But every spot on the beach, even the smallest,

[75]The bottle-nosed whale or springer, *Orca magellanica* (Gusinde 1937:37).
[76]The younger bottle-nosed whales, which form small schools.
[77]The little wood owl, *Glaucidium nanum*.
[78]The large wren, *Zonotrichia canicapilla*. In addition there exists in the Cape Horn area a second, smaller species, *Troglodytes hornensis*.
[79]This dangerous water-spirit is described more closely in Gusinde 1937:1285.

was covered with oil and grease so that the little boy slipped at every step; he could not put one foot forward without falling. The mother saw this. In a loud voice she called from the canoe: "This is my son. Let him walk up the beach!" Whereupon little Čámux no longer slipped but comfortably reached the top. Meanwhile the mother pushed away from the beach and at some distance tied the canoe to a bunch of seaweed; then she swam to the beach, walked up, and entered her family's hut with her little son. Her relatives were very happy when they saw Aiakélum. They sat down by the fire and talked for a long time.

Among the huts there were some with people who did not belong to Aiakélum's family. Húruf,[80] too, had by chance settled here. Normally he dwells far out on the open sea. When he heard that a woman had come from far away he became curious and said: "I'll take a look at her at once. Who can she be?" He entered the hut where Aiakélum was sitting. From the moment he saw her he liked her immensely; her figure entranced him and he soon started giving her amorous looks. The woman responded to him in the same way. Surreptitiously Húruf moved nearer and nearer until he was sitting very close to Aiakélum. Night had long since fallen and it was dark all around them. They had been waiting for this. The woman was sitting there with her legs pulled up (in a squatting position). Húruf gave her his hand. The woman took the man's hand and placed it on her sexual organs. After inserting his finger into her vagina the man played around there for a rather long time. His very long finger excited the woman so much that moisture flowed from her vagina. But the man continued to excite her in this way, which gave him very great pleasure. In this manner the two sat close together until far into the night. Only then did Húruf go back to his hut. It satisfied him greatly to have aroused Aiakélum so strongly, for now he was sure that she would take him for her husband. Aiakélum, in turn, could not sleep all night for sheer satisfaction. She said to herself: "Since I now must take Húruf for my husband I'll ask my family here for a large amount of oil and blubber. First I'll take this to my old husband and his kin; then I'll come right back again. My son shall stay here so that my husband will let me return soon. From now on I want to live with Húruf who loves me very much!"

The next morning this woman shrewdly and inconspicuously informed Húruf of her plan. To her folks she said: "Give me lots of oil and blubber; I want to take it to my husband and his family. You see, there they lack all that." They willingly gave her as much as she

---

[80] The powerful storm bird, *Macronectes gigantea*, conspicuous for its long, narrow wings.

wanted. She loaded everything into her canoe, then got in herself and pushed off at once. But little Čámux she left behind.

No sooner had she reached her husband's hut than she distributed the large amount of blubber and oil that she had brought. All the people were most contented. Then she informed her husband: "I'd like to stay here only for a few days; my family insists on seeing me again soon. Also, I had to leave little Čámux there since I wanted to bring the canoe filled with oil and blubber." Her husband replied: "All right, visit your family again. But come back soon and bring our child!" Quickly she got into her canoe and traveled to the region where her relatives lived. She went immediately to meet Húruf, and she has been living with him ever since. Today one still sees his long finger which he had inserted into the woman's vagina in order to arouse her desire.[81]

Informant: Not known; pp. 1233-1238.

Summary

Selfish woman travels to own family group to get food and returns with beetles for herself but with only a few berries for husband's relatives. They steal her beetles, believing them to be berries, but on finding repulsive animals they set fire to her hut in revenge.

[81]In connection with this story I was told: The big storm bird has a long, narrow wing. That wing is his very long finger with which he had excited the woman to sexual pleasure, after inserting it into her vagina. It is a well-known rule, known to the people, that if a man approaches a woman and excites her in this way they have to get married, to their own shame and as a warning to others. Boys and girls, who sometimes are informed by old people of the relationship of the sexes with each other, at the right age and on a suitable occasion, are told of that rule. But in practice it would be the individual circumstances of the two persons that counted. If the man who had thus committed an offense with a woman had no particular desire to marry her, and if she for her part likewise withdrew, the offense would remain hidden and neither of them would worry about the law. If the man insisted upon having the woman but she wanted to stay away from him and keep the incident secret, another way would remain open to the man to reach his goal. If his efforts to influence her were in vain, he would confide in a close friend of hers and reveal to this woman that he had committed an offense with the other one and had touched her in the manner described above and that she had responded to his forwardness in the way mentioned thereby demonstrating how easily she was excited by him. After that the relatives of the woman try to influence her by every means, and earnestly and reproachfully tell her that after such an occurrence it simply is the custom for the woman in question to marry the man. If she finally has no way out she stops resisting and marries the man. But if she already is married, which is most often the case, she has to leave her present husband. The latter usually agrees without resistance and resigns himself to the separation, for in this he sees the best solution for a relationship which after all is no longer sincere. Still, it may happen that the legitimate husband opposes his wife's intention of moving over to his rival. If he does not want to give her up she continues to stay with him and he watches her particularly carefully. If this husband should go away for a few days and leave his wife behind, he takes for granted that she runs to her lover's hut and sleeps with him. The husband and the other people really no longer find this an offense, for the two of them would belong together anyway

Another woman journeys to family group through waters infested with water-spirits to get food. While there she falls in love with another man. After brief return to husband's village with food she goes back to stay with lover.

Motif content

A2377.	Animal characteristics: wings.
C41.	Tabu: offending water-spirit.
D1765.	Magic results produced by command.
F420.2.	Home of water-spirits.
F851.	Extraordinary food.
J610.	Forethought in conflict with others—general.
J640.	Avoidance of others' power.
J2301.	Gullible husbands.
K330.	Means of hoodwinking the guardian or owner.
K572.	Escape from captor by means of flattery.
K1510.	Adulteress outwits husband.
K1952.2.	Better things at home.
K2060.	Detection of hypocrisy.
K2213.	Treacherous wife.
N440.+.	Secret learned. (N440. Valuable secrets learned.)
P681.	Mourning customs.
Q261.2.	Treacherous wife punished.
Q276.	Stinginess punished.
Q595.	Loss or destruction of property as punishment.
R227.2.	Flight from hated husband.
T131.5.	Exogamy.
T263.	The hypocritical wife.
T481.	Adultery.
W11.	Generosity.
W128.	Dissatisfaction.
W152.	Stinginess.

42. The Grampus

For some time Ašóulaxipa[82] had not loved her husband; she had grown tired of him. Therefore she liked to go out on the ocean alone in

---

as married people if the legitimate husband had not opposed their marriage. But they are allowed to be together in this way only when the legitimate husband is absent. The latter, however, correctly judging his wife's innermost feelings, will deliberately never let it happen that she is left alone where her lover lives. Therefore this last-mentioned concession probably never means anything in reality.

[82]The female small grampus, also called springer, *Pseudarca crassidens*.

her canoe, where she would spend a long time fishing. She always took her younger son along with her, leaving the elder son behind in the hut with his father.

Whenever she got close to a *lakúma* the cunning woman said to him from her canoe: "Oh, how nice; there I see my dear grandfather again!" Whereupon the *lakúma* let her continue unmolested and did her no harm. When she continued paddling and met another *lakúma* she called to this one, too, in a friendly tone: "Oh, how nice; there I see my dear grandfather again!" That way this one, too, let the woman continue without doing her any harm. This is how Ašóulaxipa saved herself every time. But many other women were dragged out of their canoes by the *lakúma* and pulled to the bottom of the sea.

Once a whale had stranded on a nearby island. Ašóulaxipa went there with her canoe to get some oil. As soon as her canoe touched shore she let her young son get out. But the rocky beach was completely covered with oil and was so slippery that the boy kept losing his footing. Ašóulaxipa called out in a loud voice: "Listen, you, don't let my little son slip all the time! He keeps falling and falling." There was, indeed, a man living on the island whom she secretly loved and for whom this was intended. She called in this sly way to lure him out. Soon the man came to the beach. When he saw Ašóulaxipa, he liked her very much. The two fell in love at first sight. The man said to her: "Stay with me on this island. You can be my wife." Ašóulaxipa was very pleased with this proposal and secretly rejoiced. She answered: "All right, I'll be your wife. But first let me get my elder son; he's staying with his father in the hut!" She hurried back to her hut, but did not make her intentions known. The moment no one was looking she put her elder son in the canoe and went away with him. Soon they reached the island again. Since then Ašóulaxipa has lived with that man on the island, having left her first husband forever.[83]

Informant: Not known; pp. 1261-1262.

Summary

Woman is tired of her husband. She goes with her sons to island to live with another man, avoiding dangerous water-spirits on the way.

Motif content

C41.	Tabu: offending water-spirit.
F420.5.2.1.5.+.	Water-spirit drags women into water. (F420.5.2.1.5. Water-spirit drags children into river.)

[83]What is so important in this story is the reference to the behavior of the Yamana toward a *lakúma*, which they greatly fear. It is considered to be a sea monster that endangers every canoe and pulls the passengers down into the sea. This evil water-spirit is described in more detail below (Gusinde 1937:1285-1286).

K477.	Attention secured by trickery.
K572.	Escape from captor by means of flattery.
K1510.	Adulteress outwits husband.
K2213.	Treacherous wife.
R227.2.	Flight from hated husband.
T481.	Adultery.

43. The Discontented Father-in-law

Old Tútu[84] had long been a widower. Because his unmarried children had died, too, he lived with his son-in-law. The latter had willingly received the old man in his hut, for it was his duty as son-in-law to do so. As the old man had no other relatives, his son-in-law cared for him and supported him during the last days of his life. Every day the son-in-law went to the beach, fetched mussels and meat, and occasionally brought fruits from the forest. But the old man was forever dissatisfied. Nothing was to his liking; although he ate of everything that his son-in-law brought he was always complaining about it. He used to say: "I'm very old already but I do feel like chewing something that I really like!" Then the son-in-law would look for other things and bring something new to the hut every day. But that would not please the old man, either, for after tasting it he would again say discontentedly: "I'm very old already but I do feel like chewing something that I really like!"[85]

It displeased the son-in-law that the old man was dissatisfied all the time. He did not say anything about it for that did not befit him; he had to show respect for his father-in-law. But secretly he was completely at a loss and wondered: "What might it be that the old man wants to chew and that he would really like?" He thought about it and continued to bring more things which he put before his father-in-law. The latter tasted and chewed everything but always followed it with the same discontented remark. The son-in-law then brought a few hard things. Old Tútu chewed them but he remained nonetheless dissatisfied and nothing suited him. The son-in-law again reflected; he continued to search, always bringing new and harder things.[86]

[84]This name probably belongs to the *Myiotheretes rufiventris*, a small bird with black feathers and a white spot on the head. According to this story he, as a *yékamuš*, had the habit of rubbing white soil into his hair.

[85]Note that the father-in-law avoids direct address and discussion. In the same way the son-in-law does not dare to ask openly, for which reason he stands there totally at a loss and has to do his own thinking. This agrees completely with the prevailing customs (Gusinde 1937:658).

[86]Clearly expressed is the effort of the son-in-law to please his father-in-law in the only way possible for him. Yamana customary law requires this of children-in-law.

One day he brought strips of *úri*[87] and put them before the old man. When the latter saw the *úri* fibers he began to chew them. He calmed down noticeably, cheered up, chewed on them with much pleasure, and became very contented. Now at last he no longer complained but said with great satisfaction: "This is what I like!" When the son-in-law heard these words he gave a sigh of relief and said cheerfully: "How happy and pleased my father-in-law is at last with the *úri* fibers that I brought for him. Now I shall provide him with lots of them. How could I have guessed that it's precisely the tough *úri* fibers that he likes so much!" From then on he went out every day and always brought back piles of *úri* which he put before his father-in-law. The latter would begin to chew the fibers at once; and that is all he did. After he had thoroughly chewed a large amount of fibers he took pieces of bark and sewed them together with the *úri* fibers. This is how canoes were invented. He made many such canoes and gave them to the people. Since then one always needs *úri* to sew the pieces of bark together. Such a canoe withstands the waves for a long time.

Informant: Not known; pp. 1238-1240.

Summary

Father-in-law is constantly dissatisfied with food brought by son-in-law. Finally the latter brings fibers which the old man likes. He chews and sews together pieces of bark with them. Thus canoes came about.

Motif content

A1445.1.	Origin of boat-building.
F851.	Extraordinary food.
H1553.	Tests of patience.
P265.+.	Son-in-law supports father-in-law. (P265. Son-in-law.)
W26.	Patience.
W128.	Dissatisfaction.

44. The Old Guanaco and His Daughters

A long time ago old Améra lived in Wáiawan (on the south coast of Isla Navarino). This man[88] was a widower and for that reason lived with his two daughters. Both were very pretty, especially the elder. He

---

[87]The fibers just under the bark on the stem of the *Nothophagus* species. They are pulled off in long strips and, as long as they are still soft and pliable, used for sewing together the big pieces of bark in the canoes (Gusinde 1937:445).

[88]The male guanaco, *Lama huanachus* (Gusinde 1937:34).

fell passionately in love with his elder daughter at first without her noticing it. Every day she would go to the forest and bring back large quantities of celery roots, for the old man liked them very much. He would accept them gladly and ate a lot of them, saying: "I like celery roots very much!" The next day the girl would again go into the forest and bring back lots of celery roots to put before her father.

As the days went by he fell deeper in love with his daughter, until he was so excited that whenever he saw her he could hardly eat, for she was extremely beautiful and in the hut wore no clothes at all. Therefore the old man could see how very beautiful she was. Eventually the elder daughter realized that her father had fallen in love with her. It finally reached the point where the old man was so much in love that he could not eat anything at all; he gradually grew pale and lost weight.

The younger daughter noticed it and said to her father: "My father, why do you no longer eat the celery roots that you've always liked so much?" The father replied: "I can't eat because my teeth hurt!" Then this daughter said: "That's possible. Nevertheless, you have to eat something. Every day I see you grow paler and lose more weight. Come on, at least eat something!" The father replied: "I don't feel like eating." So saying, he pulled the fur cover over his face; he was stretched out on his bed in the hut. Now the younger daughter approached him and said: "See these big piles of celery roots that you've always liked so much. At least try to eat something!" To this the old man said: "No, I really can't eat any more! I'm near death and I feel my strength leaving me." He paused a long while and then continued in a sad tone: "I'm very near death. I think it would be best if you buried me now, for I won't live much longer. Bury me very close to our hut, but in such a way that my feet and head remain in the open for the time being until I'm really dead. Also put a *yáiyi* with *ákel*[89] beside me: I want to remain that way until my *kéšpix* leaves me." At these words the two girls became very sad and cried loudly. The father calmed them down, saying: "Before you bury me there's still something I have to tell you so that you won't be deceived or frightened. Nearby there lives a man who looks exactly like me. One can't tell us apart. That is old Yéxapowa. He looks just like me and I know he's very much in love with the two of you. So when you see this man coming, don't be afraid and don't think it's me. If he wants to caress you, yield to him! I wanted to tell you this to comfort you. Now you can bury me here."

The two girls listened attentively to everything their father told them; they were very sad. Then they buried him the way he had said, so that

---

[89]The well-known short piece of gut that serves as a little bag in which the red soil used for painting is kept; cf. Gusinde 1937:430, fig. 20.

his head and feet were still uncovered; by his side they put a *yáiyi* with *ákel*. When they had finished they again cried loudly and started walking toward another camp. They walked very slowly; they were sad because they had had to say goodbye to their father.

The path to the other camp where their relatives lived went through the forest. When the two girls were far away the old man quickly got up, for in reality he was not near death at all but had only pretended in order to deceive his two daughters. From the *yáiyi* he took out some *ákel* and with it painted his entire body. Then he, too, hurried into the forest, but he took a detour and went in a roundabout way. Since he was running very fast he got far ahead of the girls and reached the path that led to the other camp. There the two girls had to pass by, so he waited for them. He said to himself: "Since I've painted myself with a lot of red earth they won't recognize me." After some time the two girls approached; he heard them crying loudly. He got up and went to meet them, calling to them in a changed voice: "What are these two girls doing here all alone and so near our camp?" He went closer to them and said: "Yes, now I recognize you! Tell me, aren't you bringing any news from my good friend, your father? How is he? We haven't seen each other for a long time." The two girls replied: "Oh, by now our father must already have died." So saying they cried again very loudly. "But how did that happen?" asked the old man. The girls replied: "He had a toothache and could no longer eat. He grew paler and paler, and lost weight. Finally he said: 'You can bury me now.' So we buried him as he asked." The old man said: "Oh, what a pity that my old friend has died." As he was saying this the younger sister told the elder: "That must be our father; I recognize his voice!" The elder sister replied: "But sister, that's impossible! Have you forgotten what our father told us before we buried him, so that we wouldn't become frightened or deceived? He said: 'Near here there lives a man who resembles me exactly, so that one can't tell us apart; that is old Yéxapowa. He looks just like me and I know he's in love with both of you. So when you see this man coming, don't be frightened and don't believe that it's me. If he wants to caress you, yield to him. I wanted to tell you this for your comfort.' That's what our father told us. Don't you remember that any more?" The younger sister said: "Yes, I remember all that, but I still think this man here must be our father!"

Although the girls were talking low the old man heard everything. Then he asked them: "Where do you want to go now?" The elder sister answered: "We want to go to the other camp where our relatives live." "Come on," said the man, "don't be so sad! Come with me, I'll show you the way." As he spoke he drew closer and closer to the older girl;

then he tenderly took her into his arms and led her behind the thick bushes, where they lay down on the soft moss and yielded to their desire. After some time Améra stood up and went to the place where the younger daughter was sitting. He embraced her, too, and withdrew behind the thicket with her, where both yielded to their lecherous desire. It was some time before they rose again and went to where the older girl was still lying. Then all three burst out laughing and continued what they had been doing. Since then they have remained in the forest with one another, and have never parted![90]

Even today the guanacos laugh and giggle in this way. The old father lives with his daughters all the time and has intercourse with them as though they were his wives. Everybody is amused by this. One can also still recognize the small spot of *ákel* where he had painted himself on that occasion. The daughters likewise have a little of this color, for when Améra embraced them some of it rubbed off.

Informant: Not known; pp. 1240-1242.

Summary

Man is in love with his elder daughter; feigns death. He then leaves grave and goes to girls, pretending to be look-alike friend of dead father. They have intercourse. Since then all three live together as husband and wives, as do all guanaco fathers and daughters.

Motif content

A2411.1.+.	Origin of color of guanaco. (A2411.1. Origin of color of mammals.)
A2425.+.	Why guanaco giggles. (A2425. Origin of animal cries.)
A2496.+.	Why young female guanacos copulate with their father. (A2496. Sexual intercourse of animals.)
H79.3.	Recognition by voice.
J154.	Wise words of dying father.
K1310.	Seduction by disguise or substitution.
K1325.	Seduction by feigned death.
K1821.2.	Disguise by painting body.
T24.1.	Love-sickness.
T24.6.	Lover refuses food and drink.
T411.	Father-daughter incest.

[90]This story is almost identical with two Selknam stories (Gusinde 1931:650; 651; Wilbert 1975:107, 109); one must conclude that the subject matter is one and the same. Here, too, it is above all the love play of the male leader of the herd with the younger, female animals that is represented. The Yamana have no more stories devoted to the guanaco, for in their economy this animal does not have even remotely the importance it has among the Selknam.

T411.1.   Lecherous father. Unnatural father wants to marry his
                           own daughter.
T411.1.2.   Father feigning death returns in disguise and seduces
                           daughter.

ETHICAL MYTHS

45. The Young Brother-in-law

On the island of Egóngo there once lived an old married couple.
They had five sons, all of whom were married. One time the sons had
gone far out to sea with their families to fish and hunt. The old parents
remained behind all alone in their hut. Not for a long time had those
five families left the island and their old parents. Their old mother was
very advanced in years. She was so frail and weak that she could no
longer hope for children at her old age. Her husband, who was
somewhat older, knew that very well. Nevertheless, whether it was that
he wanted to joke, or that he still did not want to give up all hope,
every time before sleeping with his wife he took a fresh *máku* flower[91]
and inserted it into her vagina.

He then immediately lay down on the woman to have intercourse
with her. He did this so that the *máku* flower would remain long in the
woman's vagina. And indeed, after some time both realized that the old
woman was pregnant. Soon she gave birth to a son. Such a handsome,
beautiful child the old people had never seen before. They were
ecstatic and beside themselves with joy, for the little boy really seemed
as pretty and shiny pink as the *máku* flower.[92]

This little son of theirs grew unusually quickly and in the process
became even more handsome. To the delight of his old parents he soon
began to play. The little boy also began to speak surprisingly early and

[91]Shrub common to Tierra del Fuego, *Embothrium coccineum;* cf. Gusinde 1937:702,
fig. 78.

[92]In addition to a well-proportioned body, a pink, transparent skin suggesting the
luster of blood is considered a mark of great physical beauty by the Yamana. To
emphasize this they refer, by way of comparison, to the large scarlet *Embothrium* flower,
which completely satisfies their sense of beauty. They often say, "This child resembles a
máku flower and is as lovely as one," by which they mean that they very much like the
child; cf. Gusinde 1937:701.

he asked his mother for all kinds of things. He amused himself by catching flies and mosquitoes, butterflies and beetles, dragonflies and others of this order (Hymenoptera). Each of these animals he brought to his mother and asked what it was called. The mother gave each animal a name; her little son heard it and repeated it several times. Ever since each animal bears that name. The little boy had grown considerably, and as a result was able to catch larger animals. He went to the beach and into the forest, where he caught first the small birds, later bigger ones, and finally the very largest. He brought them all to his mother and asked her what they were called. The old mother was extremely happy that her little son seemed so active and skillful; she gave each bird a name and this she told her son. He repeated the name and remembered it. Every bird bears that name to this day. Meanwhile the boy continued to grow and he showed that he was strong and brave enough also to hunt large animals. Indeed he soon killed a young sea lion, then an old, heavy sea lion, even foxes, guanacos, and dolphins; once he even killed a whale. Each of these animals he brought to his mother and asked what it was called. Every time the mother was very happy and she gave each animal a name which it bears until this day.

Now Lušwuléwa (a composite name, from *luš* = red, like the *máku* flower = wonderfully beautiful; and from *wuléwa*, the general word for boy; accordingly: "wonder child") was big enough to go hunting regularly. He brought large amounts of meat to the hut all the time and as a result his old parents were provided with lots of food. Since they were unable to eat everything that Lušwuléwa carried home they soon began to take care of the surplus; they wanted to preserve it in good condition for a later time. Lušwuléwa himself blew up many a big sea lion stomach and let it dry in the air; then he filled it with meat. In this manner he accumulated large supplies. For here in Egóngo there were many animals, and he was really a diligent and skillful hunter.

After a time the five brothers and their families returned from the long journey; they had missed their old parents very much and wanted to see them. When they had gotten close to the island a violent storm blew up and prevented them from continuing. It kept them out there on the open sea and blew so strongly that they could not move from the spot. Finally the women had to tie their canoes to thick bunches of seaweed so that the wind would not blow them out to sea.

One morning when Lušwuléwa had left the hut as usual to go hunting, he spotted those canoes out there, anchored to bunches of seaweed far from the island; they had to be tied down like that or the wind would have driven them out to the open sea. He said to himself: "I suppose they have already been sitting there for a few days. Their provisions must have gone out by now!" Without further delay he considered how he might help them. Then a thought occurred to him: "I'm sure it would be a good idea if I let those people have a well-filled sea lion stomach. If I put the stomach on the water in the right way, it may be that the current will carry it to those canoes. Then they'll have something to eat and won't die of hunger before they can continue." Instantly he ran to the hut and informed his old father: "I think my brothers are sitting in those canoes out there with their families. There's a very strong wind blowing, and for that reason they have tied their canoes to thick bunches of seaweed. I'd like to help them by letting a filled sea lion stomach drift to them with the current so that they'll get something to eat." The old man replied: "That's very good of you. Do what seems best to you. It won't be in vain if those people out there get a well-filled sea lion stomach."

Lušwuléwa at once hurried down to the beach, took a thick club, and put it on the water, carefully positioned so that the current would push it. He wanted to experiment first to make sure that the current would actually carry the club to those canoes. He followed the club with his eyes, and indeed, despite the strong wind and the high waves the club floated directly out to the open sea, precisely to the spot where the canoes were anchored. Two women happened to be sitting in the bow of their canoes trying their best to catch a few fish as all the people were terribly hungry. Suddenly the club struck very loudly against the canoe and they said to each other: "That thing out there, what could it be, and what's beating so hard against our canoe?" They leaned even farther out over the gunwale and noticed the thick club bumping against it; they wondered greatly at this. At last they took the club and threw it over the other side so that it would no longer beat against the canoe. Lušwuléwa was watching all their movements from the island and joyfully said to himself: "So that heavy club floated exactly to where the canoes are. Then I suppose a well-filled sea lion stomach will also reach them if I place it properly on the water."

He ran at once to his hut and selected a big, well-filled sea lion stomach. This he carried to the beach and positioned it precisely on the water so that the current took it immediately. The big stomach drifted off; wind and wave pushed it forward rapidly and it drifted directly toward the boats. Soon it reached there and struck violently against one of the canoes. The woman who was sitting inside became frightened at this strong blow, looked overboard, and saw to her special joy the big, well-filled sea lion stomach. She quickly seized it and tried to lift it. But she was not strong enough, as it was much too heavy. She called two men. They worked hard at it, and together they finally managed to lift the heavy, well-filled stomach into the canoe. All the people breathed a deep sigh of relief when they saw the large amount of meat; they had been suffering severely from hunger but now they had lots of food at their disposal. Although they were astonished, trying to figure out how such a big and well-filled sea lion stomach could have come to their canoes, they began to eat at once as they were very hungry, and soon stopped wondering where the stomach might have come from. So now there was much commotion out there in the canoes. From his island Lušwuléwa was watching the constant movements of the people, and very contentedly he told himself: "Then the big stomach got there all right. How those people must have thrown themselves on the meat, for they must have been very hungry!"

When the people out there had appeased the worst of their hunger they began to talk and said happily: "With all this meat we'll manage for a couple of days; we no longer have to make an effort to catch fish here. Perhaps the weather will soon improve and then we'll reach shore. But where did this big, well-filled sea lion stomach really come from? Who might have put it on the current in such a way that it reached our canoes and bumped into them? Our old father no longer has the strength to gather such amounts of meat, and even less to put such a big, full, sea lion stomach on the water; he is not able to work at all, so this big stomach certainly can't come from him! Maybe some other man happens to be staying in our father's hut. But who could that be? It would have to be a skilled hunter who could accumulate so much meat; he must also be a strong man capable of carrying this heavy load to the beach. Who might that be? Moreover, this big stomach must come from the island where our father lives, for all the meat is fresh and very well preserved!" They talked about this and that while they ate. They filled themselves completely. After some time the eldest of the brothers promised: "As soon as the weather permits I'd like to try to go over to the island where our father lives. I'll ask him how he is and who put this sea lion stomach on the water so that it bumped into our canoe. I don't doubt that this big stomach was meant for us all along." To this the others replied: "All right, do that. We are also curious to know how our father is and what man is staying with him in the hut."

The weather improved the following day with the headwind no longer blowing so strongly. The eldest of the brothers and his wife got into their canoe and left. Although they had to paddle hard they managed to keep course on the island. As they approached the island little Lušwuléwa happened to be running along the beach. He called to his father: "A canoe is approaching our island and will soon reach land. Maybe it's my brother coming here with his family." His father replied:

"That's possible." The little boy fled into the forest and hid there; after all, he was extremely handsome and for that reason did not want to be seen. Shortly after this the elder brother reached land; he and his wife left the canoe and went to his father's hut. He reported how things had gone for him, his four brothers, and their families on the long trip, how they were held back out there on the return trip by bad weather, and how a big, well-filled sea lion stomach came floating to the canoes, saving them from starvation. He also assured him with great excitement that all were wondering very much who had let them have the stomach. With laughter his old father replied: "Listen, my son, I'll explain everything to you: you have one more brother! Although you haven't seen him yet it was he who let you have the big sea lion stomach." Curiously he pressed his father: "How is that possible? Tell me, where's the boy hiding?" The father answered: "Your brother has gone into the forest again and won't return until late at night." Now the two, father and son, sat down by the fire and talked for a long time. When it had grown dark they hung a piece of hide before the entrance of the hut so as to close it; they lay down and soon fell asleep. Not until the night was far advanced did little Lušwuléwa return to the hut. In order not to wake anybody up he avoided the hut's entrance and cautiously crawled in from the side, lightly lifting a loose piece of hide. He tiptoed quietly to his bed and lay down between his father and mother. Then he crawled under a long and wide piece of fur which completely covered him. Nothing could be seen of him, not even his feet. But while he was asleep he unwittingly stirred and pushed one foot slightly out from underneath the cover.

Very early the next morning the eldest brother got up from his bed. He blew on the low fire and put a few logs on it. Then he noticed that from beneath the wide cover between his mother and father a child's foot was visible which he had not noticed the night before when he went to bed. Instantly it occurred to him that it had to be his youngest brother and he said to himself: "I'm sure he did not come home from the forest until late and stretched out on his bed here very quietly without waking anybody." Quite enchanted with that pretty little foot he thought to himself: "What a lovely little foot my new brother has! How beautiful his whole body must be! So it was he who gave us the big sea lion stomach. We certainly can be proud of such a brother!" While he was attending to the fire in the hut so that it would give a lot of heat he quietly woke his wife and said: "Look at that pretty little foot sticking out from under the cover. That must be our youngest brother my father talked about yesterday." The woman looked at that delicate food and she, too, was quite delighted. She whispered to her husband: "What a magnificent boy that must be whose foot alone is so enchanting!" Once more both stretched out on their bed. But the woman could no longer fall asleep for although she had only gotten to see his pretty foot she was thinking with great pleasure of her little brother-in-law. Later, the parents rose from their bed and ate a few mussels. But that woman was unable to either eat or talk, thinking only of her handsome brother-in-law.

The sun had long been up when little Lušwuléwa got up from his bed. Now the eldest brother and his wife saw his whole body. The woman carried on as though crazed at the sight of the exceedingly beautiful body of her little brother-in-law. She could not take her eyes off him; all day long she could eat nothing at all and at night she tossed restlessly on her bed, unable to sleep. She was quite beside herself since looking at the beautiful boy.

The following day the eldest brother finally had to say goodbye to his parents; after all, the other families were waiting for him. Again he left his father's hut and together he and his wife got into the canoe. They went out to the open sea and soon reached the place where the families in the other canoes were eagerly awaiting their return. The eldest brother told them: "Listen to this, you're going to be very surprised: we've got one more brother! Who would have guessed that, for our parents are already very old." Then all the others looked in astonishment and cried joyfully: "Is that really true? And this little brother of ours is supposed to have sent us the big sea lion stomach? No, that's quite impossible." The wife of the eldest brother said: "It's really that way! I have one more little brother-in-law. But he's so ugly, deformed, and twisted that you feel sick just looking at him; if you sit next to him you lose your appetite. The parents are just too old. What a repulsive, ugly child! I keep seeing him before my eyes!" That is what the woman said; she wanted to deceive all the other relatives, perhaps to dissuade them from going to that island. Secretly she was already planning to take the handsome brother-in-law for her husband and begin having intercourse with him; she did not want to be prevented from doing so by the other women. Meanwhile the latter were discussing what they had just learned. They said: "Since our little brother-in-law is so ugly and deformed we had better not go there so as not to lose our appetite." The brothers also discussed the matter: "How did it happen that we were given one more little brother now? Our parents are really much too old; that must be why he turned out so ugly and malformed!" In saying this, they shook their heads angrily. While they were listening to what the women were saying one of the men finally cried: "However it may be, even if our youngest brother really is so deformed and repulsive that simply can't be changed now. Soon I'll go over to the island anyway; at least I want to see our old parents." Eventually the other brothers agreed with him and said: "It would even be better if all of us would go together to the island to see how our parents are." They promptly untied their canoes from the seaweed and paddled over to the island. They disembarked and set off for their parents' hut. Little Lušwuléwa happened to be there just then. When they saw him the brothers were beside themselves with surprise; in their desire the women behaved as though mad, so crazed with love were they: their brother-in-law was exceedingly handsome and well shaped, and as magnificent as a *máku* flower! Instantly they saw through the cunning intention behind the false account of the eldest brother's wife.

Each of these women soon felt a violent desire to get together secretly with her handsome brother-in-law; each was crazy with love for him. But none of them succeeded in meeting him unnoticed in order to yield to her overwhelming desire. Each revealed her secret longing to another, and thus all five exchanged their intentions; soon each knew what was on the others' minds. Finally they spoke more openly among themselves and made a plan together to lure litttle Lušwuléwa away and amuse themselves with him. They had to try several times, but finally they managed to persuade the boy and take him along with them without the knowledge of his parents. Upon leaving the hut they only mentioned briefly: "We're going to the beach to gather mussels." But on the beach far away from the hut nothing was farther from their minds than gathering mussels. They put the beautiful child in their midst and began to play with him. He himself willingly surrendered to their lascivious doings. One after the other took his member and held it for a rather long time in her hand. Then they lay down on the youth one by one, repeating this several times. Satisfied by this love play the women gathered in the sea to cool off their voluptuous excitement in the cold water. Then Lušwuléwa followed them and they immediately touched one another under the water with their hands.

While they were busy romping around like this Lušwuléwa became especially attached to one of the women but grew increasingly indifferent toward the other four. They gradually noticed this, too, but still continued to play with him. When he and the preferred woman went farther and farther away from them in the water in order to be all alone, their jealousy erupted. Finally Lušwuléwa gave himself to that woman alone and wanted nothing more to do with the others. This they could not stand and they became furious. Together they went toward him and began splashing water on him. Slowly they pushed him farther out into the sea. They splashed him so heavily and constantly that finally he was no longer able to remain standing. Indeed he fell and drowned. Those four extremely jealous women did not permit only one sister-in-law to satisfy her desire with the handsome boy. So Lušwuléwa died because he was so handsome and well proportioned. Late at night the women returned to the hut, but without Lušwuléwa. Only much later did his parents find out that he had drowned. They were furious with those women. To have lost their pretty child made them unspeakably sad. They cried bitterly and could not reconcile themselves to having to go on living without their beautiful, clever son. These two old parents died very soon from overwhelming grief.[93]

Informant: Julia; pp. 1243-1250.

Summary

Beautiful boy is born to old couple whose five grown-up sons are away from home. He is excellent hunter and catches every kind of animal, which mother names. This is how animals got their names.

Upon return of brothers and their wives storm blows up, keeping their canoes out on sea for days. Small boy sends them meat floating in container. Eager to see their savior, eldest brother and his wife go ashore and are struck by the boy's beauty. Wife wants him for her lover and tries in vain to prevent other brothers and their wives from going ashore. Upon seeing him all the wives are almost crazed with love; they take him swimming and all start playing together. He prefers one of them, and the others drown him in their jealousy. Parents die of grief.

Motif content

A511.4.1.	Miraculous growth of culture hero.
A527.1.	Culture hero precocious.
A2571.	How animals received their names.
D1782.	Sympathetic magic.
F527.	Person of unusual color.

[93]Old Julia who lives on the Wollaston Islands told me this story which is related in the same way all over the south. It is also known in the middle and western regions, although slightly changed; this version mentions only four married brothers, and accordingly Lušwuléwa is the fifth and youngest. The many animals that he killed and brought home he did not put before his mother, as related above, but before his father, and the latter gave each its name. Both myths I heard on separate occasions and completely independently of each other; I have to thank old Mary, who lives in the west, for the second version. The main themes in this myth return in an unadulterated form in the "Story of Emienpoot" which is told among the Selknam (Gusinde 1931:661; Wilbert 1975:123).

F575.3.	Remarkably beautiful child.
F679.5.	Skillful hunter.
F963.	Extraordinary behavior of wind.
F1041.1.2.2.4.	Death from hearing of son's (sons') death.
H79.+.	Recognition by foot. (H79. Recognition by physical attributes—miscellaneous.)
J710.	Forethought in provision for food.
J1113.	Clever boy.
K2320.	Deception by frightening.
L31.	Youngest brother helps elder.
N440.+.	Secret learned. (N440. Valuable secrets learned.)
N827.	Child as helper.
P231.3.	Mother-love.
P264.+.	Beautiful child immoderately loved by sisters-in-law. (P264. Sister-in-law.)
R155.1.	Youngest brother rescues his elder brothers.
S55.	Cruel sister-in-law.
S131.	Murder by drowning.
T24.3.	Madness from love.
T71.2.	Woman avenges scorned love.
T92.	Rivals in love.
T425.+.	Sisters-in-law seduce brother-in-law. (T425. Brother-in-law seduces [seeks to seduce] sister-in-law.)
T538.	Unusual conception in old age.
T615.1.	Precocious speech.
W181.	Jealousy.

46. The Malevolent Brother-in-law

Once five brothers were living together in the hut of their brother-in-law. But the brother-in-law was an evil and dangerous person. The most disagreeable thing was that he was disgustingly stingy, for however much meat he had available he always gave his brothers-in-law only a little bit. Usually he went hunting by himself. In the forest, near the beach, he would light a big fire and try to kill the birds that sat on the beach.

One day the eldest of the five brothers had gone out to hunt birds and had unintentionally taken the same route as had his evil brother-in-law. The latter, meanwhile, had sat down on a steep hill and was warming himself by the fire. Soon this bad man discovered his brother-in-law approaching in his direction. He then made his murderous plan to kill his unsuspecting brother-in-law. From the forest he quickly fetched a sturdy *hašamáif*,[94] which he pushed into the fire. When the eldest of the five brothers got close his malevolent brother-in-law said to him: "Make yourself comfortable here by the fire and warm yourself." He even helped him sit down and gently turned him around so that the latter was facing away from the fire, as if to warm his back first; all the while the unsuspecting man was looking down from the high, steep hill. Surreptitiously the evil man reached for the burning *hašamáif*, pulled it out of the fire, brought it down on the head of his brother-in-law, and cried out: "Look out, my brother-in-law, a big *hašamáif* is falling; save yourself!" Before the unsuspecting man could turn aside the *hašamáif* had dealt him a blow that cracked his head; he died on the spot. The evil man had put the *hašamáif* into the fire so that his brother-in-law should not be able to save himself by grabbing it and warding it off, for nobody dares take a burning cudgel in his hand. Then he gave the body of his brother-in-law a powerful kick and it rolled down.

Some time later the second eldest brother went out to look for his brother who had not returned. Finally he met his brother-in-law who was still sitting on the same hill warming himself. Unsuspectingly he went toward him. He let that evil man persuade him to sit down by the fire. Here he was killed in the same way as his brother before him. Then his body too rolled down. Not long afterward the third brother set off, for his two elder brothers had still not returned and he wanted to look for them. Soon the fourth brother, too, went out to search. Indeed, these two were killed by this terrible brother-in-law in the same way as their two elder brothers. That way only the youngest brother was left.

He had been waiting for a long time, impatiently repeating: "I wonder where my four brothers can be? They've been gone a long time and none has come back. Could they have met with an accident?" Then finally he, too, went out to look for them. But he was shrewd and more careful than his brothers. Like them he started up the hill at the top of which his brother-in-law was sitting by the fire. Down at the foot of the hill he saw several bodies; they looked as though they had rolled down from the top. He said to himself in alarm: "I wonder if those are the bodies of my brothers whom someone has killed?"[95] Slowly he climbed up the hill. At the top he met his brother-in-law who was sitting by the

---

[94]A branch from the beech tree with a protruding growth, caused by the *Cyttaria* fungus; cf. Gusinde 1937:34, fig. 8; 554, fig. 66. This wood is exceedingly hard and it serves prominently as a club.

[95]It should be noted that the man did not go right up to the bodies, partly out of fear, partly out of aversion.

fire. The latter had already put a thick *hašamáif* into the fire to make it red hot. Right away he invited his brother-in-law: "Sit down by the fire here and rest comfortably. First warm your back and while you're doing that you can look down." But he replied: "I might get burned." To this the malevolent brother-in-law said: "Why are you so worried? Look at me, I even *like* to sit by the fire that way." So saying he sat down by the fire as though to warm his back, keeping his face turned away from the fire. He only wanted to allay the fear of his brother-in-law so that afterward the latter would follow his example. The youngest brother had already looked into the fire and seen the thick glowing *hašamáif*. While the evil man kept his face turned away from the fire he seized the *hašamáif*, pulled it quickly from the fire, swung it, and brought it down on his unsuspecting brother-in-law. The glowing *hašamáif* smashed his head and he died on the spot. Thus this man took revenge on his degenerate brother-in-law for the murder of his brothers.

Informant: Julia; pp. 1250-1252.

Summary

Evil man kills his four brothers-in-law one by one by luring them to sit by fire, then crushing their heads. Finally the last remaining brother kills man in the same way.

Motif content

K815.	Victim lured by kind words approaches trickster and is killed.
K832.	Dupe induced to look about: seized and killed.
K912.2.+.	Men lured into trap one by one and killed. (K912.2. Men lured into serpent pit one by one and killed.)
K959.4.	Murder from behind.
K1641.	Ambushed trickster killed by intended victim.
K2211.1.	Treacherous brother-in-law.
L10.	Victorious youngest son.
Q285.	Cruelty punished.
Q411.6.	Death as punishment for murder.
Q581.1.	Unusual murder avenged in like manner.
S116.4.	Murder by crushing head.
W152.	Stinginess.

47. A Ghost Story

Once five brothers were living together in the same hut with their brother-in-law. The latter was a malevolent, evil person who, whenever he had a chance, caused his brothers-in-law every conceivable harm. Finally he grew disgusted with them. He wanted to kill them. One day he invited the youngest of the five brothers to accompany him up a steep cliff to catch cormorants. When they reached the cliff the evil brother-in-law lit a big fire. While the other went off to gather firewood the evil man put much wood on the embers and among it hid a thick *hašamáif,*[96] covering it well to get it red hot. After some time the young brother-in-law came back and threw down his burden of wood. The *hašamáif* was now glowing brightly; the fire was close to the edge of the cliff. The malevolent man said to his brother-in-law: "Why don't you climb down this wall and see whether any cormorants are sitting there." The other one climbed down, not suspecting what his malevolent brother-in-law was planning. When he was standing exactly below the fire this evil person pushed the burning *hašamáif* over the edge of the rock so that it fell right on the head of his young brother-in-law. The latter died instantly and his body rolled down to the beach. The murderer went back to his hut. He pretended to be very sad, and the others thought that their youngest brother had met with an accident on the cliff because of carelessness.

Not long afterward the brother-in-law invited the second youngest of the five brothers: "Would you like to accompany me to that cliff? I'm going to hunt for cormorants there." The other at once got up and went with him. When they reached the top the evil man again lit a big fire near the edge of the cliff. When the other was not looking he pushed a thick *hašamáif* into the embers and covered it with firewood. When it was completely red hot the evil man said to his brother-in-law: "Why don't you try to climb down this cliff a ways. I'm sure there are some cormorants sitting in the holes there." Unsuspectingly the young man climbed down. When he was standing exactly below the fire that bad person pushed the glowing *hašamáif* over the edge of the cliff. It fell right on the head of his brother-in-law killing him instantly; the body rolled down to the beach. That bad man now went home to his hut, crying loudly and pretending to be very sad. The others thought their second youngest brother had met with an accident because of carelessness.

After some time the evil man invited the third of the five brothers to accompany him to the cliff. The latter immediately went with him. There this bad person killed his unsuspecting brother-in-law in the same way as he had killed his two younger brothers. Again he came back crying sadly so that also the two surviving brothers-in-law became very

[96]A bulging growth of wooden tissue on the beech tree branch, caused by the *Cyttaria* fungus; cf. p. 141 n. 94.

sad. Not long afterward he went with the second eldest of the five brothers to that rock wall and killed him in the same manner.

Thus there was only the eldest brother left. One day the evil man said to him: "Would you like to accompany me to that cliff to hunt cormorants?" His brother-in-law replied: "Oh, yes, we can go at once." The two of them left. But the eldest brother suspected something, for how could all four of his brothers have met with accidents so quickly, one after the other? When the two reached the cliff they made a fire. After some time the malevolent man told his brother-in-aw: "Why don't you climb down that cliff? I'm sure there are cormorants sitting in those holes there. Get them." But the other replied: "That looks very dangerous to me. I wonder if this isn't the place where somebody killed my four brothers?" In the fire a thick *hašamáif* was already glowing. That man had secretly hidden it there. Again the eldest brother repeated: "No, I won't go there, it's much too dangerous for me." The other replied: "How worried you are. There's absolutely no danger. Come on, go." The eldest brother said: "You go on and stand there first; then you'll see how dangerous it is." Finally that awful man climbed down. When he was standing below the fire the other pushed the glowing *hašamáif* so that it fell over the edge of the cliff. He called out a warning: "*Hašamáif kakáta šúen, álum*; there's a *hašamáif* coming, my brother-in-law!" But the latter could not get out of the way in time; the *hašamáif* fell right on his head and killed him on the spot.

The *késpix*[97] of the five dead people got together and built a canoe. In it they went to their nephew's hut. They called him out and pretended to be real people still. The nephew suspected nothing for he had not yet heard that the five men had died. His name was Alaánama.[98] The men invited him into their canoe and he got in. They went to a distant island to hunt birds. They were lucky there, and while the five *késpix* hunted, Alaánama cut up the birds they had killed. He also made many *kéti*.[99] In the sausages he made for his uncles he used the entrails and the contents of the guts; in the *kéti* he was going to eat himself, however, he used only good parts. The uncles, too, had in their turn made a few sausages while on the island. These they gave to their nephew who pretended to eat them. But he only put the ones he had made for himself into his mouth, and gave his uncles the *kéti* he had made expressly for them. All five ate them, failing to notice how much offal they were swallowing at the same time. Then they all went back again to the nephew's hut. There the *késpix* now

[97] Apparently their souls.
[98] The sea leopard, *Lobodon carcinophagus*, rare in the Cape Horn region.
[99] A kind of sausage. In Gusinde 1937:584 it is shown how it is made.

lived with Alaánama. Every time they went bird hunting the nephew made the sausages in the same way and his uncles did not notice anything.

After a long time the ghosts left, each in a different direction. They left their nephew alone in the canoe. At his leisure he looked for a thick cudgel and put it in the canoe. When the ghosts returned later they asked him: "Where were you?" To this he replied: "I went very far. Look at this cudgel. I brought it from where I was; you can find this wood only in that far away place." Now all six got into their canoe and went to another island. When they were close to shore they hit such strong surf that their canoe went completely to pieces. They lost no time making a new one, and no sooner had they finished it than the five *késpix* flew off, each in his particular direction. When they returned later they asked their nephew again: "Where have you been in the meantime?" He replied: "I was very far away." Then he gave his uncles those bad sausages, the kind he had always made for them. They ate them and noticed nothing. Soon all six left that place too and went to another island. When they got there a violent surf came up and their canoe was broken. So again they had to build a new one. They had hardly finished when the nephew said plaintively to his uncles: "Now it's about time for me to return to my mother's hut. She has a lovely voice and I love to listen to it. Besides, I'm sure my mother is very worried about me; she may even believe me dead." The ghosts told him: "All right, let's go to your mother's hut." They loaded much meat and blubber into their canoe, as well as a few sea lions they had not yet cut up, and with this they set off.

Soon they were near the beach where the nephew's mother had her hut. They tied the canoe to a thick *Macrocystis* stem. Alaánama secretly hid a fat sea lion in this bunch of seaweed. He put it aside for his own use, for he was planning to stay with his mother from now on and let his uncles travel on alone. All six got out by the shore. When they walked up to the hut they heard the lovely voice of their nephew's mother. They approached very slowly. The five *késpix* went and stood very close to the entrance and looked into the hut, but the nephew stayed behind. He said to himself: "Those two that are standing right in the middle of the entrance I'm going to shove into the hut with a strong push." He ran quickly and gave the two ghosts in front such a violent push that they were shoved inside. He himself hurried in after them and held them firmly. The other three *késpix* flew up and left. In the hut Alaánama took some dog dung, human urine and feces, and rubbed it into the faces of the ghosts. They both were behaving like crazy, and Alaánama wanted to calm them down this way so that they might slowly become people again. Over several days the nephew treated his

uncles in this strange manner and also gave them urine to drink.[100]
Thereupon the two *késpix* calmed down and by and by became human
beings.[101] Now the nephew watched them less carefully and allowed
them more freedom; he even permitted them to leave the hut. One day
when they had left to look for *amáim*, berries, they again became as
mentally disturbed as before. They turned into real *késpix* and flew
away. Their nephew soon became aware of this and returned to the hut
alone, crying and lamenting. He cried again and again: "Oh woe, now
my two uncles have left forever!"[102]

Informant: William; pp. 1252-1255.

Summary

Evil man kills his four brothers-in-law one by one by inducing them to climb
down cliff, then throwing red hot club at them. Finally the last surviving
brother kills evil man in this same way.

The five ghosts go to live with nephew who gives them bad food to eat,
keeping the best pieces for himself. Thinking them mentally disturbed he
attempts to cure two of them, the others having escaped, but in the end these
two also escape.

Motif content

D562.2.	Transformation by urine.
D1500.1.37.	Urine used in medicine.
E320.	Dead relative's friendly return.
E379.4.	Ghost as confederate of man.
E541.	Revenants eat.
E545.	The dead speak.
E545.13.	Man converses with dead.
E599.+.	Ghosts build canoe. (E599. Other actions of revenants.)
E599.+.	Ghosts go hunting. (E599. Other actions of revenants.)
E599.5.+.	Ghost flies. (E599.5. Ghost travels swiftly.)
E722.1.+.	Soul appears like the body it left at death. (E722.1. Form of soul as it leaves body at death.)

[100]In fact, even very recently a person who was mentally disturbed or mentally not
normal was treated in exactly this way by the other people, above all by his relatives.
They would pour a large quantity of urine into his mouth, which he had to swallow.
Through this they wanted to restore his mental equilibrium.

[101]By this is meant that their behavior again became somewhat rational and human.

[102]The first part of this story agrees in its essential features with what old Julia who
lives in the south told me in 1920 (Gusinde 1937:1250). Not until 1923 did old William
who is from the east tell me the complete story above.

The peculiarity of the second part of this story is demonstrated by the fact that it is
solely in this story that actual souls appear, returning to those everyday circumstances
and to those people which they had left at death. Also the behavior of the souls
themselves is not that of mentally normal people.

E752.1.3.+.	Souls of dead captured. (E752.1.3. Souls of dead captured on leaving corpse.)
F556.	Remarkable voice.
F601.	Extraordinary companions.
F959.1.	Madness miraculously cured.
J261.	Loudest mourners not greatest sorrowers.
J1434.	Strenuous cure for madness.
J1772.9.	Excrements thought to be meat and therefore eaten.
K912.2.+.	Men lured into trap one by one and killed. (K912.2. Men lured into serpent pit one by one and killed.)
K917.	Treacherous murder during hunt.
K1641.	Ambushed trickster killed by intended victim.
K2210.+.	Treacherous nephew. (K2210. Treacherous relatives.)
K2211.1.	Treacherous brother-in-law.
Q411.6.	Death as punishment for murder.
Q581.1.	Unusual murder avenged in like manner.
R211.	Escape from prison.
S115.4.	Murder by crushing head.
S183.	Frightful meal.
W152.	Stinginess.
Z221.	Eldest brother as hero.

48. The Treacherous Bachelor

Once there was a bachelor. He proved himself to be very skillful at catching fish, always bringing home many big ones. In the same camp there lived another man who was married to a beautiful woman. He had no luck at all at fishing. One day he asked the bachelor: "Where do you catch all these big fish?" The bachelor answered: "I always find them over there by that island!" The married man asked: "Would you take me there some time?" The bachelor immediately replied: "Come on!" And the two went to the island. First they ran along the beach until they were standing opposite the island, which was a great distance away. Indeed one could see on this island a lot of fish entrails, small balls of grass with which the insides of the fish had been cleaned, and also well sharpened mussel shells with which the bellies of the fish had been cut open.[103] The married man asked: "You told me you could reach this island with one single jump. But it's too far away! I couldn't reach it in one jump!" The bachelor replied with a laugh: "It only looks

[103] As is well known every man cleans and dresses the larger animals immediately on the spot where he caught and killed them.

as though the island is far off; actually it is quite close. If you get a good running start you can easily jump across. You'll certainly reach the island. Be brave!" Upon hearing these words the other actually started running, intending to jump. He came running bravely but in the end he stopped short. He stopped suddenly and did not jump. Then the bachelor urged him even more: "Come on, don't be frightened! The island is really not as far away as it seems. Just try once more!" The other tried again; he started running very fast and from far away and actually jumped. But the island was too distant after all: the man fell into the water and hit his head against a rock, killing himself instantly. "Now you can get fish, as many and as big ones as you'd like!" said the bachelor, laughing mockingly. Then he added: "You may stay there forever!" He left the dead man lying in the water and went contentedly to the latter's hut. The wife was sitting by the fire. Joyfully the bachelor told her that her husband after smashing his head near the island had died on the spot. Both burst out laughing with delight. They had secretly been lovers for a long time. Now at last the husband was dead. They caressed each other and indulged in their desire. Late at night the woman's eldest son came back to the hut. He had approached it very quietly. But when he entered unexpectedly and saw his mother lying next to the bachelor, he became furious. He drove the harpoon he was holding through the bachelor's body, just punishment for the culprit.[104]

Informant: Not known; pp. 1256-1257.

Summary

Bachelor in love with beautiful woman tricks her husband into killing himself by attempting impossible jump. Dead man's son then kills bachelor upon finding him with the woman.

Motif content

F575.1.	Remarkably beautiful woman.
F634.	Mighty fisherman.
K891.	Dupe tricked into jumping to his death.
K2213.	Treacherous wife.
P233.6.	Son avenges father.
Q241.	Adultery punished.
Q411.6.	Death as punishment for murder.
Q461.3.	Impaling as punishment for adultery.
T92.10.	Rival in love killed.
T481.	Adultery.

[104]This story is told in the south. Its structure resembles that of the following story which is told in the west.

49. A Bachelor

Here in the west there once lived a bachelor who always had lots of firewood in his hut. Not far away he had found a low stone slab with sharp edges standing upright. He knocked sticks and tree trunks against the edges to split them. Some distance from him lived a married man who always had trouble splitting and cutting wood. One day he came to the place where the bachelor was busy splitting wood. The bachelor took a stick and broke it. It looked as though he was beating the stick against his knee, for he had placed himself so that both his legs were around the sharp stone slab, concealing it; when he struck he bent one leg somewhat and thus the stick split on the slab. The married man stood a little apart from the bachelor and asked: "How can you split the sticks on your own knee?" The bachelor replied laughingly: "As you can see, it's very easy. If I strike hard enough any stick splits, no matter how thick it is. One only has to approach it with courage. You try it, too!" The man tried at once and struck his knee. He gave a scream and complained: "But it hurts terribly!" The bachelor laughed and tried to calm him down: "But that's impossible! Watch how I'm standing. Just strike hard!" Again the bachelor took a thick stick and brought it down against the sharp stone slab which he had hidden between his legs. Just as the stick came down he inconspicuously bent one leg and the stick split on the stone slab. "So from this you can see that it is possible!" laughed the bachelor. "You only have to hit hard, then your knees don't hurt. Courage now! Begin bravely!" The married man once again took a stick and struck it against his knee. It hurt terribly but the stick did not split. He wailed loudly with pain after each blow. As though displeased the bachelor shouted to him: "Come on now, bring your arm far back and strike with all your might!" Finally the other swung a thick stick with all his strength and brought it down on both his knees. They were smashed terribly and much blood flowed; he lay there and soon died. The cunning bachelor burst into loud laughter. He mocked the man, saying scornfully: "All right, then! Just go on splitting wood on your knees!" The bachelor then hurried to that man's hut and told the wife everything that had just happened. They had long been meeting as lovers; now both were happy that the husband was no longer alive. They moved close together and immediately had intercourse. Soon the dead man's son came to the hut. When he saw the bachelor on his mother's bed he became furious and thrust his harpoon right through him. The bachelor died immediately. This is how the son avenged his father.

Informant: Not known; pp. 1257-1258.

Summary

Bachelor in love with married woman tricks her husband into killing himself by trying to split wood against his own knees. Dead man's son then kills bachelor upon finding him with mother.

Motif content

J2401.	Fatal imitation.
K890.	Dupe tricked into killing himself.
K2213.	Treacherous wife.
P233.6.	Son avenges father.
Q241.	Adultery punished.
Q411.6.	Death as punishment for murder.
Q461.3.	Impaling as punishment for adultery.
T92.10.	Rival in love killed.
T481.	Adultery.

50. The Skillful Slinger

Once there lived a bachelor who had fallen very much in love with another man's wife. He himself was a *wetawémuwa*, that is, an excellent slinger (*wetáwa* really means the stone thrown by the sling, but also denotes the sling itself), but the other man was stupid and clumsy. He thought long about how he might make the latter's wife his own.

One day he said to the married man: "Why don't we go down to the beach and practice a bit with our slings!" The other replied: "I can't handle the sling very well." The bachelor insisted: "That's precisely why you have to practice. I'll be glad to help you!" They both went to the open beach and chose a target. They began throwing stones at the target with their slings. The bachelor scored a hit every time but the other always missed. Finally the married man said timidly: "It's strange that you hit the target every time. How come you always succeed?" The bachelor answered: "You must rub some blood on your hand. Look at my hand!" He held out his hand covered with blood. Thereupon the married man asked: "But where will I get blood?" The bachelor replied: "That you have to get from your own body, preferably from between your legs. Look closely how I do it!" He reached down between his legs with his forearm and quickly pulled back the palm of his hand close to his genitals; this hand he held under the other man's eyes and it was actually completely covered with blood. Earlier the bachelor had secretly smeared fresh cormorant blood between his legs. Thereupon the married man promised: "I'll do the same thing." Cautiously he gave himself a few light scratches and wailed at once: "Oh, but it hurts!" The bachelor laughed and urged him on: "You must scratch more strongly. Bring your hand down once quickly and hard past your genitals, then you won't feel the pain!" The other actually seized his genitals with all his might and pulled them off completely. A terrible pain set in and much blood flowed. He died soon afterward. The bachelor who had caused all this laughed scornfully. He said to himself: "Now you'll certainly hit the mark with your sling!" Since the married man was now dead he took the latter's beautiful wife.

Informant: Not known; pp. 1258-1259.

Summary

Bachelor in love with married woman tricks her husband into killing himself by tearing off genitals. Then he takes over dead man's wife.

Motif content

F661.	Skillful marksman.
J1919.5.	Genitals cut off through ignorance.
J2401.	Fatal imitation.
J2650.	Bungling fool.
K890.	Dupe tricked into killing himself.
T11.3.2.	Dream about a marriage with another's wife.
T92.10.	Rival in love killed.

51. The Cormorant Visitors

A long time ago an unusually severe winter set in; lots of snow fell and it was icy cold. Worst hit were the Wollaston Islands where snow piled up high and remained for a long time. Isolated there on an island sat a woman who had been alone for quite some time. She no longer had fire, for there were no *šewáli* (firestones) left. She also had hardly anything left to eat. So she found herself in great distress, for the long winter was extremely severe. One night she was lying on her bed still awake, when she saw a big black bird enter her hut and sit down in the middle of it. Soon it began to talk exactly like a Yamana. The woman listened closely and assured herself that the bird was really speaking her own language. Amazed, she said to herself: "But how is that possible?

That bird speaks just like the Yamana. Isn't that strange!" Unnoticed she lifted her head a bit. She discovered a great number of these birds in the middle of her hut; they were sitting around the fire which they themselves had lit again, warming themselves. They were all shivering with cold in the frosty air. The woman drew up a bit closer behind the birds, where it was very dark since they themselves were obscuring the light from the flames. That is how close they were to the fire. Now the woman could understand exactly what these birds were saying. Indeed, all spoke just like Yamana, and Marutuwérelakípa[105] caught every word clearly. Each bird spoke of its long journeys far out on the open sea, of the harbors it visited, of the rocks and islands it had flown by, of the animals it had hunted down, of the many dangers it had escaped. Meanwhile all were warming themselves comfortably by the fire. The woman was listening attentively. Since the birds spoke just like Yamana she believed everything they said. She was keeping herself in deep shadow and all the birds had their backs to her. She was so extremely happy and pleased, and finally convinced herself that those birds had to be people after all. She gave a sigh of relief and said to herself: "How nice that at last some of my people have come here. Now I'm no longer so completely alone!" Then she moved even closer to sit in the circle of birds; she wanted to tell them how long she had been sitting here alone and how much she wanted to warm herself by the fire she had been without for so long. But as she was pushing herself into the circle of birds to sit down she bumped her arm against one of them. She just had time to see that all the birds were scraping and cleaning skins. The woman was now brightly illuminated by the flames, and when the birds spotted her in their midst they became very frightened. They rose quickly, extinguished the fire, snatched up all their skins, and flew away. Only a whale was left behind; it was too heavy for them. The startled woman followed the birds with her eyes. But they were gone. Now she no longer doubted that all those creatures really were birds, namely *touwíšiwa.*[106] She saw the big whale which the birds had left for her, and thus did not have to die of hunger. But still she was very sad that she was all by herself again on the island and without fire. She cried for a long, long time. Then she, too, turned into a bird, the *marutuwérelakípa* out there on the open sea.

Informant: Julia; pp. 1259-1260.

[105]This name identifies a sea bird of average size. I was not able to determine the species zoologically as the Indians were unable to describe it clearly enough. This type of bird appears also in the next two stories.

[106]The iridescent cormorant, *Phalacrocorax olivaceus.*

Summary

Woman isolated on island during severe winter has no food or fire. One night she finds many birds in her hut, sitting around fire and talking in Yamana language. When she joins them they leave, taking fire with them but leaving food for her. Alone again she cries, and then turns into bird.

Motif content

A2452.	Animal's occupation: hunting.
B172.	Magic bird.
B200.+.	Birds with human traits. (B200. Animals with human traits.)
B211.3.	Speaking bird.
B235.+.	Birds have meeting, discuss their journeys. (B235. Secrets discussed in animal meeting.)
D531.	Animals provide food for men.
B772.+.	Marooned woman abandoned by birds. (B772. Shipwrecked man repulsed by animals.)
D150.+.	Transformation: woman to bird. (D150. Transformation: man to bird.)
F982.	Animals carry extraordinary burden.
N455.+.	Overheard animal conversation. (N455. Overheard [human] conversation.)

52. The Bird from the High Seas

Once Marutuwérelakípa[107] came with her family to a small lonely island, and the fire went out for all of them. Sadly they sat there not knowing what to do, for they did not even have *šewáli* (firestones) with them. They suffered badly from the cold, because there was exceedingly heavy snow and the winter was unusually severe. Full of despair they huddled in their cold hut. One evening when it had grown very dark many *touwíšiwa*[108] quite unexpectedly arrived and sat there on the beach. They talked to one another just as the Yamana speak and had a lively conversation. As soon as they arrived they said: "Here we'll make a fire and rest!" And indeed, it was not long before a bright fire was blazing. All this the people saw and heard. The women moved closer, for they wanted to warm themselves by the fire. Now they could understand very clearly what the *touwíšiwa* were saying. They were

---

[107]A sea bird of average size. This bird plays the principal role also in the preceding story.

[108]The magnificent *Phalacrocorax olivaceus*.

talking about their long journeys, about the frequent bad weather, about the islands and bays they had visited; they also remarked how comfortable they were feeling there by the fire and that they were going to continue their traveling the following day. They felt so snug and comfortable by the fire that they kept shaking themselves all the time.

Meanwhile the women had gotten quite close to the birds. They were delighted with the gleaming embers and planned to steal a few firebrands. Very cautiously some of them extended their hands toward the fire. But when they wanted to take a few burning logs and pull them away from the hearth the compact flock of *touwišiwa* suddenly flew up. All flew high up into the air and soon were out of sight. Although the women became very frightened they soon calmed down at the thought of the fire they had been without so long. But when they looked more closely at the fire which they already considered theirs, it was only dry grass and not real fire at all. Disappointed, they said to one another: "What is this? After all, we did see fire and reached for it; now we're only holding dry grass in our hands!" Others said: "Those birds did have real fire, we all saw it. They talked just as we do. They also said: 'Tomorrow we'll catch a lot of fish and then make a fire again on that other island there!' They were all feeling so comfortable here by the fire, which all of us clearly saw. And now we have nothing but dry grass in our hands!" They grew extremely sad, for again they were without fire. But the birds never came back to this island; nor did they ever again appear in that region.

Informant: Mary; pp. 1260–1261.

Summary

Isolated on island and without fire during severe winter some people find many birds on beach, sitting around fire and talking in Yamana language. When people try to join them birds leave, and fire turns out to be only dry grass.

Motif content

A1415.	Theft of fire.
A2434.2.	Why certain animals are absent from countries.
B172.	Magic bird.
B200.+.	Birds with human traits. (B200. Animals with human traits.)
B211.3.	Speaking bird.
B235.+.	Birds have meeting, discuss their journeys. (B235. Secrets discussed in animal meeting.)
F882.	Extraordinary fire.

F964.   Extraordinary behavior of fire.
N455.+.   Overheard animal conversation. (N455. Overheard [hu-
                           man] conversation.)

53. The Braggart

Several families once went to an island to hunt sea lions, for they had
long been lacking blubber and oil. Martúwux-yélluwa went with them.
He was very unpopular with all people for he wanted to be number one
everywhere; he thought he knew everything best; he considered himself
more clever than the rest; he was a braggart and an egoist. Long ago
people had all grown tired of him, for he always wanted to be the one to
give orders. They were secretly considering playing a trick on him to
make him look ridiculous. One day some men said to him: "See that rock
over there by the point, the one that juts out from that island? A large
sea lion just crawled up on it. You really should harpoon it. You're the
only one who knows how to throw the harpoon with precision." These
words flattered Túwux[109] very much. He took his harpoon and ran
quickly to that point, which was far away. He went by himself, leaving
all his belongings in his hut. After he had gone very far the people
packed their own things, loaded them into their canoes, and extinguished all the fires in the huts. They also loaded all that man's things
into his wife's canoe. She put out the fire in their hut and took
everything that belonged to her and her husband. Everybody left and
went to the campsite they had just come from, leaving absolutely
nothing behind on the island. Departing they said to one another:
"Now he may stay here forever! After all, the island itself will never
disappear." Toward evening the man returned to the place where his
people's huts had been. But he saw to his dismay that they had all gone.
They had taken everything along: canoes, hides, fire and firewood,
even his own weapons and tools. Sadly he sat down in his hut, of
which only the framework was still standing; everything inside was
missing, even the fire. He was cold and hungry.

When the people reached the old camp everybody went silently into
the huts. But the father of the man they had deserted on the island soon
realized that his son had not come with them, for nobody had spoken
to him about his son. That seemed very suspicious to him and he

[109]The night heron, *Nycticorax obscurus*.

suspected something bad. His daughter-in-law did not tell him anything either, for she was staying in the hut of her own kin.

Once he was sitting in his hut with only his grandson. A long time had passed, and he had not been able to find out anything about his son. The old man said to the little boy: "My little grandson! You see that a long time has already gone by. I'm going to give you some good advice, but be cunning: sneak around unobserved in the other people's huts and listen carefully to what they say. Maybe you'll be able to find out something about your father. Possibly they've killed him or some other accident has befallen him. Who knows how and when and where. But be cunning so that no one will notice what you are up to! You can also lie down on a bed in another hut, at night when it gets dark, and pretend to be asleep. Listen carefully to what the people are saying! Then, in the morning come to my hut and tell me what you heard. But be cunning when you do so!" "All right," said the boy, "I'll be clever and do as you've told me."

He went unnoticed into the hut of his mother's relatives, sat down by the fire, and played. The sisters-in-law of the man they had left on the island had gone out on the ocean at sunset to fish with torches in the dark. They did not return until late. When they entered the hut they did not know that the little boy had crawled under the hides. They immediately sat down by the fire, for although they had had a fire in the canoe, they were very cold. One of them said: "How cold it is tonight; although we had a fire in the canoe we were terribly cold!" To this the other replied: "But how do you think that conceited braggart is feeling whom we left on the island without anything at all? He doesn't even have a fire; he must be trembling terribly with cold." The other sister-in-law said: "He well deserved it. Why does he always want to be the best and the most clever!" The cunning grandson heard all this because he was not asleep and was well hidden.

The following morning he got up from the bed and acted quite unconcerned. Not until then did the two sisters-in-law realize that the little boy had slept there. Soon he went and sat outside by the entrance of the hut, for the sun was shining warmly. His grandfather watched him from his own hut. After some time he called to him loudly: "Where are you hiding, my little grandson? Oh, now I see you! You're sitting there in front of your aunts' hut. Come here a minute! I'll pick the lice off you again, for you always have lots of them on your head. Come quickly now!" The little boy got up and went to his grandfather's hut. He squatted very close to him so that he was able to whisper into his ear imperceptibly, and the grandfather acted as though he was picking lice from his head. The little boy told him that the night before his father's two sisters-in-law had not returned from fishing until late, that they had been very cold although they had a fire in the canoe, but that their brother-in-law there on the island probably was shivering terribly with cold and frost since they had left him behind without anything, even without fire, as punishment for his having wanted always to be the best and the most clever. The old man said: "Now I understand everything!"

Quickly he began to peel off bark and built himself a canoe. He loaded a lot of firewood on board. After this he took a burning piece of wood from his hearth and made a fire with it in the new canoe. He then said to the other people: "I'm going to the eternal island which never disappears! If I like it there I'll stay." The others said: "What strange ideas this old man has! What's he going to do on that island? Who knows whether someone hasn't finally told him that we deserted his son there in order to play a trick on him." And one of those two sisters-in-law said to the other: "Do you remember? That night when we ˜came back from fishing, the old man's grandson must have overheard what we were saying: then he told his grandfather every-thing." The old man took a few relatives with him and they all went to the island.

In his distress the man who had been left on the island had begun to tame a few birds, for after all he had nothing to eat. The tame birds in their turn attracted other birds so that he was able to obtain enough meat and did not die of hunger.

When the old man arrived at the island with his canoe he got out. He thought: "I wonder how I'm going to find my son here? Where can he be? This island is so big! Maybe he has already died of hunger and cold." Then he saw a lot of bird droppings on the ground and said to himself: "Maybe my son has tamed these birds for himself." He felt the droppings; they were cold so he continued walking. Then he again felt the bird droppings on the ground and noticed that they were warmer. So he said to himself: "My son must be around here!" He continued walking in the direction where the bird droppings became warmer and warmer. When he touched them again and found them to be soft and warm he said to himself: "My son must be here!" He walked yet a little farther and soon heard loud snoring. Joyfully he said: "That's my son snoring!" He walked up to him and shook him awake. The latter became very frightened, got up cautiously, and suddenly went for the old man's throat, for he thought someone wanted to kill him. Quickly the old man said: "Take a good look: I'm your father! Don't be fright-ened!" Then the son recognized his father and was very happy to see him there. Soon he told him how all the others had deserted him, how he had been able to save his life only with great difficulty, and how much he had suffered without fire. The father comforted him. Soon they got into the canoe and went back to the camp.

Before they reached shore and got out the man said to his father: "I'm going to stay in the canoe a bit longer. But you can call all the people together and invite them to our hut; entertain them for a long time. Then I'll leave the canoe, sneak up to the hut, and scrape away the earth from outside so that all the poles will become loose and shaky. But you must keep talking to the people. When I'm finished with my task I'll secretly give you a sign; then run out quickly because the hut will collapse and kill everybody inside."

The two now did exactly that. The old man called the people together and everyone came to his hut. Here he spoke with them for a long time. But meanwhile on the outside his son was loosening the ground where the hut was standing. Soon he signaled his father, and the latter quickly came out. Then the whole hut collapsed and crushed everybody inside. Anyone that tried to escape was killed by the two. This is how all those who had left Martúwux-yélluwa on the island perished, including his own wife.

But today Túwux is much appreciated; he is very popular among the people, because his call always announces an imminent visit, the (visitor's) canoe coming from the direction whence he comes flying.[110]

Informant: Not known; pp. 1262-1266.

Summary

Unpopular braggart is tricked into going hunting by fellow villagers, who then break camp, leaving him alone on island. The man's father, with the help of the man's son, finds out and goes to rescue him. In revenge they kill all the villagers.

Motif content

B147.2.+.	Night-heron's call announces the coming of visitors. (B147.2. Birds furnish omens.)
B771.	Wild animal miraculously tamed.
C450.	Tabu: boasting.
F677.	Skillful tracker.
H79.3.	Recognition by voice.

---

[110]My informants had a discussion in which they expressed their opinions of this story. All agreed: "The punishment was very just for those people who had left that man on the island without anything. But he, too, had to have his punishment, as he was a conceited braggart and a troublesome know-it-all."

J2353.1.	Foolish boasts get man into trouble.
K750.	Capture by decoy.
K811.	Victim lured into house and killed.
K874.	Deception by pretended lousing.
K910.	Murder by strategy.
K1616.	Marooned man reaches home and outwits marooner.
K2213.	Treacherous wife.
K2218.	Treacherous relatives-in-law.
L430.	Arrogance repaid.
N455.9.+.	Location of sought man learned from overheard conversation. (N455.9. Location of sought object learned from overheard conversation.)
N827.	Child as helper.
P233.	Father and son.
P291.	Grandfather.
Q288.	Punishment for mockery.
Q330.	Overweening punished.
Q411.	Death as punishment.
Q467.5.	Marooning as punishment.
R153.3.	Father rescues son(s).
S116.	Murder by crushing.
S145.	Abandonment on an island.
W34.	Loyalty.
W117.	Boastfulness.

TALES ABOUT SHAMANS, SPIRITS, AND OGRES

54. The Revenge of the Sparrow Hawk

Once Yookalía[111] came to a camp where he met a beautiful girl. He liked her very much, so he stayed. But he himself was not popular and had only a few friends among those people. Eventually he fell deeply in love with the girl. He frequently went to her hut to offer his love, but to no avail. Still he kept coming to her hut, and finally she let herself be persuaded and promised to become his wife. Yookalía was extremely happy over this and both now lived together. But one night when he

---

[111]The sparrow hawk, *Milvago chimango*.

came quietly to her bed and revealed his intention to sleep with her, the girl energetically pushed him back and would have nothing to do with him any more. That made him very sad, for he realized now that the girl no longer wanted to be his wife. He complained to the other people but they laughed at him. He simply had no friends there; nobody knew him well enough. Whenever they had a chance these people would always make fun of him, even the girl he loved.

The men often went out to hunt guanacos but they never took Yookalía along. Every time they killed a guanaco they filled a twisted piece of gut with its blood and made a sausage which they brought back to the hut. But for Yookalía they made another sausage, for they wanted to make fun of him. With a pointed stick they poked around in their noses until blood flowed; this blood they gathered up in a piece of gut and prepared a *kéti* (a special kind of sausage). This sausage they brought back to the hut to give to Yookalía. He roasted it over the fire and ate it. The others looked on and secretly laughed. The men did not give Yookalía anything else to eat; therefore he kept growing paler and thinner. Although he asked for something different, the people gave him nothing else, and when he asked for more of the same, they did not give him any.

Yookalía had now grown very weak and thin indeed. One day the people returned from hunting and, as usual, gave him the blood sausage. Since he was very hungry he ate it, and the others secretly laughed. But two good friends that he now had among the women finally felt sorry for him. They told Yookalía: "Listen, what you're eating is a sausage made of human blood. The people made this kind of sausage for you with blood from their noses!" He became furious, threw the remainder away, and would no longer eat anything.

Since the people had treated him so badly he decided to leave their camp. He had very good arrows and a beautiful bow. Without anybody noticing he pushed his weapons outside the hut from within. Then he told his two good friends: "Now paint me nicely because I'm returning to my parents! The people here don't like me. But they'll get their punishment. You two will be rewarded for having treated me well." The two women painted him beautifully. Unobtrusively he took his weapons which he had earlier pushed out of the hut and, before anyone realized it, he had left.

He went in the direction of his father's place. But he had to go past the hut of a bad, evil-minded woman. As Yookalía came closer the woman wanted to kill him. But the younger Yoálox who goes around everywhere hid Yookalía and he was saved. He continued on. Wherever he spent the night he made a big fire to warm himself. That way all the places he had passed were marked.

When he was close to his father's hut his younger brother, who was standing by the entrance, saw him. Instantly he called into the hut: "Far in the distance there I see a man; I'm sure it is my brother!" To this the mother said: "That man in the distance can't possibly be your brother. Surely he died long ago. I haven't heard from him in a long time." Gradually the man came closer and closer; he was walking slowly as he was very weak and worn out. But when he entered the hut his mother recognized him at once and was happy that he had come. Since he was so pale and thin his mother asked him: "Why are you so pale and so thin?" He replied: "Those people there treated me very badly; even my bride made a fool of me. They only fed me sausages of human blood, nothing else. Therefore I grew thinner and thinner, and finally I fled." Sympathetically the mother asked: "But how was this possible?" He replied: "Two good friends among the women told me everything. Then I wouldn't eat anything any more and left."

The father sat on his bed and heard everything. He became very indignant that those people had treated his son so badly. Then he lay down and soon fell asleep. In his dream he wanted to kill a whale, let it wash ashore, and then spoil its meat so that everyone who had treated his son badly would be punished. Now he was dreaming, and he killed a big whale in his dream. Then he let it be stranded near the camp of those people; in his dream he recognized all those who had mistreated his son. Finally he placed himself personally inside the whale. He wanted to watch those who came and to see what pieces each would receive. Now at last would be punished all those who had given his son the sausage made of human blood.

The next morning a man from that camp saw the big whale lying on the beach. He quickly called the people. They came hurrying. Each got a big piece of blubber; all ate and were very contented. Yookalía's bride, too, got her piece; his two good friends also got their pieces, and all were very contented. But the old *yékamuš*, Yookalía's father, who was sitting inside the whale, saw exactly which piece of blubber was given to whom. When all the people had eaten plenty he suddenly transformed all the consumed pieces of blubber except for those that had been eaten by Yookalía's two friends. Suddenly the pieces of blubber began to move in everyone's stomach as though they were coming alive again. They were strongly pulled toward the place where the whale was lying; and along with them they were also pulling the bride and all those people who had given Yookalía human blood. The individual pieces assembled themselves perfectly on their own accord. The whale came alive again and swam off with the people who had remained stuck to it. Only Yookalía's two good friends were spared.

Even today one can still see all those people sticking to the whale's back.[112] That is how the old *yékamuš* avenged his son, Yookalía, because those people had given him sausages of human blood.[113]

Informant: Not known; pp. 1266-1268.

Summary

Man who is always ridiculed and mistreated by bride and villagers leaves camp and returns to parents. His father, a powerful shaman, avenges son's disgrace: he places himself inside stranded whale which villagers eat, then makes the swallowed pieces of meat come alive and assemble into whale again, leaving people stuck to its body.

Motif content

A2310.+.	Why parasites cling to whale's back. (A2310. Origin of animal characteristics: body covering.)
B16.2.+.	Devastating whale. (B16.2. Devastating wild animals.)
B175.+.	Magic whale. (B175. Magic fish.)
D2060.	Death or bodily injury by magic.
E31.	Limbs of dead voluntarily reassemble and revive.
E32.	Resuscitated eaten animal.
E780.	Vital bodily members.
F1034.+.	Shaman concealed in body of whale. (F1034. Person concealed in another's body.)
G550.	Rescue from ogre.
H88.	Identification by tokens left as trail.
K515.	Escape by hiding.
K959.2.	Murder in one's sleep.
K1210.	Humiliated or baffled lovers.
K2213.	Treacherous wife.
K233.6.+.	Father avenges son. (P233.6. Son avenges father.)
P233.8.	Prodigal son returns.
Q72.	Loyalty rewarded.
Q285.	Cruelty punished.
Q288.	Punishment for mockery.
Q551.2.1.+.	Magic adhesion to whale as punishment. (Q551.2.1. Magic adhesion to object as punishment [for opposition to holy person].)
Q551.3.	Punishment: transformation.
S183.	Frightful meal.

[112]This refers to the many parasites, above all the common *Balanus psittacus* (Gusinde 1937:577, 591), with which every older whale appears to be covered.

[113]This story shows close similarities to two Selknam stories, entitled "The Revenge of Elankáiyink" (Gusinde 1931:642; Wilbert 1975:92) and "How Hačámšes Took Revenge" (Wilbert 1975:98).

S400.   Cruel persecutions.
T75.   Man scorned by his beloved.
T75.2.1.   Rejected suitor's revenge.
T288.   Wife refused to sleep with detested husband.
W34.   Loyalty.

55. The Disrespectful Son-in-law

Once there was a son-in-law who lived in the hut of his father-in-law; he had taken both of the old man's daughters for his wives. But this son-in-law did not treat his father-in-law too respectfully. Whenever morning dawned and a beautiful day announced its arrival the old man would say joyfully "*Yaléakumáala!*" Upon hearing this the son-in-law would mumble: "*Taléakumáala!*"[114] He would whisper it quickly so that the old man could not understand it clearly and would fail to notice that his son-in-law was deliberately making fun of him. For a long time the son-in-law kept on in this very way always greeting his old father-in-law with the same words.

Finally one day the younger daughter said to her father: "Listen, father. You always say: '*Yaléakumáala.*' But your son-in-law answers mockingly: '*Taléakumáala,*' thereby making fun of you!" When he heard this the old man became furious. He immediately started considering how to take full revenge on this disrespectful son-in-law. He lay down and fell asleep. In his dreams he wanted to make a whale drift ashore and place himself inside it in order to punish his son-in-law. He was a great *yékamuš.* For that reason he succeeded: in his dream he killed a whale; at once it drifted close to the camp and he placed himself inside it.

The following morning the son-in-law got up from his bed. As he looked out of the hut he saw many *dášalux*[115] hovering in the air. He said to himself: "Where did all these *dášalux* come from? There must be a dead whale floating around near here, for there are many birds. I'll go at once and see what it can be!" He went back into his hut and told his wives everything. They replied: "Good, you go and see whether it really is a whale floating around nearby!" He ran out and climbed a small hill. From there he saw how a whale was drifting closer and closer toward land, with many birds hovering above it in the air. These birds

---

[114]Literal translation: "A lovely day" (is to be expected), and (it will be) "a cross-eyed day." Both forms together have a pleasant ring.
[115]The large albatross, *Diomedea melanophrys*, from the sea.

were talking; he heard them saying: "Just come closer, my brother-in-law; after all, the old father-in-law is 'cross-eyed.' What a 'lovely day,' my son-in-law. Certainly, my 'cross-eyed' father-in-law!" They were talking thus like human beings. This amazed him; he looked around but could not see anyone. He climbed down from the hill because the whale was coming closer. He heard the conversation loud and clear now. Then he said to himself: "There must be people here for I can hear their voices! But I don't see anyone. Where can they be? Whence may they have come? Where are they hiding? One only hears their conversation!" He continued walking and was now very close to the whale. Here, too, he saw nothing but birds and said to himself: "Where are the people that I hear talking around here? I only see birds everywhere!"

He took his knife and cut himself a big piece of blubber from the whale. This he loaded on his shoulders, quickly turned around and walked toward his hut. But strange: on the way this piece of blubber grew larger and larger; it finally grew so large and so heavy that he had to cut it in half; it had become so big that he was no longer able to carry it. One half he put in the swampy water and the other half he again loaded on his shoulder. But after a short time this piece, too, grew very large; soon he was no longer able to continue with this one, either. Again he divided it into two parts and put one half of it in the swampy water; the other half he continued to carry. But also this half grew very large, so that again he had to make two pieces out of it. All this repeated itself five times, and then once more. At last he reached his hut.

His family soon arrived and all ate of the pieces of blubber. During the meal he told them where he had found the whale, how he had cut a big piece of blubber and loaded it on his shoulder, how this piece had grown bigger and bigger on the way, that he had to cut it in half, and all this six times. He also informed them where in the swampy water he had buried the other halves. Everyone was very happy over this and said: "Tomorrow we'll go where the whale is lying!"

The next morning many people went to that place and set up their huts close to the whale. Each cut a big piece of blubber for himself and ate with relish. It was a long time since they had eaten blubber. The little grandson of the old *yékamuš* had crawled up on the whale and plunged his knife deeply into it. Then his grandfather, who was sitting inside, called to him in a low voice: "Little grandson, don't stab too deeply!" Although the little boy heard the voice and was very surprised he, nevertheless, continued to carve. Then he heard the same voice again: "Little grandson, please don't cut so deeply!" Now he became very frightened and ran to his mother; he told her everything. But she instructed him not to say anything and to stay in the hut.

The people remained in this place for some time and ate well. Then they went back to their former camp. The two daughters of the old *yékamuš* began to paint themselves and put on their feather ornaments as a sign of grief. They thought their old father had died. The others, too, painted themselves, and all gathered for the *yamalašemóina*. When they began to cry and to chant, all the pieces of blubber started to move; they came alive again and moved toward the whale on the beach; each piece put itself in place all by itself and soon the whale had been pieced together again. Also the son-in-law felt himself drawn toward the whale as though by a strong power; he was lifted up on the back of the whale against his will. But now the old *yékamuš* came out of the whale, because the animal began to live and move again; it slid down the beach into the water and took with it the son-in-law who was sitting on its back.

Even today one can still see the son-in-law riding on the back of the whale. But those pieces of blubber that the son-in-law put into the swampy water on his way to the camp became bigger and bigger, exactly obeying the wish of the old *yékamuš*. Whenever the old man wanted it, his two daughters went to fetch one piece after the other. Accordingly, they had blubber from that big whale for a very long time.[116]

Informant: Not known; pp. 1269-1271.

Summary

In order to punish disrespectful son-in-law shaman hides inside beached whale which is found by son-in-law. Meat from whale which the latter carries home magically grows so that he has to cut it in half six times on the way. After all have eaten their fill, shaman makes pieces of meat come alive again and assemble into whale. Son-in-law is also drawn to whale. He still sits on whale's back as its dorsal fin.

Motif content

A2350.+.	Why dolphin has high dorsal fin. (A2350. Origin of animal characteristics: trunk.)
B16.2.+.	Devastating whale. (B16.2. Devastating wild animals.)
B175.+.	Magic whale. (B175. Magic fish.)
B211.3.	Speaking bird.
C170.+.	Tabu: showing disrespect for father-in-law. (C170. Tabu connected with husband's or wife's relatives.)

[116]The so-called whale in this story is actually a dolphin, which is characterized by a long, high dorsal fin. This is supposed to indicate the disrespectful son-in-law. The basic plot and individual motifs coincide with those used in the Selknam story "The Revenge of Elankáiyink" (Gusinde 1931:639; Wilbert 1975:92).

D1812.5.0.2.	Omens from flight of birds.
D2061.	Magic murder.
D2106.	Magic multiplication of objects.
E31.	Limbs of dead voluntarily reassemble and revive.
E32.	Resuscitated eaten animal.
E780.	Vital bodily members.
F983.	Extraordinary growth of animal.
F1034.+.	Shaman concealed in body of whale. (F1034. Person concealed in another's body.)
K959.2.	Murder in one's sleep.
P211.	Wife chooses father's side in feud. Must choose between husband and father.
P681.	Mourning customs.
Q395.	Disrespect punished.
Q551.2.1.+.	Magic adhesion to whale as punishment. (Q551.2.1. Magic adhesion to object as punishment [for opposition to holy person].)
Q551.3.	Punishment: transformation.
W187.	Insolence.

56. The Sensitive Sparrow

Long ago a dead whale once drifted ashore on the coast. The nearest inhabitants lit four big fires to inform the other people. The others saw the fires and said: "A whale has stranded; quickly, let us go there!" They took their canoes and went to where the whale was. Within a short time many people came together. Héšpul,[117] too, came with his people; he led his group and brought them to the place where the whale was lying. Although many people had already arrived Héšpul was not recognized by anyone when he and his group got there. Despite the fact that he was the headman of his group, the people entertained the newcomers well and treated them in a much friendlier manner than they did Héšpul himself. Nobody knew him.

This indifferent behavior toward him by the other people hurt Héšpul very much. He felt gravely offended becasue they did not respect and wait on him as a powerful *yékamuš* should be. He did not say anything, but soon began considering how he might take revenge on those who were paying him so little attention. One beautiful, clear day, just when the sun was at its highest point, he let it become completely dark. The people were very frightened and wondered in amazement:

[117]This little sparrow, of the family Tyrannidae, is *Taeniptera pyrope*.

"What is this? What can it mean? Where's this darkness coming from all of a sudden?" At the same time they were seized by great fear. Then Héš-pul declared: "It is I who sent you this darkness because you are not treating me with the respect that properly befits a *yékamuš!* I am Héšpul, the great *yékamuš!*" The people looked at one another, rather embarrassed. Then they asked him: "How long is this darkness going to last?" He answered harshly: "It will last forever!" The people became very sad and began to cry. After some time they begged: "Please take away this darkness! If it stays the way it is now we'll be unable to see and we'll die of hunger. If you do that we'll also wait on you particularly well!" A few went to his hut and said: "Listen, we didn't know you! So don't be offended by our behavior. Now we'll pick out the best pieces of meat and the best blubber for you. Forgive us and take away this darkness. After all, now we know that you're a powerful *yékamuš!*" Héšpul answered: "All right, I'll forgive you for this mistake, but know now that I'm a powerful *yékamuš.*"

Then the people left his hut. He rubbed white paint all over his body and painted the red line across his face; finally he put the feather headdress on his head and soon began to sing his song of the east. As he was thus singing, it slowly dawned in the east. As he continued chanting it grew lighter and lighter, until finally it was as light as when the sun is at its peak. The people were happy and gave a sigh of relief. They immediately prepared a big feast. They gave Héšpul the tastiest pieces of meat and selected the best blubber for him. All were cheerful and contented.

Thus Héšpul even today still chants his "song of the east," "Pit, pit, pit," every morning. But it grows light very slowly, since the people of that time had not honored him sufficiently. All are happy as soon as it is light again and heave a deep sigh of relief following the dark night. Héšpul, the powerful *yékamuš,* continues to be highly revered even today.

Informant: Alfredo; pp. 1271-1272.

Summary

Powerful shaman (sparrow) is offended when no one recognizes him at a large gathering of people. He therefore makes sun go away and darkness descend. Frightened, everyone begs forgiveness, and sun slowly returns. Since then it only grows light very slowly every morning.

Motif content

A1179.2.	Origin of dawn.
A2426.2.+.	Sparrow's song. (A2426.2. Cries of birds.)

B34.	Bird of dawn.
B755.	Animal calls the dawn. The sun rises as result of the animal's call.
D1766.	Magic results produced by religious ceremony.
D2146.1.3.	Day produced by magic.
D2146.2.1.	Night produced by magic.
D2173.	Magic singing.
Q36.	Reward for repentance.
Q395.	Disrespect punished.
Q552.20.1.	Miraculous darkness as punishment.
W116.	Vanity.

57. The Makers of Stone Points

Once several families had a camp, and among them there lived two unpopular men. It was not long before the two noticed that the others were planning to kill them. So they left, quickly and secretly. Eventually the people noticed that they were gone; they pursued them in the hope of catching them again. But the two men were already far away; they had run quickly. Unexpectedly they came to Kaluwélla-waia, a narrow inlet which cuts deeply into the coast (in the west). It was impossible to go around it because its shores were steep and covered with dense vegetation; nor was there a crossing (fjord) that they could have used. Strangely, though, there were many big fish in the water, pressed closely together with their backs slightly above the surface. In their distress the two men set out to walk across on these fish, first one, then the other. The first walked over the fish with great caution; he reached the other shore and then jumped onto a cliff; he was saved. But the second man trod with less caution so that one of the fish moved; he slipped, fell, sank down into the water, and was eaten alive by the big fish. His companion saw this from the shore and became very sad. But he had to hurry along and soon he came to Aniawáia (bay east of Puerto Olla). Here he found a large camp where many people had erected their huts. He told them how the people in the other camp had intended to kill him, how he had run away, how he had saved himself in Kaluwéllawaia, and how his friend had slipped and been eaten alive by the big fish. When the people heard this they became very sad and promptly began their *yamalašemóina*. For a long time they painted themselves, as they always do when they are in mourning. They also decided to make many *yékus* with which to kill those big fish.

One day when their mourning ceremony had come to a close, several men and a woman got into a canoe to go where certain stones can be found that are used for making points. They paddled all day long and did not reach the place until evening. They disembarked. The men rapidly built a hut and the woman gathered mussels on the beach. Then all sat down by the fire and ate a lot, because the men had to fortify themselves for the job that lay ahead.

The following morning they got up early. But before they went into the forest they said to the woman: "You get into the canoe and go far out on the channel; tie it to seaweed and stay there until we get back to the beach. For here in this region lives a man who is as handsome as *máku;*[118] he is so handsome that he might easily ensnare you! Therefore you had better go out on the channel and stay there to avoid becoming seduced by this good-looking man." The woman was very serious and strong-willed; she had never had anything to do with other men, nor did she show any inclination for this. Therefore she replied: "I'll do everything you told me!"

When the men had once more eaten their fill, they went into the forest and climbed the mountain. They got to the place where the suitable stone is found and promptly made stone points. From up there they often looked down to the channel where they saw the canoe far from the beach tied to seaweed; the woman was sitting inside. Reassured they said: "Just look at that! She's a good, serious woman; that handsome Hulušénuwa[119] won't get anywhere with her!"

Indeed, Hulušénuwa soon did come to the beach; he really was as good-looking as *máku*. Seeing the woman sitting there in the canoe alone he beckoned her to come ashore, intent on having intimate relations with her. He enticed her for a long time with flattering words. The woman looked at him frequently and noticed more clearly how wonderfully handsome this man Hulušénuwa was. She heard his alluring calls and felt more and more attracted to him: he was exceedingly handsome and enticed her very seductively with sweet words. But in spite of all this the woman controlled herself; she remained steadfast in her canoe and did not untie it from the *(Macrocystis)* seaweed.

Toward evening the men came down from the mountain and approached the beach. Handsome Hulušénuwa noticed them and hid in the forest. The men came out of the forest and called the woman. She

[118]Here again the reference is to the scarlet flower of the *Embothrium coccineum* shrub; cf. Gusinde 1937:702, fig. 78.

[119]The smaller of the two species of wren in Tierra del Fuego, *Troglodytes hornensis* (Gusinde 1937:42). It plays a part also in narrative 17 of this volume.

untied the canoe and came paddling toward shore. The men loaded all
the *yékuš* on board; they had brought very many. Then they
themselves got in and returned to the camp. When they arrived the
woman went to the other women and told them what had happened to
her. She said: "Where we were today there lives an extremely
handsome man, he is as handsome as *máku!* He can charm every single
one of us women, that's how magnificent he is. He greatly attracted
me, too. I felt a strong desire to yield to him. But I made a big effort
and did not give in to my desire. In fact I remained in the canoe far out
on the channel. None of you could do that, for this man is exceedingly
good-looking!" All the women listened very attentively. Then they said
laughingly: "We could manage that, too, just like you!" Another
woman said loudly: "Me he couldn't seduce under any circumstances.
I wouldn't let myself be ensnared by him!" Her own husband heard
that. So he told her: "All right, why don't you go with us tomorrow;
then we'll see how you behave!"

The following day the men went out again, this time taking that
other woman along. They got to the well-known place and disembarked. The men quickly built a hut and the woman looked for mussels
which they roasted over the fire; they ate, giving themselves strength.
But before they went into the forest the husband said to his wife: "Now
you must get into the canoe and go far out on the channel. Tie the
canoe to a bunch of seaweed and remain there until we come back.
We'll call you when you can come paddling back to the shore!" The
woman replied: "All right, I'll leave at once!" The men hurried into the
forest and climbed the mountain.

But the woman remained on the beach for some time, undoubtedly
waiting for that handsome man. And indeed Hulušénuwa soon arrived.
The woman was captivated just by looking at him. She ran toward him
and threw herself into his arms. She forced him down on the sand and
here they yielded long to their lust. Meanwhile the men had long since
reached the place where the stones for the *yékuš* are, and here they
were busily working away. Although they looked down from time to
time across the wide waterway they could not see the canoe.
Repeatedly they told one another: "There we are! The canoe is most
likely still lying by the shore. That's probably how it is: that woman
has let herself be tempted by Hulušénuwa, and the two are now having
fun together on the beach." After some time the men went down the
mountain and soon reached the beach. Here they saw the evil doings of
the two who were still embracing each other, lying on the beach. When
Hulušénuwa noticed the approaching men he ran away in a great
hurry. But the woman remained lying there, totally out of her senses

with desire. When her own husband got there he kicked her. Only then did she recognize him and said: "Cool me off, for I'm still full of desire. Hulušénuwa is so wonderfully handsome that I am beside myself!" The man walked some distance away and heated a sharp stone point. With this he quickly returned to where his wife was lying. With all his strength he pushed this red hot stone point into her vagina and slit open her stomach to the navel. In this condition he left her. He was boiling with rage.

The men got into the canoe without the woman and returned to the camp where the women were waiting on the beach. They saw that there were only men sitting in the canoe and asked: "What? Are only the men coming back? Where can the woman be? Aha! She must have let herself be seduced by that handsome man; she yielded to him and stayed behind with him. So then she did let herself be tempted by him, after all!" The men disembarked. They said that the woman had let herself be ensnared by that man out there and that she had died from wanton lust. But they did not mention that her furious husband had slit her stomach open.

The following day the men went back to that place for they needed still more *yékuš*. But the woman whom they had left behind the day before was no longer there: handsome Hulušénuwa, who is himself a clever *yékamuš*, had completely cured and taken her for his wife. Since then both live together amusing themselves with each other.

Informant: Not known; pp. 1273-1276.

Summary

Man escapes pursuers by walking across fjord to friendly camp on backs of fish; his companion slips, falls, and is eaten by fish. Expedition of many men and a woman is sent out to collect stones for stone points to kill man-eating fish. While men are working woman is enticed by handsome man but resists him. Another woman on second expedition gives in to temptation and her enraged husband slits open her stomach. Handsome man cures her and takes her for his wife.

Motif content

B16.2.+.	Man-eating fish. (B16.2. Devastating wild animals.)
B470.	Helpful fish.
B523.	Animal saves man from pursuer.
B555.	Animals serve as bridge across stream.
D2161.2.	Magic cure of wound.
F575.2.	Handsome man.
H473.	Test of wife's obedience.
P681.	Mourning customs.

Q241.	Adultery punished.
Q411.0.1.	Husband kills returning adulteress.
Q451.	Mutilation as punishment.
R210.	Escapes.
R220.	Flights.
R243.	Fugitives aided by helpful animal.
S112.2.+.	Murder with hot stone. (S112.2. Murder with hot iron.)
T254.6.	Disobedient wife punished.
T331.+.	Woman unsuccessfully tempted by man. (T331. Man unsuccessfully tempted by woman.)
W31.	Obedience.

58*a*. The Cannibals

Some people from the central group had once their camp in Hamanáulum.[120] They had observed that many other families had already gone west. A rumor was going around: "In Wáiman[121] there is a whale lying on the beach." So the people said to themselves: "We will also go there to get a lot of meat and blubber for ourselves. We'll just get another good night's rest!" And so, the next morning they got into their canoes. They traveled day and night, so as to reach the whale as soon as possible. There were ten families and a *yékamuš*. Because they also traveled at night—and these nights were very dark—they could not see the coast line very well and actually went past the whale! They continued paddling on and on. They had long since reached Hapananúši[122] and finally entered a harbor there; they were all very tired. They got out to scout and inquire about the whale they had been looking for all this time.

Many people had built a large camp here, but they were cannibals. It was their custom to eat everybody who came from the east. In order to kill them with ease they would permit only one stranger to enter a hut and stay there overnight, for each family could easily overpower one stranger in their hut and quickly kill him.

When these ten families arrived they were distributed over ten different huts. The *yékamuš* was sent to yet another hut. He went inside; an old woman was sitting on her bed near the fire making a small basket. When the *yékamuš* had entered, her husband said to him:

[120]A short beach about three kilometers west of what is today Ušuáia.
[121]This denotes the entire west of the Yamana territory, particularly the northern shore of Beagle Channel (Gusinde 1937:205).
[122]Name for the neighboring territory of the Halakwulup.

"Sit down here by the fire! You must be very hungry?" To this the *yékamuš* replied: "Yes, I'm very hungry, for we traveled far in search of the beached whale without finding it. Where can the whale be?" Then the man took his knife and grabbed his wife by her left breast; it was long and fleshy and he cut it off. He promptly hung it by the fire to roast it. The *yékamuš* saw this. Horrified he said: "Are you by any chance going to roast this piece for me?" The other man answered: "Yes, it's for you. You are very hungry, aren't you?" To this the *yékamuš* said very indignantly: "I'll never eat human flesh! What do you think we are? We came to look for that whale which we were told was stranded here in the west. We don't eat human flesh!" So saying he left the hut and looked around outside until he found a piece of meat. With this he returned to the hut, put it on the fire and roasted it; then he ate.

There was also a basket hanging in this hut containing ten small children. When they saw the *yékamuš* they happily jumped around in their basket, singing: "*Yárum hapánana, yárum hapánana,*" meaning: "Today we'd like to eat this man." But the two old people replied, likewise very happily: "*Hamašúnna hapánana, hamašúnna hapánana.*"[123]

The *yékamuš* then inferred what that was supposed to mean and realized the serious danger he and his people were in! Since he was a great *yékamuš* he caused a profound sleep to come over all the people in this camp by secretly throwing a piece of fat into the fire. While it was burning, they fell asleep at once and slept so soundly that no one moved any more. Quickly the *yékamuš* ran to his own people and told them that they were in grave danger. Everybody quickly grabbed their things. They stole from the cannibals whatever they could get their hands on, loaded everything into their canoes, and were gone. They hastened to get back again to the east, their homeland.

When they were already far away a dog began to bark so loudly that those people woke up and noticed that all their belongings had been stolen. Far in the distance they caught sight of the thieves hurrying away. Quickly they prepared to pursue them. When the people saw

[123]The word *hapánana*, as used here by the Halakwulup, was described to me as having no meaning whatsoever. The children wanted to make clear to the old people that they would prefer to eat the man that day, while the old people wanted to put off the feast until the next day. But so that the stranger would not realize what they intended to do with him they only emphasized the adverbs "today" and "tomorrow," together with a completely meaningless word. This was sufficient for both the old people and the children, who understood one another. Whether it is related to *hapona* I can't determine.

The same meaningless word was also the reason for characterizing themselves as the Hapánana Yamana and their territory as Hapananúši (Gusinde 1937:957).

that the cannibals were coming after them they were overwhelmed by fear. They hid in Asúsiwaia.[124] But the Hapananúši people spotted them, and with the sling threw a big *šewáli* (firestone). It fell very close to the hiding place of the fugitives and burst with an explosion like thunder. One can still hear it thundering in that region.[125] In order to flee more quickly and easily, the fugitives tossed a large part of the stolen goods overboard. They continued paddling again, eastward all the time, past Lapatáia and Hamanáulum, until they finally got to Ušuáia where they had had their previous camp. But the Hapananúši people were still throwing big rocks after them.

Thus even today in that whole region, but especially in Asúsiwaia, Lapatáia, and Hamanáulum, one can still see large boulders scattered around; all these the Hapananúši people threw after the thieves with their slings. The things the thieves had stolen also turned into rocks and are still lying around where the fugitives had tossed them overboard.

Informant: Not known; pp. 1282-1284.

Summary

Group of people traveling in search of beached whale inadvertently get to village of cannibals. From behavior of villagers shaman realizes danger. He puts cannibals to sleep by magic, and his people escape. Cannibals pursue, throwing large rocks after them which can still be seen in that region today.

Motif content

A977.	Origin of particular stones or groups of stones.
D471.	Transformation: object to stone.
D1364.	Object causes magic sleep.
D1964.4.+.	Magic sleep induced by shaman. (D1964.4. Magic sleep induced by druid.)
D2149.1.	Thunderbolt magically produced.
F968.	Extraordinary thunder and lightning.
G11.18.	Cannibal tribe.
K811.	Victim lured into house and killed.
K910.	Murder by strategy.
R220.	Flights.
S183.	Frightful meal.

[124]This small bay is situated west of Bahía La Romanche, in the northwestern arm of the Beagle Channel.

[125]This refers to the thunderlike noises caused by icebergs colliding or large chunks of ice breaking off from the glaciers.

58b. The Cannibals

Once (in the olden days) several families had their camp in the eastern corner of Bahía Ušuáia. When they heard that a whale had beached in the west, three of their men got into a canoe and departed in a westerly direction. Two of them were *yékamuš*, the third one was not. Those two were *Héšpul*[126] and Yookalía.[127] Their canoe was extremely fast. Rapidly it went past Puerto Olla.[128] Farther and farther their canoe advanced until they reached Hapananúši,[129] a place inhabited by the Halakwulup, a dangerous, evil folk. The three Yamana saw the huts of these people, left their canoe, and went ashore. The two *yékamuš* were invited into one hut; the third man was called into another.[130] When the two *yékamuš* entered the hut all the children there cheered exultantly. They shouted loudly: *"Yárum káiya,* quickly now!" That means (in their language): "We want to eat these two at once!" But the older people replied: *"Hamašúnna,* not until tomorrow!"

The two *yékamuš* soon grasped the meaning of these words. One of them also saw how a woman surreptitiously cut off part of her breast and put it on the glowing charcoal to roast, for she wanted to invite those two to eat. Héšpul became very upset at this. He pulled the piece of flesh from the fire and threw it out of the hut in a wide arc. Then he said furiously: "I didn't come here to eat human flesh!" He took his *yékuš* and cut off a piece of whale meat, which he put on the glowing embers. Thick smoke was formed which caused the people in the hut to fall asleep, for he was a *yékamuš.*[131] All the people, even the snapping dogs, were overcome by a profound sleep.

Now Héšpul said to his companion who was sitting next to him: "We'll see quickly which pieces of blubber are the best. These we'll put aside for ourselves!" They looked around, cut out the best parts of blubber and the nicest pieces of meat for themselves, and carried them

---

[126]*Taeniptera pyrope*, a small sparrow of the Tyrannidae family. It plays an important part in other stories as a mythological personage.

[127]*Milvago chimango*, the sparrow hawk.

[128]This small harbor is situated on the north shore exactly opposite Punta Divide; thus it lies on the borderline between the central and western Yamana groups.

[129]The waterways west of the Darwin Channel as far as the last projecting arm of the Brecknock Peninsula. In the parlance of the central and eastern Yamana the inhabitants of this remote region are known as "Halakwulup."

[130]It was the deliberate intent of those evil people to separate the three visitors from one another in order to be able to overpower them more easily individually.

[131]With his supernatural knowledge as shaman he deliberately made his adversaries harmless in this way.

to their canoe. Soon their canoe was filled to the top and they hurriedly departed. They paddled diligently and kept going all night until they got to Asúsiwaia early in the morning.

As they went past this small harbor they heard the Halakwulup hurl big rocks after them with their slings. Each stone that fell caused a loud crash. The three Yamana threw many pieces of blubber into the water to lighten the canoe and to advance more rapidly. They paddled with all their might and soon reached Ušuáia. Here they noticed that the Halakwulup had been unable to get close to them after all, and had since turned back. From then on Héšpul stayed in Ušuáia.

The Halakwulup sat down together and decided: "The three Yamana men came here to kill us; they took our meat and escaped into their territory. Now we'll build a very large hut and provide for ourselves. Afterward we'll build a long canoe and alone, without the women, we shall go to the Yamana, to capture, and kill them." Thus began the *čiéxaus*. From the Halakwulup it later came to the Yamana.[132]

To imitate what the Halakwulup had planned, the Yamana catch live birds and bring them into the Big Hut where they leave them.[133] These birds remind one of the Yamana whom the Halakwulup had intended to capture.

Informant: Not known; pp. 956-958.

Summary

Three men traveling in search of beached whale inadvertently get to village of cannibals. From behavior of villagers shaman realizes danger. He puts cannibals to sleep by magic, and they escape. Cannibals pursue in vain. Thus began the *čiéxaus* ceremony.

Motif content

A1530.	Origin of social ceremonials.
D1364.	Object causes magic sleep.
D1964.4.+.	Magic sleep induced by shaman. (D1964.4. Magic sleep induced by druid.)
F1035.	Disintegration: man eats himself up or dismembers himself.
G11.18.	Cannibal tribe.
R220.	Flights.

[132]It was there in the west that Halakwulup and Yamana came into contact. From the former the latter learned the puberty rites which in time also came to be adopted among the central and eastern Yamana.

[133]This custom is not taken too seriously. It is more the fancy of some participant or other to catch a bird and thus meet the demands of that custom.

59. The Water-spirits

In the old days some people went to Kaluwéllawaia. There are many *lakúma* there but these people did not know that. Soon the *lakúma* came out, and all the people lost their canoes; they barely saved their lives by swimming to a beach but there was no wood there. For a long time they were without fire and finally ran out of food. But on the other side was a beautiful place with plenty of food. One day a man saw something floating on the surface of the water; it was quite wide and flat. Soon more such pieces appeared. He looked closely and saw that they were *lakúma* lying there next to one another. They became so numerous that they stretched from one shore to the other. They lay very quietly. One of the men said: "If we run quickly over them we'll get to the other shore!" He did so. He ran quickly, and reached the opposite shore. Right after him the two other men and the women and children also tried it. But they walked much too slowly and all the *lakúma* submerged; they disappeared into the water taking all the people with them. The *lakúma* will seriously harm anybody who comes within their reach.

Only the one man, who was a great *yékamuš*, saved himself. He went to the other people, called them together, and reported everything. He said: "Now we must make many *yékuš* and kill those *lakúma* down there!" The men went to work. They advanced against the *lakúma* and killed many of them. The latter were lying on the bottom. Nowadays, when you come to this palce you will see many flat stones on the bottom. These are all those *lakúma* which on that occasion went slowly under with the people flattening themselves out and which are still lying in the water there in that spot.

Informant: Whaits; pp. 1286-1287.

Summary

People stranded in desolate place try to walk across water to opposite shore on backs of flat water-spirits lying side by side. One man succeeds, the others are taken by water-spirits. In revenge other people kill many of them. Today one still sees water-spirits as flat stones on bottom of sea.

Motif content

A977.	Origin of particular stones or groups of stones.
D231.+.	Transformation: water-spirit to stone. (D231. Transformation: man to stone.)
F420.2.	Home of water-spirits.

F420.5.2.	Malevolent water-spirits.
F420.5.2.1.	Water-spirits lure mortal into water.
F420.5.2.7.3.	Water-spirit wrecks ship.
F842.	Extraordinary bridge.
Q411.6.	Death as punishment for murder.
Z356.	Unique survivor.

60. The Disobedient Girl

A girl who is *túri* is not allowed to eat berries. Now once there was a *túrikipa* who felt very much like eating berries. She secretly ran away, sat down in the forest, and ate lots of *amáim*. Actually the girl did not eat and swallow the berries; she only put them into her mouth, squeezed out the juice with her teeth, and threw the solid parts away.[134] None of her family knew about this.

When soon afterward the family of this *túrikipa* was crossing a wide waterway a big *lakúma* emerged and threatened the people. In their fear they promptly threw many mussels, birds, and chunks of meat into the water, but the *lakúma* did not let go of the canoe. The girl kept herself hidden on the bottom of the canoe, not looking up once. The people threw their dog overboard but the *lakúma* was not satisfied with that, either. In their despair the people hurled a small girl into the water; the girl sank very quickly. Still the *lakúma* did not release the canoe. Finally the people pushed that big girl, the *túrikipa*, overboard. The *lakúma* seized her eagerly and dived with her as quickly as lightning. Soon the entrails (of that girl) surfaced. This made the people very sad. Before long the *lakúma* itself appeared on the surface again, laid itself flat, and became very wide. Then the people discovered on its back a large number of mussels, of a size bigger than they had ever seen before.[135] The men reached for them and got a few. Their shells were particularly sharp. In their fury the men quickly cut up the *lakúma* with them, ripped out its entrails, and dismembered it completely. The *lakúma* died immediately and sank to the bottom of the sea. In that instant and without anyone paddling the canoe moved from the spot, and soon reached shore. The people breathed a sigh of relief. But the girl was lost, for she had eaten of the berries when *túrikipa*.

[134] In this way the girl thought she would be able to get around the wording of the unequivocal and definite prohibition.

[135] It is known that on the back of an old whale there are numerous parasites, mainly of the *Balanus* and *Coropula* types. This passage refers to them.

Informant: Whaits; pp. 1287-1288.

Summary

Menstruating girl eats berries, contrary to tabu. Subsequently water-spirit refuses her family's canoe passage across water, until she is thrown overboard. Water-spirit eats girl, then is killed in turn by people.

Motif content

C140.+.	Food tabu during menses. (C140. Tabu connected with menses.)
C929.5.	Death by being swallowed for breaking tabu.
D1523.2.	Self-propelling (ship) boat.
D22136.8.	Ship moved by sacrifice.
F402.1.11.2.	Evil spirit kills and eats person.
Q411.6.	Death as punishment for murder.
S260.1.	Human sacrifice.
S263.4.+.	Sacrifice to water-spirit who has stopped boat in midstream. (S263.4. Sacrifice to river-god who has stopped boat in midstream.)
W126.	Disobedience.

61. The Ogre Who Fell in Love with a Woman

Once a *hánnuš* fell in love with Maxutuwérelakipa. She was an extraordinarily beautiful woman, and cunning and sly besides. For her part, she wanted nothing to do with the *hánnuš* and drove him away whenever he drew close to caress her. At first he was disappointed, but later it annoyed him very much to have gone so often and in vain to Maxutuwérelakipa's hut. Finally he threatened to kill her if she did not yield to him.

This woman lived on an island. It was winter then. When the *hánnuš* threatened he would soon return with many other *hánnuš* to finish her off she thought seriously of defending herself. She hastened to build a sturdy hut for herself and covered it with strong pieces of bark. She kept the entrance particularly low and narrow. Opposite the entrance she left a hole and placed some brushwood in front of it, so that nobody would notice it. She knew how to make fine and solid *sírsa* (forks to catch crabs with); she always had a supply of them.

One evening the *hánnuš* showed up at the woman's place again bringing several companions along. She was well prepared, however. Upon seeing the *hánnuš* coming toward her hut, which was covered with large pieces of bark, she quickly crawled outside through the narrow opening in the back. When the *hánnuš* entered he could not find her. He turned toward the entrance and looked out. While he was bending over to ease himself through the door the woman stood up in her hiding place and thrust a crab fork vigorously into his backside. The *hánnuš* gave a loud scream of pain and scurried out through the narrow entrance. Immediately another *hánnuš* squeezed himself into the hut to see what had happened. But he did not find Maxutuwérela-kipa, either. As he likewise bent over to crawl out, the woman, with a powerful thrust, drove a *sírsa* also into his backside. He could not help screaming loudly and with the *sírsa* sticking in his behind he instantly squeezed out through the narrow entrance. The rest of the *hánnuš* were amazed at this. Still a third ventured into the hut, looked around for the woman, and was just as unable as the others to find her. He went to the entrance and from within called to the other *hánnuš:* "I can't find the woman here!" As he bent down to exit Maxutuwérelakipa from her hiding place drove a crab fork into his backside, too. He could hardly move on account of the pain, so deeply had the *sírsa* penetrated. Yet he forced himself, dragging the *sírsa* stuck in his behind until one of the other *hánnuš* could free him from it. He was screaming terribly. The rest of the *hánnuš* were very uneasy. They conferred with one another and decided: "We had better get away from here quickly, all of us!" So they got up and hurried back into the heart of the forest.

Cunning Maxutuwérelakipa over there on the island had long since carried all her things to another place on the beach. When the *hánnuš* were far enough away she crawled out of her hiding place and hurried down to the beach. It was a harsh winter and the channel was frozen over. She stepped on the thick ice cover and found it resistant. But as she advanced the ice cracked behind her. By the time she had reached the middle of the channel the fleeing *hánnuš* reached the top of a nearby mountain. From there they saw Maxutuwérelakipa. They became furious and rushed down from the mountain to the beach in order to kill that miserable woman who had outwitted them all. But Maxutuwérelakipa called jeeringly to the *hánnuš:* "Just come after me, while I wait for you here!" The first *hánnuš* ran out on the ice thinking that it was still the large, continuous cover of solid immovable ice over which the woman had advanced. But since she had broken up the compact sheet into small cakes of ice those first *hánnuš* immediately went under. The small ice floes could not carry the big, heavy creatures. When the other *hánnuš* on the shore saw the first ones drown they stayed behind; they hurled many threats at Maxutuwérelakipa and then turned back.

Informant: Not known; pp. 1291-1292.

Summary

Woman rejects ogre suitor. He returns with other ogres to kill her but she throws crab forks into their behinds then escapes over thin ice. Some ogres pursue her, but fall through ice and drown.

Motif content

F575.1.	Remarkably beautiful woman.
G500.	Ogre defeated.
J1111.	Clever girl.
K811.+.	Victims lured into house and wounded. (K811. Victim lured into house and killed.)
K893.1.+.	Woman leads pursuers to edge of thin ice, swerves suddenly; they fall through. (K893.1. Man leads pursuers to edge of thin ice, swerves suddenly; they fall through.)
L311.	Weak (small) hero overcomes large fighter.
T70.	The scorned lover.
T75.2.1.	Rejected suitors' revenge.

62. The Boy and the Ogre[136]

Once there was a blind man who lived with his wife. Each slept on his own bed, separated from the other by the fire. One night a *hánnuš* sneaked into the hut, approached the woman, and forced her to copulate. The old man noticed faint noises as the *hánnuš* left and asked his wife: "What is that strange rustling sound?" She replied: "There's nothing here; don't get so upset for nothing!" In due time, however, the old man realized that his wife was pregnant. Indeed, she soon gave birth to a son. The blind man did not love this son at all; he knew that the boy did not come from him. And then the son was an unusual creature, too. In just a few days he grew a lot bigger; he was able to walk and climb, and worked diligently for his parents almost immediately. He especially helped the blind man a lot, because he believed him to be his own father.

Occasionally when the boy walked through the forest he would see strange signs on the trees here and there. He often wondered: "Where might these signs have come from? My blind father surely hasn't put

[136]*See also Koppers 1924:200-201.*

them there." One day as he spoke these words a *hánnuš* looked out from behind a tree and said in a friendly tone: "It is I who put those signs there!" The little boy was dumbstruck for he was afraid of the *hánnuš*. The latter continued: "So my own son is afraid of me?" The little boy wondered at this and ran back to the hut. The words of the *hánnuš* had hurt him, so he asked his mother: "It isn't really possible that I have two fathers, is it?" His blind father also heard his question; angrily he explained to the little boy that one night his mother had slept with a *hánnuš*. But the mother denied this and assured him: "It isn't so. Only in my dreams did a *hánnuš* once come to my bed!" The small boy continued to work diligently for the blind old man, but he did not love the *hánnuš* who was his real father.

One day the little boy was busy again in the forest. His father, the *hánnuš*, approached him, took him into his arms and carried him to the place where his large *hánnuš* family lived. It was a big cave. Here many *hánnuš* were gathered, but all were strange-looking creatures: some had four eyes, others only one; some had no heads, others had their faces on their chests; these had only one leg, those only one arm, and others were deformed in other ways. Now all came running to stare at the stranger. After some time the old *hánnuš* led his son back to the place in the forest whence he had taken him. But the small boy was very uneasy and later told the Yamana in great detail how he had fared among the *hánnuš* people. He continued working diligently for the blind old man.

Informant: Not known; pp. 1292-1293.

Summary

Woman has a child by ogre. Small boy rejects his ogre father and regards mother's husband as his father, working hard for him, although his love is not returned.

Motif content

F511.1.+.	Giant with face on chest. (F511.1. Person unusual as to his face.)
F531.1.1.1.	Giant with one eye in middle of forehead.
F531.1.3.3.1.	One-legged giant.
F531.1.6.7.	One-armed giant.
F531.6.2.1.	Giants live in mountains or caves.
F655.	Extraordinary perception of blind man.
G310.+.	Ogres leave signs on trees. (G310. Ogres with character-istic methods.)
G360.	Ogres with monstrous features.

G361.3.	Headless ogre.
K2213.	Treacherous wife.
N440.+.	Secret learned. (N440. Valuable secrets learned.)
N731.	Unexpected meeting of father and son.
N832.	Boy as helper.
P231.5.+.	Foster father reveals fact that son is offspring of supernatural father. (P231.5. Mother reveals fact that son is offspring of supernatural father.)
R11.	Abduction by monster (ogre).
T232.2.	Adulteress chooses loathly paramour.
T615.	Supernatural growth.
T675.1.+.	Child prefers foster father. (T675.1. Children prefer foster mother.)
T681.	Each likes his own children best.

63. The Two Rival Shamans

Once there were two brothers. They were clever *yékamuš*. For a long time they had been living together peacefully but one day they became real enemies. The people who at that time lived together with these two brothers in Agáia-wáia (a strip of coast in Ponsonby Sound) split into two groups, each group joining the *yékamuš* of its liking. Both groups left that place. They went to a long channel in the west; one settled on the southern shore, the other on the northern. The enmity between the two brothers and the antagonism of the two groups persisted; each *yékamuš* felt that he was more capable than the other and each group praised most the one they had joined. Finally by that long channel there[137] one said to the other: "Now I'll prove to you that I can do more and that I'm stronger than you!" One of them left his hut (in his dream), got into his canoe, and went to the center of the channel. Here he met his brother who had come from the opposite shore. Instantly he began to fight against the latter, hurling a pointed *yékuš* into his heart. Then he returned to shore and went into his hut. The other brother had likewise dreamed: he left his hut, got into his canoe, and went to the middle of the channel. Here he met his brother who had come from the opposite shore. Instantly he began to fight against the latter, hurling a pointed *yékuš* into his heart. Then he returned to shore and went into his hut. The following morning both of the *yékamuš* woke up. Each

---

[137]All this happened in a vision or in a state of dreaming, and each of the two adversaries was as aware of what was happening as though it were taking place in everyday life. That is precisely the special way of shamans.

was feeling very weak and faint, and each said to the people around him: "I'm going to die soon; there is a lot of blood flowing from my mouth and nose. Last night I was fatally wounded by my brother!" Indeed, this *yékamuš* died even before the sun reached its peak. The people at once lit a signal fire informing the group on the other side that a *lóima* would soon be sung. At exactly the same time the people on the other shore also lit a signal informing the group on the opposite shore that a *lóima* would soon be sung there, too. From each shore a canoe promptly departed with messengers who were to carry the news to the other side. The two canoes met in the middle of the channel and one told the other: "Our *yékamuš* has just died; his brother killed him!" Now all the people soon knew what had occurred and that those two *yékamuš* had been equally strong.

Informant: Not known; pp. 1392-1393.

Summary

Two brothers fight in order to determine who is the greater shaman. Both die at the same time, and their respective followers realize that both were equally powerful.

Motif content

D615.1.+.	Contest between magicians. (D615.1. Transformation contest between magicians.)
D1719.1.	Contest in magic.
F1068.2.2.	Fight in dream with real result.
H217.	Decision made by contest.
K66.	Dream contests.
P251.5.3.	Hostile brothers.
S73.1.	Fratricide.

64. The Nagging Wife

A *yékamuš* was married to a woman who was very jealous of him. He concerned himself intensively with the welfare of his fellowmen, and that displeased her. Once when they were making a journey in their canoe she said scornfully: "I thought you were a capable *yékamuš!* Other people you provide with all kinds of food; but for me you won't let either a whale or any other kind of fish be stranded; you get me neither birds nor crabs. You ought to take much better care of your wife!" The *yékamuš* became very annoyed at these words and without answering he lay down. Although he kept his eyes closed his wife continued nagging him. She did not stop until the shaman was snoring loudly. She steered her canoe toward Káawaia. Meanwhile the *yékamuš* slept, and he called forth two *lakúma* from far away (in the west). Finally the *lakúma* arrived in Káawaia, seized the canoe, and lifted the bow high up. Fearfully the woman called her husband who was still asleep: "Get up and help me in this danger; after all, you are a *yékamuš!*" He replied very calmly: "Try to manage on your own. Often enough you have given me to understand that I am powerless!" She implored him: "Don't be so stubborn and help me, lest the *lakúma* kill me!" When his wife had been trembling there for some time the man got up but he still did not move a finger. The woman was in terrible fear. At last he ordered her: "Paint both *lakúma* with white paint!" She replied: "Impossible, I'll never be able to do that!" Then he told her: "Give me the paint." He approached the bow with it, leaned over, and painted both *lakúma;* one was on the right side and the other on the left. The *lakúma* let this happen without any resistance. Afterward the *yékamuš* straightened himself, stretched out both arms, and laughed: "Hi, hi . . ." The two *lakúma* slowly lowered the canoe and dived down. Instantly they sent a favorable wind for the canoe so that it soon reached its destination. The woman had completely changed her mind and ruefully confessed to her husband: "Until today I have made fun of you and had a very low opinion of you; now I know that you are truly a capable *yékamuš!*"

Informant: Not known; pp. 1428-1429.

Summary

Wife of shaman nags and belittles him constantly but repents after he has saved them from dangerous water-spirits.

Motif content

D2165.	Escapes by magic.
F404.+.	Shaman summons water-spirits in sleep. (F404. Means of summoning spirits.)
F405.+.	Means of combating water-spirits: painting them white. (F405. Means of combating spirits.)
F420.5.2.7.4.	Water-spirit holds ship back.
Q288.	Punishment for mockery.
T253.	The nagging wife.
T257.	Jealous wife or husband.

65. The Origin of the Men's *Kína*[138]

Up in the north of the Isla Grande and also on the large, beautiful plain of Yaiyióxan[139] the women were the first to perform the *kína*. At that time women were in sole control: they commanded the men, who were subordinate, just as today the women obey the men. Also, the men sat behind in the stern of the canoe and the women sat up front in the bow. The men did all the domestic chores according to the instructions of the women: they looked after the children, kept the fire going, cleaned the skins. That is the way it was to remain forever. For that purpose the women invented the Big Hut and everything that goes on inside it. They told the men: "We are looking for Tánuwa! Maybe we'll be able to find her; maybe she'll come out of the earth and enter the Big Hut!" The men believed this. They had to move on every time the women broke camp.

But they did not find Tánuwa in that region, and so they moved to another place, traveling along the north coast of the Isla Grande as far as the northeastern tip. Whenever they stopped to rest they built the *kína*-hut and performed again. From there they wandered south along the east coast of the Isla Grande. Wherever they performed, a large, level plain was formed. They searched every place for evil, powerful Tánuwa, continuing south until they were near Cabo San Pablo. From here on they no longer followed the coast, and this is why even today one finds only forested, mountainous country south of this cape. The women then took a southwesterly direction, crossed the mountain range, and on the south coast of Isla Grande reached the Beagle Channel near Puerto Harberton. From here they moved west. Wherever they built their *kína*-hut and performed, as for example at Puerto Brown, the surface of the earth changed, and level, open country was formed. They wandered along the (north) coast of the Beagle Channel continuing westward until they finally came to Yáiaašága.[140] Here they performed their *kína* for a long time. The women came out of the Big Hut, alone or in groups, with their bodies completely painted and wearing *hílix* (masks) over their heads. A *yékamuš* would call to the men: "That is Súna-yáka!" or "That is Wasénim-yáka!" And many more spirits came out. The men believed that this was really the case. But in actual fact it was the women who had painted themselves and concealed their faces with masks so that no man could recognize them.

[138]*See also Martial 1882-1883:214.*
[139]This is the name for the level area surrounding Bahía Thetis.
[140]Today generally called "Boca del infierno," doubtless derived from that myth. This place is located on the peninsula that extends southward into Bahía Ušuáia.

In spite of much performing and searching the women were unable to find Tánuwa and get her to come out of the earth. So they decided to travel no farther and to stay here in Yáiaašága. This area is very nice and level. They liked it very much and said: "This is where we'll stay! Now we'll deceive the men and tell them: 'We have found Tánuwa; she came out of the ground just now and is with us in the Big Hut!' " Promptly the women rolled a few dry skins into a thick roll and began thrashing the ground with it until it rang. They screamed, shouted, and cried as though frightened to death. The men heard them, ran into their huts, and hid there filled with fear. They whispered quietly to one another: "Indeed, our wives have now discovered Tánuwa! For they never screamed so long and so loud when the spirits appeared." When the terrible screaming began and the earth thundered the men said to themselves with great conviction: "That must be Tánuwa coming out of the earth. The women have found her after all!" The women continued to perform there in Yáiaašága. The men were kept in fear and subjugation, and continued to do all the chores assigned them by the women.

Lem, the sun-man, was an excellent hunter. He was always sent out to hunt, and he brought back plenty of game. All those women in the *kína*-hut needed a lot of meat. One day while out hunting Lem killed a big guanaco[141] which he threw over his shoulder. Walking toward the camp he went past a lagoon and heard the voices of two girls. He became curious and said to himself: "What can these two be doing here?" He quietly sneaked up, and, hidden in the bushes, saw the two girls washing off the paint in which the "spirits" were supposed to appear. In doing so they kept practicing how to imitate the voices and the movements of his two daughters (Lem's daughters[142]), for the latter played an important part in the *kína*-hut. The girls were saying: "We want to practice well, so that we can act exactly like Lem's daughter. Then we'll help her sing, and deceive the men with her." They continued to practice while talking about the activities of the women in the *kína*-hut.

Suddenly Lem jumped out of his hiding place and stood right in front of the girls to block their escape. Very sternly he snapped at them: "What are you doing here?" Frightened, they fell silent. Then he ordered them: "You have to tell me everything—what you are doing here, what you were talking about, and what takes place in the *kína*-hut. I know much already, for I was listening to you." Then the girls

---

[141]It should be pointed out that in the central part of the Yamana territory guanacos are very rare and are hardly ever hunted by the Indians.

[142]Old Whaits only mentioned "a daughter of the sun-man" at this point.

blushed with shame and broke out in a cold sweat. Finally they told Lem everything, confessing: "It is the women themselves who paint their bodies and put on masks; then they come out of the house and show themselves to the men. There are no others (spirits) there. It is the women themselves who scream and yell to frighten the men; Tánuwa doesn't do these things." The girls gave him still other information. Then Lem said: "In return for this I'll give you some advice: stay here at the lagoon and don't go back either to the camp or to the kína-hut, for something bad is going to happen now!" So the two girls stayed and eventually changed into little ducks.[143]

Angrily Lem picked up his guanaco again and set out toward camp, all the while considering how to take revenge on the women. When he reached his hut he threw the guanaco to the ground and said fretfully: "So that's why I'm dragging all that game home every day, so that my daughters can make fun of me and deceive us men! They take away our meat as though it were for Tánuwa, and then proceed to eat it themselves in the kína-hut!" All the women who were standing near his hut listened in surprise and wondered: "What has happened? What is Lem saying? Why is he so furious?"

Téšurkipa[144] happened to be sitting nearby, working on a harpoon point. Hearing Lem's excited words she said to herself: "Somebody must have told him about the activities of the women! Perhaps he eavesdropped on the girls who went to the lagoon to wash." She blushed with shame, for she presumed that the deceit of the women had been revealed. Then she thought: "How can I silence Lem so that he

[143]As long ago as January 1920 old Whaits told me this part in a somewhat different version: The sun-man was an excellent hunter. Although he always brought back much game from the hunt, there was soon a shortage of meat again, and thus he had to go hunting constantly. The reason was that his meat was stolen by the women. One day as he was walking toward the camp carrying a heavy guanaco he happened past a lagoon where two girls were bathing. Without being seen he sneaked up and listened to their conversation. Then he heard them saying: "Lem is always bringing back much meat from the hunt. Today he is on his way home again, and surely he won't return empty-handed. But the clever women steal all the meat from him and carry it to the kína-hut where all of them eat it together, which Lem doesn't know." When the sun-man suddenly stepped out of his hiding place the girls caught sight of him and fearfully ducked below the surface of the water. But he called to them: "I've already seen you and recognized you; come on out!" Fearfully they approached. Lem told them: "What are you talking about here? I was listening to you!" They stammered: "We only said: 'Lem is always bringing home much meat, but there it is stolen from him and therefore he has to go hunting again every day!' " Lem now ordered them: "Since you know who is stealing my meat you have to tell me who they are!" Trembling, the girls revealed to him: "All the women who gather in the kína-hut steal the meat you bring, and eat it. That's why they stay so long in the kína-hut playing and frightening the men!" On Lem's advice the two girls who had revealed the secret to him remained in the lagoon. They turned into ducks, and are very timid.

[144]Today a type of sparrow with yellow feathers, rarely seen there.

keeps quiet and the other men don't find out?" There were many men lying in the hut in front of which the woman was sitting, and although covered up they were awake. She alone was sitting up, for after all she did not have to crawl under cover.[145] When Lem entered the hut the woman spoke to him in words intended to gloss over everything and make him keep silent: "We women gave the men a terrible fright just now! We all came into the hut and the men immediately crawled under the covers, thinking that we were Kalampáša." She said this in order to embarrass Lem and distract him, so that he would say nothing further and to keep the men from finding out anything.

Then she ran at once to the *kína*-hut and told the women: "Lem knows everything that goes on here!" The women became very upset at these words. They stood up, screamed loudly, painted themselves, put on masks, and went again to the hut in which all the men had gathered, intending to really frighten them now. But this time several men, without being seen, peeped out from under the furs with which they were covered, saying: "Now we won't let ourselves be scared; we'll watch closely to see if it really is our wives who're coming!" Keeping their hands over their faces they peeked through their fingers. While the women were dancing and screaming, sometimes even right into the ears of the men, the latter were watching attentively but remaining completely motionless. When after a long spell of dancing the women departed the men threw aside their covers again and said to one another: "That person was my daughter.—That one was your wife.— That one was my wife; I recognized her. So then it wasn't Kalampáša but only our women!" Thus the deception of the women was revealed. Lem told the men in detail what he had seen and heard by the lagoon. Now the men wanted to confirm this by getting more information, and they debated what to do. Immediately they sent the fastest man among them to run after the women. He ran after them and dashed into the Big Hut: the women were sitting around the fire and each had leaned her mask against the wall behind her, so that the little man could clearly recognize the face of each and every one of them. His name was Šalalakína; today he is a little bird.[146] He slipped into the Big Hut and went around behind the backs of the women who were squatting there. He pushed over all the masks in the process and escaped on the other side of the wide entrance. Seeing this the women guessed that a fast runner among the men must have run through there, for how else could

---

[145]During the Kalampáša-play the people in the camp had to gather in a big dwelling hut, if possible, and here await the visit of the serpent Kalampáša. This event has already been described in Gusinde 1937:1330.

[146]This timid, nimble bird lives in swampy regions. It has chocolate-covered feathers and a beautiful voice.

all the masks have fallen! They gnashed their teeth in shame and anger, and gave loud screams. Meanwhile little Šalalakína was telling the men: "I sneaked into the hut and ran quickly from one side to the other, pushing over all the masks. But I didn't see Tánuwa. Only women are sitting there in the Big Hut." The men were listening.

They believed that they had to get even more evidence, however, for they wanted to know whether the women were deceiving them with all their talk about Tánuwa. Therefore they now sent off this man, now that one, who could run particularly fast, first the smaller ones, then the bigger. Each sneaked in on one side, dashed through, and escaped on the other. Soon the women noticed this and picked up their bows and arrows. After each man who ran through the hut and pushed over their masks they shot an arrow which stuck in his backside and became a tail. Particularly easy targets were the heavy animals (which were men at that time), and that is why they have a tail to this day. The women threw a harpoon after the otter, and for that reason it has a wide tail to this day. After the fox they threw an *uškútta*-shrub[147] that was lying there, with all its leaves and twigs; it stuck in his backside and that is why the fox has a bushy tail. This way each of the men who ran through the Big Hut was driven out by the women.

Finally when there were no more fast runners among the men they rested. Then they armed themselves with clubs and slings, with harpoons and spears, with bows and arrows, and marched on the Big Hut. The women were overcome with terrible fear. But the men stormed forward and a raging battle began, the men falling furiously on the women. Only two of the latter were able to escape unharmed; all the others were badly beaten and turned into animals, and one can tell from all of them that they received some hard blows on that occasion. During the battle Lem poured masses of water on the *kína*-hut to put out the fire, for it had started to burn. He poured so much water that it became a mighty wave. This wave went far out into the ocean, taking with it the big sea animals, for there is no room for them on land (no way for them to move around). Even today one sees this wave: it is the heavy surf breaking against the high outlying rocks. With his sling Lem threw a large bucket *(túku)* filled to the brim with water into the fire so that a strong hissing sound was heard. This sound, too, went out into the ocean, and can be heard even today through the mighty rumble of the waves.

All the women were killed or transformed; some fled; only the small children were unharmed. Soon after this furious battle Lem the

[147]This is the winter pepper tree, *Drimys winteri* (Gusinde 1937:28).

sun-man went up to the sky, and so did his brother Akáinix, the rainbow, and the latter's wife Hánuxa, the moon-woman. Since that time the men alone perform in the *kína*-hut, in the same tradition and manner as did the women before them.

Informant: Mašemikens; pp. 1337-1342.

Variant version

A long time ago we men took the *kína* away from the women. Way up in the north of the Isla Grande, in the region of Yaiyióxan, the women performed the first *kína*. Who knows whether they were Selknam women or not? Perhaps in those days the Selknam were not yet as different from us Yamana as they obviously are today. On their wanderings from the north down here the women were looking for Tánuwa everywhere, but could not find her. In vain did they try in the various places where they built their Big Hut. Finally they came to Yáiaašága. They liked it there and decided to stay. They immediately lied to all the men, pretending finally to have found Tánuwa there. They made noise, screaming, jumping, and dancing excitedly. The men were to believe that all this was done by Tánuwa; however, that was not the case. The only thing that Tánuwa really caused is the large heaps of stones, boulders, and rubble which can still be seen west of Ušuáia. It was Tánuwa who lifted, stirred, and moved those masses. For if she herself had raved as wildly and waved her arms as excitedly as those women did in the *kína*-hut, the entire area would have been destroyed. All the noise and frenzy came from the women themselves, who made the men believe that it was Tánuwa raging so fiercely.

One day when Lem was returning home from the hunt he overheard two girls by a lagoon. While he was hiding among the tall reeds the girls were talking to each other: "Let's practice some more." So saying they trilled over and over again: "Lo lo lo lo. . . ." Finally they said: "Now we can do it just like the women in the *kína*-hut!" As they were about to stop practicing Lem stood up in his hiding place and walked toward them. He was angry and spoke to them harshly and reproachfully: "So then it's our own women who are deceiving us men with

---

[148]A certain type of *kína*-spirit. Bridges (1933:113) says about this identification: "Certain men or beings supposed to be the sons of a certain kölapöša, who acted parts in the *ceena* drama." Here, as in the other version of this myth, the reader is again referred to the *kalampáša*-performance (Gusinde 1937:1330, 1340).

their singing! Nor do the *ušamína*[148] descend from above into the *kína*-hut! That's something I shall tell the men about immediately!" The girls were trembling with fear and confusion, but Lem ordered them: "Now tell me everything!" Helplessly they revealed to him: "In the *kína*-hut there is nobody but our women; they alone are the ones who do everything. The men, however, are deceived and deluded." Lem was satisfied with that and assured the girls: "All right, I'll save you two. Stay hidden here by this lagoon, then you'll escape with your lives!" When Lem had reached the camp he threw the guanaco he had hunted angrily on the ground and said aloud: "As far as the meat is concerned the women are cheating me and all the men!" These words frightened Téšurkipa, who hurried to the *kína*-hut and told the women: "Lem must have found out something (about our deception)!" The women were overcome with terror and noisily prepared a spirit appearance (the *kalampáša mátu*). But the men looked out from under their fur covers and clearly recognized their painted and masked wives.

Soon the great battle began in Yáiaašága. The men drove the women out of the *kína*-hut and the latter all turned into animals. The men threw harpoons or spears at the women; that's why animals have tails.[149] The man attacking the *čilawáiakipa* had no spear handy, so he used his sling and threw the next best thing at her, a winter pepper tree with twigs and leaves. That is why the fox has a bushy tail. The *yékeslef*[150] ran away without taking off her mask. She took refuge in the water and is still wearing the mask. The *haféim*[151] did the same, and to this day one can recognize the mask that she wore on that occasion on her head. Likewise the *tepérakipa*.[152] The *wémarkipa* (*Larus glaucodes*) was hit by many arrows, which can be seen from the many dark lines and dots on her wings. The *ašóula* (the small grampus, *Pseudorca crassidens*) happened to be away when the battle began. Returning later to this place he noticed how few people there were and said: "Something must have been going on here. How I would like to have helped in this fight!" He pulled a glowing club from the big fire, and while doing so burned himself under his arms and in other places: these are the light-colored spots that he has had ever since.

[149]In the first version of this myth the same Mašemikens said that it was the women who had thrown various weapons after the running men, which are still recognizable today as tails.

[150]The squid (*Loligo subulata*). Probably this is also what Bridges (1933:646) means by "a species of cuttlefish with a hard bill or horn." On the pointed end of its long, cigar-shaped body the cuttle fish mentioned above has two broad triangular fins. These are taken to be the "mask" which it supposedly wore at the time.

[151]A trunkfish, about as long as a hand, with short thorns all over its body.

[152]The shape of the mouth of this ursine seal, *Arctocephalus australis* (Gusinde 1937: 41), is taken to be a mask that it once wore.

The big spears and harpoons that were thrown by our men at that time can still be seen lying by the lagoon in Yáiaašága, although overgrown by high grass. Everyone who goes there notices them. Among them are huge boulders, also thrown by our men against the women on that occasion. In the big battle all the women who had pretended *kína* were turned into animals—land animals, birds, and sea animals. At the same time, Lem, too, left this earth, for as a servant to the women he had also been involved in the *kína*, as it were, since he had to provide them with meat. His brother Akáinix and the latter's wife Hánuxa also went with him up to the sky, as did several others, and they all became stars. Since then the men rule in the *kína*-hut, and no woman may approach it without permission, much less join in the meeting.

Informant: Mašemikens; pp. 1342-1345.

Summary

In primeval times women lead the people on wanderings around island. They keep men in subjugation by occasionally dressing up as dangerous spirits and enacting certain ritual. On each ritual occasion ground is leveled, creating present-day plains in Yamana territory.

One day Sun-man overhears conversation revealing women's deception. He tells men; they verify it by sending several fast runners (animals) through women's ceremonial hut. Women shoot arrows after them, hence the long tails of these animals today. Men attack hut and defeat women in furious battle. They take over spirit ceremony, and since then they rule the women.

Motif content

A711.	Sun as man who left earth.
A736.1.	Sun and moon as man and woman.
A736.5.	Children of the sun.
A738.+.	Sun is excellent hunter. (A738. Attributes of sun.)
A738.2.2.	Sun endowed with wisdom and passion.
A751.8.	Woman in the moon.
A753.+.	Moon and rainbow married. (A753. Moon as a person.)
A791.	Origin of the rainbow.
A901.+.	Topographical features caused by experiences of ancestors. (A901. Topographical features caused by experiences of primitive hero.)
A925.1.	Origin of high sea waves.
A925.5.	Origin of mournful sound of sea.
A977.	Origin of particular stones or groups of stones.
A990.+.	Origin of plains. (A990. Other land features.)
A1372.9.	Why women are subservient to men.
A1472.	Beginning of division of labor.

A1530.+.	Origin of secret society. (A1530. Origin of social ceremonials.)
A1620.+.	Why tribe lives in certain place. (A1620. Distribution of tribes.)
A1630.	Wandering of tribes.
A2257.+.	Animal characteristics from battle. (A2257. Animal characteristics from duel.)
A2260.	Animal characteristics from transformation.
A2378.1.	Why animals have tail.
A2378.6.1.	Why fox has bushy tail.
A2378.9.+.	Why otter has broad tail. (A2378.9. Nature of animal's tail—miscellaneous.)
A2412.1.+.	Markings of seal. (A2412.1. Markings of mammals.)
A2412.1.+.	Markings of whale. (A2412.1. Markings of mammals.)
A2412.2.	Markings on birds.
A2412.4.	Markings on fish.
A2433.2.2.	Animals that inhabit water.
C420.	Tabu: uttering secrets.
C422.	Tabu: revealing identity of certain person.
D100.+.	Transformation: women to animals. (D100. Transformation: man to animal.)
D161.3.+.	Transformation: women to ducks. (D161.3. Transformation: man to duck.)
D293.	Transformation: man to star.
F565.3.	Parliament of women.
F679.5.	Skillful hunter.
F681.	Marvelous runner.
F873.0.1.	Battle rage.
F1084.	Furious battle.
H580.	Enigmatic statements.
H1280.	Quest to other realms.
H1370.+.	Quest for spirit. (H1370. Miscellaneous quests.)
J421.	Subordination of weak to strong.
J421.+.	Subordination of strong to weak by deception. (J421. Subordination of weak to strong.)
J613.	Wise fear of the weak for the strong.
J623.	Prevention of hostility by inspiring fear in enemy.
J624.	Uniting against a common enemy.
J647.	Avoiding enemy's revenge.
J1050.	Attention to warnings.
J1681.	Cleverness in dealing with the enemy.
K515.	Escape by hiding.
K1200.	Deception into humiliating position.
K1821.2.	Disguise by painting body.
K1821.3.	Disguise by veiling face.

K1828.	Disguise as deity (or spirit).
K2060.	Detection of hypocrisy.
K2213.	Treacherous wife.
K2214.1.	Treacherous daughter.
K2320.	Deception by frightening.
K2350.+.	Fast runners sent through enemy's camp to gather information. (K2350. Military strategy.)
L300.+.	Triumph of the oppressed. (L300. Triumph of the weak.)
N440.	Valuable secrets learned.
N455.	Overheard (human) conversation.
P555.	Defeat in battle.
Q261.2.	Treacherous wife punished.
Q411.4.	Death as punishment for treachery.
T148.	Matriarchy.
W11.5.	Generosity toward enemy.

66. How a Shaman Rescued His People

Once there were two *yékamuš* who must be counted among the most skillful ever. The people in the west were then in great distress, for bad weather had made it impossible for a long time either to hunt sea lions or gather mussels. The *yékamuš* saw the desperate situation, and one of them fell into a sleep so as to be active in his dreams. The next morning the *yékamuš* told his people: "Move farther west, and stay on the south shore!" All the families broke camp at once and set off. The following night the *yékamuš* dreamed once more and the next morning he said: "(In my dream) I saw two whales approaching us. They are sisters. Both are pregnant; each has a nearly full-grown calf in her womb. Out there in the ocean an *ašóula* (the small grampus, *Pseudorca crassidens*) approached and threatened them. The two sisters implored it insistently: 'Don't kill us! If you do, the calves within us will also die, and so you would be killing four living beings all at once!' The *ašóula* was not to be moved, however, and mercilessly killed the two whales. Soon they'll be in sight, and they'll be washed ashore here." The people were extremely happy over what their *yékamuš* had told them. And indeed, that same evening the tide washed up two huge whales there on the level coast. They were females, and when the people cut them open they found the calves inside of them. Their astonishment perdured for a long time.

Informant: Nelly Lawrence; pp. 1388-1389.

Summary

Shaman saves his people from starvation through magic knowledge of food supply.

Motif content

D1711.	Magician.
D1810.0.2.	Magic knowledge of magician.
D1814.1.	Advice from magician (fortune-teller, etc.)
F969.7.	Famine.
J157.	Wisdom (knowledge) from dream.
N845.	Magician as helper.
S100.	Revolting murders or mutilations.
S185.+.	Cruelty to pregnant whale. (S185. Cruelty to pregnant woman.)
W155.	Hardness of heart.

THE MOTIF INDICES

Motif Distribution by Narrative

A. MYTHOLOGICAL MOTIFS

a. Gods (A220.2. — A240.1.) 1; 3; 4; 8.
b. Demigods and culture heroes (A511.4.1. — A592.2.1.+.) 1; 3; 9; 10; 11; 12; 13; 14; 15; 17; 18; 20a; 20b; 21; 32; 33; 34; 35; 40; 45.
c. Cosmogony and cosmology (A711. — A791.) 1; 2; 3; 4; 5; 6; 21; 65.
d. Topographical features of the earth (A900.+. — A990.+.) 1; 6; 7; 32; 33; 34; 35; 37; 58a; 59; 65.
e. World calamities (A1005. — A1040.) 1; 2; 6; 7; 8.
f. Establishment of natural order (A1111. — A1191.) 21; 32; 56.
g. Creation and ordering of human life (A1200. — A1630.) 3; 7; 9; 10; 11; 12; 13; 14; 15; 16; 17; 18; 20a; 20b; 37; 43; 52; 58b; 65.
h. Animal characteristics (A2210. — A2585.) 3; 4; 6; 7; 17; 18; 19; 21; 22; 24; 25; 26; 27; 28; 29; 30; 31; 33; 35; 37; 38; 39; 40; 41; 44; 45; 51; 52; 54; 55; 56; 65.

B. ANIMALS

a. Mythical animals (B16.2.+. — B34.) 54; 55; 56; 57.
b. Magic animals (B147.2.+. — B175.+.) 6; 7; 51; 52; 53; 54; 55.
c. Animals with human traits (B200.+. — B299.1.) 6; 7; 19; 22; 23; 31; 32; 51; 52; 55.
d. Friendly animals (B314. — B555.) 19; 32; 33; 34; 35; 51; 57.
e. Marriage of person to animal (B600.+. — B670.+.) 17; 18; 19; 23; 31.
f. Fanciful traits of animals (B736.1. — B772.+.) 31; 51; 53; 56.
g. Miscellaneous animal motifs (B871.2.+. — B874.3.) 19; 40.

C. TABU

    a. Tabu connected with supernatural beings (C41. — C94.3.) 23; 41; 42.
    b. Sex tabu (C114. — C170.+.) 17; 26; 27; 28; 29; 30; 55; 60.
    c. Speaking tabu (C420. — C450.) 22; 32; 53; 65.
    d. Miscellaneous tabus (C871.+.) 23.
    e. Punishment for breaking tabu (C920.2. — C987.) 28; 30; 60.

D. MAGIC

    a. Transformation (D100.+. — D681.) 1; 5; 7; 17; 18; 19; 21; 24; 26; 27; 28; 29; 30; 31; 33; 34; 35; 36; 37; 38; 47; 51; 58a; 59; 63; 65.
    b. Magic objects (D932. — D1691.) 7; 12; 20a; 24; 32; 34; 35; 47; 58a; 58b; 60.
    c. Magic powers and manifestations (D1711. — D2188.) 4; 6; 7; 11; 18; 19; 20a; 24; 31; 33; 40; 41; 45; 54; 55; 56; 57; 58a; 58b; 60; 63; 64; 66.

E. THE DEAD

    a. Resuscitation (E1. — E121.) 20a; 20b; 33; 54; 55.
    b. Ghosts and other revenants (E257.+. — E599.5.+.) 2; 18; 20b; 47.
    c. The soul (E772.1.+. — E780.) 47; 54; 55.

F. MARVELS

    a. Otherworld journeys (F30.) 2.
    b. Marvelous creatures (F402.1.11.2. — F681.) 1; 3; 4; 5; 7; 8; 13; 17; 24; 27; 30; 31; 32; 33; 34; 35; 37; 38; 40; 41; 42; 45; 47; 48; 50; 53; 57; 59; 60; 61; 62; 64; 65.
    c. Extraordinary places and things (F701. — F882.) 4; 23; 24; 41; 43; 52; 59; 65.
    d. Extraordinary occurrences (F911.4. — F1084.) 1; 2; 5; 40; 45; 47; 51; 52; 54; 55; 58a; 58b; 63; 65; 66.

G. OGRES

a. Kinds of ogres (G11.18. — G371.) 18; 19; 33; 34; 58a; 58b; 62.
b. Falling into ogre's power (G475. — G477.) 33; 34.
c. Ogre defeated (G500. — G550.) 33; 34; 54; 61.
d. Other ogre motifs (G630.+.) 33.

H. TESTS

a. Identity tests: recognition (H30. — H88.) 27; 40; 44; 45; 53; 54.
b. Tests of truth (H217.) 63.
c. Marriage tests (H473.) 57.
d. Tests of cleverness (H580.) 65.
e. Tests of prowess: quests (H1223.1. — H1385.) 17; 23; 25; 37; 65.
f. Other tests (H1553.) 43.

J. THE WISE AND THE FOOLISH

a. Acquisition and possession of wisdom (knowledge) (J21.50. — J157.) 4; 10; 11; 12; 15; 44; 66.
b. Wise and unwise conduct (J261. — J1050.) 10; 11; 12; 13; 15; 18; 28; 30; 31; 32; 41; 45; 47; 65.
c. Cleverness (J1111. — J1681.) 24; 37; 39; 45; 47; 61; 65.
d. Fools (and other unwise persons) (J1772.9. — J2650.) 10; 11; 12; 15; 26; 30; 36; 41; 47; 49; 50; 53.

K. DECEPTIONS

a. Contests won by deception (K66.) 63.
b. Thefts and cheats (K330. — K477.) 17; 40; 41; 42.
c. Escape by deception (K500. — K572.) 18; 33; 41; 42; 54; 65.
d. Capture by deception (K700. — K778.) 23; 53.
e. Fatal deception (K800. — K959.4.) 4; 19; 25; 33; 39; 40; 46; 47; 48; 49; 50; 53; 54; 55; 58a; 61.
f. Deception into self-injury (K1000.) 33.

g. Deception into humiliating position (K1200. — K1210.) 54; 65.

h. Seduction or deceptive marriage (K1310. — K1335.) 29; 44.

j. Deceptions connected with adultery (K1500. — K1569.9.) 27; 30; 31; 36; 38; 41; 42.

k. Deceiver falls into own trap (K1600. — K1641.) 4; 23; 25; 46; 47; 53.

l. Deception through shams (K1700. — K2060.) 4; 19; 23; 26; 31; 33; 37; 38; 41; 44; 65.

m. Villains and traitors (K2210.+. — K2218.) 19; 23; 25; 30; 41; 42; 46; 47; 48; 49; 53; 54; 62; 65.

n. Other deceptions (K2320. — K2350.+.) 45; 65.

L. REVERSAL OF FORTUNE

a. Victorious youngest child (L10. — L31.) 20a; 20b; 45; 46.

b. Unpromising hero (heroine) (L112.2.2.) 32; 33; 34; 35; 40.

c. Triumph of the weak (L300.+. — L311.) 32; 33; 34; 35; 61; 65.

d. Pride brought low (L430.) 53.

M. ORDAINING THE FUTURE

a. Curses (M411.1. — M416.) 10; 11; 12; 28.

N. CHANCE AND FATE

a. The ways of luck and fate (N131.+.) 31.

b. Unlucky accidents (N360.) 4.

c. Lucky accidents (N440. — N681.0.1.+.) 3; 4; 17; 22; 27; 28; 31; 32; 34; 36; 38; 40; 41; 45; 51; 52; 53; 62; 65.

d. Accidental encounters (N731.) 62.

e. Helpers (N800.+. — N845.) 1; 3; 13; 14; 17; 18; 24; 32; 33; 34; 35; 45; 53; 62; 66.

P. SOCIETY

a. The family (P211. — P291.) 1; 3; 4; 5; 9; 10; 11; 12; 13; 15;

19; 20a; 20b; 23; 24; 25; 26; 30; 31; 35; 43; 45; 48; 49; 53; 54; 55; 62; 63.
b. Government (P555.) 65.
c. Customs (P665. — P681.) 4; 31; 34; 37; 40; 41; 55; 57.

Q. REWARDS AND PUNISHMENTS

a. Deeds rewarded (Q2. — Q83.1.) 4; 20a; 20b; 40; 54; 56.
b. Deeds punished (Q211. — Q395.) 4; 18; 19; 22; 23; 24; 25; 27; 28; 29; 30; 32; 36; 37; 38; 39; 41; 46; 48; 49; 53; 54; 55; 56; 57; 64; 65.
c. Kinds of punishment (Q411. — Q595.) 18; 19; 24; 25; 27; 29; 30; 32; 35; 36; 38; 39; 41; 46; 47; 48; 49; 53; 54; 55; 56; 57; 59; 60; 65.

R. CAPTIVES AND FUGITIVES

a. Captivity (R9.1. — R11.) 1; 33; 62.
b. Rescues (R153.2. — R155.2.) 20a; 31; 45; 53.
c. Escapes and pursuits (R210. — R245.) 23; 31; 37; 40; 41; 42; 47; 57; 58a; 58b.
d. Refuges and recapture (R315.) 19.

S. UNNATURAL CRUELTY

a. Cruel relatives (S0. — S73.1.4.) 18; 19; 20b; 24; 25; 30; 37; 39; 45; 63.
b. Revolting murders or mutilations (S100. — S185.+.) 18; 19; 23; 24; 25; 33; 35; 45; 46; 47; 53; 54; 57; 58a; 66.
c. Cruel sacrifices (S260.1. — S263.4.+.) 60.
d. Abandoned or murdered children (S302.1. — S325.0.1.) 33.
e. Cruel persecutions (S400.) 54.

T. SEX

a. Love (T11.3.2. — T92.10.) 17; 19; 28; 35; 36; 38; 44; 45; 48; 49; 50; 54; 61.
b. Marriage (T117.11. — T148.) 3; 16; 17; 35; 40; 51; 65.

    c.   Married life (T210.1. — T292.) 4; 17; 19; 30; 31; 35; 36; 40; 41; 54; 57; 62; 64.

    d.   Chastity and celibacy (T310.1. — T331.+.) 17; 35; 57.

    e.   Illicit sexual relations (T410.+. — T481.) 26; 27; 28; 29; 30; 31; 33; 36; 38; 41; 42; 44; 45; 48; 49.

    f.   Conception and birth (T538. — T589.2.) 18; 45.

    g.   Care of children (T615. — T685.) 18; 27; 45; 62.

U. THE NATURE OF LIFE

    a.   Nature of life—miscellaneous (U243.) 40.

W. TRAITS OF CHARACTER

    a.   Favorable traits of character (W10. — W34.) 13; 14; 24; 31; 38; 41; 43; 53; 54; 57; 65.

    b.   Unfavorable traits of character (W116. — W187.) 6; 7; 17; 18; 20b; 22; 32; 33; 37; 39; 41; 43; 45; 46; 47; 53; 55; 56; 60; 66.

X. HUMOR

    a.   Humor of disability—physical (X137.) 23.

    b.   Humor of lies and exaggeration (X1503.) 15.

Z. MISCELLANEOUS GROUPS OF MOTIFS

    a.   Heroes (Z221. — Z293.) 40; 47.

    b.   Unique exceptions (Z311. — Z356.) 33; 59.

Topical Motif Index

A. MYTHOLOGICAL MOTIFS

a. Gods A220.2. — A240.1.

A220.2.	The sun-god and his family. (1); (3).
A220.2.+.	Rainbow is sun's brother. (A220.2. The sun-god and his family.) (4).
A221.	Sun-father. (3).
A225.	Son of the sun. (1); (3).
A227.	Two sun-gods. (1).
A240.1.	Moon-goddess. (8).

b. Demigods and culture heroes A511.4.1. — A592.2.1.+.

A511.4.1.	Miraculous growth of culture hero. (45).
A512.4.	Sun as father of culture hero. (1).
A513.	Coming of culture hero (demigod). (9); (13).
A515.1.	Culture heroes brothers. (10); (11); (15); (20a); (20b).
A515.1.+.	Culture heroes two brothers and a sister. (A515.1. Culture heroes brothers.) (9); (12); (13); (14); (17).
A515.1.+.	Culture heroes two brothers and several sisters. (A515.1. Culture heroes brothers.) (21).
A515.1.1.2.	Twin culture heroes—one foolish, one clever. (15).
A515.2.	Father and son as culture heroes. (1).

A515.4.   Culture hero has faithful attendant. (3).

A520.+.   Culture heroine as leader of people. (A520. Nature of the culture hero [demigod].) (13).

A522.2.   Bird as culture hero. (32); (33); (34); (35).

A524.2.   Extraordinary weapons of culture hero. (12); (14); (17); (34); (35).

A525.1.+.   Culture hero argues with his elder brother. (A525.1. Culture hero fights with his elder brother.) (10); (11); (12); (15); (20a).

A526.2.   Culture hero as mighty hunter. (1); (11); (40).

A526.7.   Culture hero performs remarkable feats of strength and skill. (32); (33); (35).

A527.+.   Remarkably clever culture heroine. (A527. Special powers of culture hero.) (9); (13); (14).

A527.1.   Culture hero precocious. (45).

A527.3.   Culture hero as magician. (11).

A530.   Culture hero establishes law and order. (9).

A531.   Culture hero (demigod) overcomes monsters. (33).

A531.4.   Culture hero conquers sea monster. (34).

A535.   Culture hero swallowed and recovered from animal. (40).

A541.   Culture hero teaches arts and crafts. (9); (10); (13); (14).

A545.   Culture hero establishes customs. (9); (11); (12); (15).

A545.+.   Culture hero establishes customs pertaining to child-birth. (A545. Culture hero establishes customs.) (18).

A545.+.   Culture hero establishes customs pertaining to menstruation. (A545. Culture hero establishes customs.) (17).

A560.   Culture hero's (demigod's) departure. (21); (33).

A566.2.   Culture hero ascends to heaven. (1); (3); (21).

A592.2.1.+.   Wife of culture hero gives birth to boy. (A592.2.1. Daughter of culture hero gives birth to boy.) (18).

c. Cosmogony and cosmology A711. — A791.

A711.	Sun as man who left earth. (1); (3); (65).
A720.2.	Formerly great heat of sun causes distress to mankind. (1); (2); (6).
A722.+.	Sun's night journey. Goes to otherworld. (A722. Sun's night journey. Around or under the earth.) (3).
A727.	Raising the sun. (1).
A727.1.	Sun originally so hot that it threatens all life. (1).
A733.5.	Sun dries out earth with its heat. (1).
A736.	Sun as human being. (1); (3).
A736.1.	Sun and moon as man and woman. (65).
A736.5.	Children of the sun. (65).
A738.+.	Sun is excellent hunter. (A738. Attributes of sun.) (65).
A738.1.	Physical attributes of sun. (3).
A738.2.+.	Sun as benevolent leader. (A738.2. Mental powers and disposition of sun.) (3).
A738.2.+.	Sun as evil tyrant hated by people. (A738.2. Mental powers and disposition of sun.) (1).
A738.2.2.	Sun endowed with wisdom and passion. (65).
A739.2.	War with the sun. (1).
A745.+.	Moon has son. (A745. Family of the moon.) (5).
A750.+.	Why moon is red. (A750. Nature and condition of the moon.) (5).
A751.5.5.+.	Moon spots are scarifications. (A751.5.5. Moon spots are tattoo marks.) (5).
A751.8.	Woman in the moon. (5); (65).
A753.+.	Moon and rainbow married. (A753. Moon as a person.) (65).
A761.	Ascent to stars. People or animals ascend to sky and become stars. (1); (21).
A791.	Origin of the rainbow. (4); (65).

d. Topographical features of the earth A900.+. — A990.+.

A900.+.	Indentations on mountain top from primeval flood. (A900. Topography—general considerations.) (7).

A900.+.	Why mountain tops are bare today: scorched by sun. (A900. Topography— general considerations.) (1); (6).
A901.	Topographical features caused by experiences of primitive hero. (35).
A901.+.	Topographical features caused by experiences of ancestors. (A901. Topographical features caused by experiences of primitive hero.) (65).
A911.	Bodies of water from tears. (37).
A920.2.	Origin of sea channels. (35).
A925.1.	Origin of high sea waves. (65).
A925.5.	Origin of mournful sound of sea. (65).
A930.1.	Creator of rivers. (32); (35).
A934.2.	Rivers formed where certain stones are placed. (35).
A934.9.	Stream unexpectedly bursts from side of mountain. (32).
A955.6.+.	Islands from stones cast by hero. (A955.6. Islands from stones cast by giantess.) (35).
A955.11.	Islands originally form continent, later separated. (35).
A977.	Origin of particular stones or groups of stones. (58a); (59); (65).
A977.1.	Giant responsible for certain stones. (33).
A977.5.	Origin of particular rock. (34); (35).
A990.+.	Origin of glaciers. (A990. Other land features.) (6).
A990.+.	Origin of plains. (A990. Other land features.) (65).

e.   World calamities A1005. — A1040.

A1005.	Preservation of life during world calamity. (7); (8).
A1006.1.	New race from single pair (or several) after world calamity. (7); (8).
A1010.2.+.	Great flood lasts two days. (A1010.2. Great flood lasts eight months.) (7).
A1015.+.	Moon-woman causes flood. (A1015. Flood caused by gods or other superior beings.) (8).

A1016.3.	Flood caused by melting of ice after great spell of cold. (7).
A1018.	Flood as punishment. (8).
A1018.3.	Flood brought as revenge for injury. (6); (7); (8).
A1021.	Deluge: escape in boat (ark). (7).
A1022.	Escape from deluge on mountain. (7); (8).
A1029.6.	Survivors of flood establish homes. (7).
A1030.	World-fire. (1); (2).
A1031.3.	Evil demons set world on fire. (2).
A1036.+.	Earth restored after world-fire. (A1036. Earth recreated after world-fire.) (2).
A1038.+.	Men hide from world-fire. (A1038. Men hide from world-fire and renew race.) (2).
A1040.	Continuous winter destroys the race. (6).

f.   Establishment of natural order A1111. — A1191.

A1111.	Impounded water. (32).
A1179.2.	Origin of dawn. (56).
A1191.	All things receive names. (21).

g.   Creation and ordering of human life A1200. — A1630.

A1200.	Creation of man. (18).
A1275.	Creation of first man's (woman's) mate. (16).
A1313.2.	Origin of female sex organs. (16).
A1313.2.+.	Origin of shape of vagina. (A1313.2. Origin of female sex organs.) (17).
A1335.	Origin of death. (20a); (20b).
A1346.	Man to earn bread by sweat of his brow. (11); (15).
A1351.	Origin of childbirth. (18).
A1352.	Origin of sexual intercourse. (16).
A1352.3.	Former intercourse by navel. (16).
A1355.	Origin of menstruation. (17).
A1372.9.	Why women are subservient to men. (3); (7); (65).
A1404.	Gods teach people all they know. (9).

A1414.3.+.   Origin of fire—culture hero strikes rocks together. (A1414.3. Origin of fire—children strike rocks together.) (10).
A1415.   Theft of fire. (52).
A1445.1.   Origin of boat-building. (43).
A1446.   Acquisition of tools. (9); (12); (13).
A1457.1.+.   Origin of the sinker. (A1457.1. Origin of the fish hook.) (37).
A1459.1.   Acquisition of weapons. (9); (13).
A1459.1.+.   Origin of arrowhead. (A1459.1. Acquisition of weapons.) (13).
A1459.1.+.   Origin of harpoonpoint. (A1459.1. Acquisition of weapons.) (14).
A1472.   Beginning of division of labor. (65).
A1520.   Origin of hunting and fishing customs. (9); (11); (12).
A1530.   Origin of social ceremonials. (58b).
A1530.+.   Origin of girls' initiation ceremonial. (A1530. Origin of social ceremonials.) (17).
A1530.+.   Origin of secret society. (A1530. Origin of social ceremonials.) (65).
A1595.+.   Origin of body paint: imitation of designs on animals and birds. (A1595. Origin of tattooing.) (17).
A1620.+.   Why tribe lives in certain place. (A1620. Distribution of tribes.) (65).
A1630.   Wandering of tribes. (65).

h.   Animal characteristics A2210. — A2585.

A2210.   Animal characteristics: change in ancient animal. (22).
A2230.   Animal characteristics as punishment. (25).
A2238.   Animal characteristics: punishment for greed. (24).
A2257.   Animal characteristics from duel. (4).
A2257.+.   Animal characteristics from battle. (A2257. Animal characteristics from duel.) (65).
A2260.   Animal characteristics from transformation. (65).

A2536.+.   Bird as sign of spring. (A2536. Animals of good omen.) (6).

A2545.+.   Why people treat bird respectfully. (A2545. Animal given certain privilege.) (6).

A2571.   How animals received their names. (21); (45).

A2585.   Why there is enmity between certain animals and man. (25).

B. ANIMALS

a. Mythical animals B16.2.+. — B34.

B16.2+.   Devastating whale. (B16.2. Devastating wild animals.) (54); (55).

B16.2.+.   Man-eating fish. (B16.2. Devastating wild animals.) (57).

B34.   Bird of dawn. (56).

b. Magic animals B147.2.+. — B175.+.

B147.2.+.   Night-heron's call announces the coming of visitors. (B147.2. Birds furnish omens.) (53).

B172.   Magic bird. (6); (7); (51); (52).

B175.+.   Magic whale. (B175. Magic fish.) (54); (55).

c. Animals with human traits B200.+. — B299.1.

B200.+.   Birds with human traits. (B200. Animals with human traits.) (51); (52).

B211.2.7.+.   Speaking sea lion. (B211.2.7. Speaking sea-beast.) (19).

B211.3.   Speaking bird. (23); (31); (51); (52); (55).

B235.+.   Birds have meeting, discuss their journeys.

(B235. Secrets discussed in animal meeting.) (51); (52).

B263.5.   War between groups of birds. (22).

B266.1.+.   Thirsty animals fight over well. (B266.1. Thirsty cattle fight over well. (22).

B266.1.+.   Thirsty cormorants fight over well. (B266.1. Thirsty cattle fight over well.) (22).

B299.1.   Animal takes revenge on man. (6); (7); (23).

d.   Friendly animals B314. — B555.

B314.   Helpful animal brothers-in-law. (19).

B450.+.   Helpful hummingbird. (B450. Helpful birds.) (32); (33); (34); (35).

B470.   Helpful fish. (57).

B523.   Animal saves man from pursuer. (57).

B531.   Animals provide food for men. (51).

B551.+.   Sea lion carries girl across water. (B551. Animal carries man across water.) (19).

B555.   Animals serve as bridge across stream. (57).

e.   Marriage of person to animal B600.+. — B670.+.

B600.+.   Marriage of woman to sea lion. (B600. Marriage of person to animal.) (19).

B610.   Animal paramour. (19).

B610.1.   Girl's animal lover slain by spying relatives. (19).

B621.+.   Sea lion as suitor. (B621. Beast as suitor.) (19).

B631.   Human offspring from marriage to animal. (19).

B651.1.   Marriage to fox in human form. (18).

B652.   Marriage to bird in human form. (17); (18); (23).

B670.+.   Marriage of falcon to albatross. (B670. Unusual mating between animals.) (31).

f.   Fanciful traits of animals B736.1. — B772.+.

      B736.1.   Bird sheds tears. (31).

      B755.   Animal calls the dawn. The sun rises as result of the animal's call. (56).

      B771.   Wild animal miraculously tamed. (53).

      B772.+.   Marooned woman abandoned by birds. (B772. Shipwrecked man repulsed by animals.) (51).

g.   Miscellaneous animal motifs B871.2.+. — B874.

      B871.2.+.   Giant sea lion. (B871.2. Giant wild beasts.) (19).

      B874.   Giant fish. (40).

C. TABU

a.   Tabu connected with supernatural beings C41. — C94.3.

      C41.   Tabu: offending water-spirit. (41); (42).

      C94.3.   Tabu: mocking animal. (23).

b.   Sex tabu C114. — C170.+.

      C114.   Tabu: incest. (17); (26); (27); (28); (29); (30).

      C140.   Tabu connected with menses. (17).

      C140.+.   Food tabu during menses. (C140. Tabu connected with menses.) (60).

      C141.   Tabu: going forth during menses. (17).

      C170.+.   Tabu: showing disrespect for father-in-law. (C170. Tabu connected with husband's or wife's relatives.) (55).

c. Speaking tabu C420. — C450.

C420.	Tabu: uttering secrets. (65).
C422.	Tabu: revealing identity of certain person. (65).
C429.1.	Tabu: mentioning secret water spring. (22); (32).
C450.	Tabu: boasting. (53).

d. Miscellaneous tabus C871.+.

C871.+.	Tabu: refusing a request from wife's relatives. (C871. Tabu: refusing a request.) (23).

e. Punishment for breaking tabu C920.2. — C987.

C920.2.	Death of wife for breaking tabu. (30).
C929.5.	Death by being swallowed for breaking tabu. (60).
C987.	Curse as punishment for breaking tabu. (28).

D. MAGIC

a. Transformation D100.+. — D681.

D100.+.	Transformation: man to crustacean. (D100. Transformation: man to animal.) (38).
D100.+.	Transformation: women to animals. (D100. Transformation: man to animal.) (65).
D150.	Transformation: man to bird. (26); (33); (36); (37).

E.   THE DEAD

a.   Resuscitation E1. — E121.

E1.   Person comes to life. (20a); (20b).
E31.   Limbs of dead voluntarily reassemble and
                     revive. (54); (55).
E32.   Resuscitated eaten animal. (54); (55).
E35.ˇ   Resuscitation from fragments of body.
                     (33).
E50.   Resuscitation by magic. (20a).
E58.   Resuscitation by weeping (tears). (20b).
E121.   Resuscitation by supernatural person.
                     (20a).

b.   Ghosts and other revenants E257.+. — E599.5.+.

E257.+.   Ogre seeks firewood to roast boys. (E257.
                     Ghosts seek firewood to roast man.) (18).
E320.   Dead relative's friendly return. (47).
E323.   Dead mother's friendly return. (20b).
E361.   Return from the dead to stop weeping.
                     (20b).
E379.4.   Ghost as confederate of man. (47).
E381.   Ghost summoned by weeping. (20b).
E440.   Walking ghost "laid." (20b).
E481.   Land of the dead. (2).
E494.   Ball game in lower world. (2).
E541.   Revenants eat. (47).
E545.   The dead speak. (47).
E545.13.   Man converses with dead. (47).
E599.+.   Ghosts build canoe. (E599. Other actions
                     of revenants.) (47).
E599.+.   Ghosts go hunting. (E599. Other actions of
                     revenants.) (47).
E599.5.+.   Ghost flies. (E599.5. Ghost travels quick-
                     ly.) (47).

c.   The soul E722.1.+. — E780.

E722.1.+.   Soul appears like the body it left at death.

F. MARVELS

a. Otherworld journeys F30.

b. Marvelous creatures F402.1.11.2. — F681.

F547.3.+.	Red penis. (F547.3. Extraordinary penis.) (17).
F547.3.1.	Long penis. (17); (27).
F556.	Remarkable voice. (47).
F565.1.	Amazons. Women warriors. (1).
F565.3.	Parliament of women. (1); (4); (13); (65).
F565.3.+.	Parliament of women overthrown. (F565.3. Parliament of women.) (3); (7); (8); (65).
F575.1.	Remarkably beautiful woman. (3); (4); (17); (31); (48); (61).
F575.2.	Handsome man. (3); (4); (5); (57).
F575.3.	Remarkably beautiful child. (45).
F601.	Extraordinary companions. (47).
F611.3.2.	Hero's precocious strength. Has full strength when very young. (24).
F617.	Mighty wrestler. (4).
F621.2.	Trees pulled up by giant. (33).
F634.	Mighty fisherman. (37); (48).
F655.	Extraordinary perception of blind men. (62).
F660.	Remarkable skill. (34); (35); (40).
F660.+.	Skillful craftsmen. (F660. Remarkable skill.) (13).
F661.	Skillful marksman. (32); (34); (35); (50).
F667.	Skillful tracker. (53).
F679.5.	Skillful hunter. (17); (24); (38); (40); (45); (65).
F681.	Marvelous runner. (65).

c.   Extraordinary places and things F701. — F882.

F701.	Land of plenty. (24).
F830.+.	Extraordinary sling. (F830. Extraordinary weapons.) (4).
F841.	Extraordinary boat (ship). (23).
F842.	Extraordinary bridge. (59).
F851.	Extraordinary food. (24); (41); (43).
F873.0.1.	Battle rage. (65).
F882.	Extraordinary fire. (52).

d.   Extraordinary occurrences F911.4. — F1084.

F911.4.	Jonah. Fish (or water monster) swallows a man. (40).
F912.2.	Victim kills swallower from within by cutting. (40).
F913.	Victims rescued from swallower's belly. (40).
F915.	Victim speaks from swallower's body. (40).
F921.	Swallowed person becomes bald. (40).
F932.7.+.	Ocean boils. (F932.7. River boils.) (1).
F950.	Marvelous cures. (40).
F959.1.	Madness miraculously cured. (47).
F961.1.	Extraordinary behavior of sun. (1); (2).
F963.	Extraordinary behavior of wind. (45).
F964.	Extraordinary behavior of fire. (52).
F968.	Extraordinary thunder and lightning. (58a).
F969.7.	Famine. (66).
F982.	Animals carry extraordinary burden. (51).
F983.	Extraordinary growth of animal. (55).
F989.15.	Hunt for extraordinary (magic) animal. (40).
F1034.+.	Shaman concealed in body of whale. (F1034. Person concealed in another's body.) (54); (55).
F1035.	Disintegration: man eats himself up or dismembers himself. (58b).
F1041.1.2.2.4.	Death from hearing of son's (sons') death. (45).
F1041.21.6.1.	Wounding self because of excessive grief. (5).
F1068.2.2.	Fight in dream with real result. (63).
F1084.	Furious battle. (65).

G.   OGRES

a.   Kinds of ogres G11.18. — G371.

G11.18.	Cannibal tribe. (58a); (58b).

G31.+.	Children flee from stepmother who turns cannibal. (G31. Children flee from father who turns cannibal.) (18).
G61.	Relative's flesh eaten unwittingly. (19).
G72.1.	Woman plans to eat her children. (18).
G81.	Unwitting marriage to cannibal. (18).
G304.2.5.+.	Monster bursts from heat. (G304.2.5. Troll bursts when sun shines on him.) (33).
G310.+.	Ogres leave signs on trees. (G310. Ogres with characteristic methods.) (62).
G312.	Cannibal ogre. (34).
G332.	Sucking monster. (33).
G334.	Ogre keeps human prisoners. (33).
G346.	Devastating monster. (33).
G352.+.	Sea lion as ogre. (G352. Wild beast as ogre.) (34).
G360.	Ogres with monstrous features. (62).
G361.3.	Headless ogre. (62).
G371.	Stone giants. (33).

b. Falling into ogre's power G475. — G477.

G475.	Ogre attacks intruders. (34).
G477.	Ogre kills men and rapes women. (33).

c. Ogre defeated G500. — G550.

G500.	Ogre defeated. (61).
G510.4.	Hero overcomes devastating animal. (34).
G511.	Ogre blinded. (33); (34).
G512.0.1.	Hero kills trouble-making evil strong men. (33).
G512.3.	Ogre burned to death. (33).
G512.9.	Animal kills ogre. (34).
G550.	Rescue from ogre. (54).

d. Other ogre motifs G630.+.

G630.+.	Stone man's eyes, palms, and soles like foreigner's. (G630. Characteristics of ogre.) (33).

H. TESTS

a. Identity tests: recognition H30. — H88.

H30.	Recognition through personal peculiarities. (40).
H31.	Recognition by unique ability. (40).
H32.	Recognition by extraordinary prowess. (40).
H79.+.	Recognition by foot. (H79. Recognition by physical attributes—miscellaneous.) (45).
H79.+.	Recognition by long penis. (H79. Recognition by physical attributes—miscellaneous.) (27).
H79.3.	Recognition by voice. (44); (53).
H88.	Identification by tokens left as trail. (54).

b. Tests of truth H217.

H217.	Decision made by contest. (63).

c. Marriage tests H473.

H473.	Test of wife's obedience. (57).

d. Tests of cleverness H580.

H580.	Enigmatic statements. (65).

e. Tests of prowess: quests H1223.1. — H1385.

H1223.1.	Quest to recover one's honor through feats. (23); (25).
H1242.+.	Oldest brother alone succeeds on quest. (H1242. Youngest brother alone succeeds on quest.) (25).
H1280.	Quest to other realms. (65).

H1370.+.   Quest for spirit. (H1370. Miscellaneous
                    quests.) (65).
H1381.3.1.   Quest for bride. (17).
H1385.   Quest for lost persons. (37).

f.   Other tests H1553.

H1553.   Tests of patience. (43).

J.   THE WISE AND THE FOOLISH

a.   Acquisition and possession of wisdom (knowledge) J21.50. —
     J157.

J21.50.   "Idleness begets woe; work brings happi-
                    ness." (10); (11); (12); (15).
J53.+.   Ambush betrayed by movements of birds.
                    (J53. Army saved from ambush by obser-
                    vation of birds' movements.) (4).
J154.   Wise words of dying father. (44).
J157.   Wisdom (knowledge) from dream. (66).

b.   Wise and unwise conduct J261. — J1050.

J261.   Loudest mourners not greatest sorrowers.
                    (47).
J421.   Subordination of weak to strong. (65).
J421.+.   Subordination of strong to weak by de-
                    ception. (J421. Subordination of weak to
                    strong.) (65).
J610.   Forethought in conflict with others—gen-
                    eral. (41).
J613.   Wise fear of the weak for the strong. (65).
J623.   Prevention of hostility by inspiring fear in
                    enemy. (65).
J624.   Uniting against a common enemy. (65).

J640.	Avoidance of others' power. (41).
J641.	Escaping before enemy can strike. (18).
J647.	Avoiding enemy's revenge. (65).
J652.	Inattention to warnings. (28); (30); (31).
J702.	Necessity of work. (10); (11); (12); (15).
J710.	Forethought in provision for food. (45).
J715.	Kindness unwise when it imperils one's food supply. (32).
J910.	Humility of the great. (13).
J1050.	Attention to warnings. (65).

c.   Cleverness J1111. — J1681.

J1111.	Clever girl. (61).
J1113.	Clever boy. (45).
J1341.	Retort from underfed servant (child). (24); (37); (39).
J1434.	Strenuous cure for madness. (47).
J1681.	Cleverness in dealing with the enemy. (65).*

d.   Fools (and other unwise persons) J1772.9. — J2650.

J1772.9.	Excrements thought to be meat and therefore eaten. (47).
J1820.	Inappropriate action from misunderstanding. (26).
J1919.5.	Genitals cut off through ignorance. (50).
J2079.	Absurd wishes—miscellaneous. (10); (11); (12); (15).
J2133.5.1.	Wife carried up tree to sky in bag in husband's teeth. (30).
J2301.	Gullible husbands. (41).
J2353.1.	Foolish boasts get man into trouble. (53).
J2401.	Fatal imitation. (49); (50).
J2431.	A man undertakes to do his wife's work. (36).
J2650.	Bungling fool. (50).

*Thompson 1955-58: 4, 493.

K. DECEPTIONS

a. Contests won by deception K66.

K66.   Dream contests. (63).

b. Thefts and cheats K330. — K477.

K330.   Means of hoodwinking the guardian or
                        owner. (41).
K330.+.   Women induce owners to give up food.
                        (K330. Means of hoodwinking the guard-
                        ian or owner.) (17).
K477.   Attention secured by trickery. (40); (42).

c. Escape by deception K500. — K572.

K500.   Escape from death or danger by deception.
                        (18).
K515.   Escape by hiding. (54); (65).
K515.6.   Escape by hiding in the earth. (33).
K572.   Escape from captor by means of flattery.
                        (41); (42).

d. Capture by deception K700. — K778.

K700.   Capture by deception. (23).
K750.   Capture by decoy. (53).
K778.   Capture through the wiles of a woman.
                        (23).

e. Fatal deception K800. — K959.4.

K800.   Killing or maiming by deception. (19).
K810.   Fatal deception into trickster's power. (4);
                        (25).

K811.	Victim lured into house and killed. (53); (58a).
K811.+.	Victims lured into house and wounded. (K811. Victim lured into house and killed.) (61).
K812.	Victim burned in his own house (or hiding place). (33).
K815.	Victim lured by kind words approaches trickster andd is killed. (25); (46).
K832.	Dupe induced to look about: seized and killed. (39); (46).
K839.2.	Victim lured into approach by false token. (25).
K874.	Deception by pretended lousing. (53).
K890.	Dupe tricked into killing himself. (49); (50).
K891.	Dupe tricked into jumping to his death. (48).
K893.1.+.	Woman leads pursuers to edge of thin ice, swerves suddenly; they fall through. (K893.1. Man leads pursuers to edge of thin ice, swerves suddenly; they fall through.) (61).
K910.	Murder by strategy. (40); (53); (58a).
K912.2.+.	Men lured into trap one by one and killed. (K912.2. Men lured into serpent pit one by one and killed.) (25); (46); (47).
K917.	Treacherous murder during hunt. (47).
K926.	Victim pushed into water. (39).
K952.	Animal (monster) killed from within. (40).
K958.	Murder by drowning. (39).
K959.2.	Murder in one's sleep. (54); (55).
K959.2.1.	Woman's father and brothers kill her husband in sleep for having married against their wishes. (19).
K959.4.	Murder from behind. (39); (46).

f. Deception into self-injury K1000.

K1000.	Deception into self-injury. (33).

g.   Deception into humiliating position K1200. — K1210.

K1200.	Deception into humiliating position. (65).
K1210.	Humiliated or baffled lovers. (54).

h.   Seduction or deceptive marriage K1310. — K1330.

K1310.	Seduction by disguise or substitution. (44).
K1325.	Seduction by feigned death. (44).
K1330.	Girl tricked into man's room (or power). (29).

j.   Deceptions connected with adultery K1500. — K1569.9.

K1500.	Deception connected with adultery. (27).
K1501.	Cuckold. Husband deceived by adulterous wife. (30); (31); (36); (38).
K1510.	Adulteress outwits husband. (41); (42).
K1514.	Adulteress gets rid of husband while she entertains lover. (36); (38).
K1514.18.	Adulteress makes excuse to go and attend to bodily needs: meets lover. (36).
K1521.	Paramour successfully hidden from husband. (27); (38).
K1550.	Husband outwits adulteress and paramour. (38).
K1550.1.	Husband discovers wife's adultery. (27); (30); (31); (36); (38).
K1551.+.	Husband spies on adulteress and lover. (K1551. Husband returns home secretly and spies on adulteress and lovers.) (36).
K1558.1.	Husband castrates paramour. (27).
K1569.2.	Husband surprises wife and paramour. (36).
K1569.9.	Husband kills surprised paramour. (38).

k.   Deceiver falls into own trap K1600. — K1641.

K1600.	Deceiver falls into own trap. (4).

K1616.   Marooned man reaches home and outwits marooner. (23); (53).

K1641.   Ambushed trickster killed by intended victim. (25); (46); (47).

l.   Deception through shams K1700. — K2060.

K1700.   Deception through bluffing. (37).

K1821.2.   Disguise by painting body. (44); (65).

K1821.3.   Disguise by veiling face. (65).

K1828.   Disguise as deity (or spirit). (65).

K1860.   Deception by feigned death (sleep). (4).

K1868.   Deception by pretending sleep. (26); (31).

K1871.2.   Sham cure by pretended extracting of object from patient's body. (33).

K1952.2.   Better things at home. (41).

K2010.   Hypocrite pretends friendship but attacks. (19); (23).

K2050.   Pretended virtue. (38).

K2060.   Detection of hypocrisy. (41); (65).

m.   Villains and traitors K2210.+. — K2218.

K2210.+.   Treacherous nephew. (K2210. Treacherous relatives.) (47).

K2211.0.2.   Treacherous younger brother. (30).

K2211.1.   Treacherous brother-in-law. (19); (25); (46); (47).

K2212.   Treacherous sister. (19).

K2212.2.   Treacherous sister-in-law. (19).

K2213.   Treacherous wife. (23); (41); (42); (48); (49); (53); (54); (62); (65).

K2214.1.   Treacherous daughter. (65).

K2218.   Treacherous relatives-in-law. (53).

n.   Other deceptions K2320. — K2350.+.

K2320.   Deception by frightening. (45); (65).

K2350.+.   Fast runners sent through enemy's camp to
                        gather information. (K2350. Military strat-
                        egy.) (65).

L.   REVERSAL OF FORTUNE

a.   Victorious youngest child L10. — L31.

L10.   Victorious youngest son. (46).
L13.+.   Compassionate elder son. (L13. Compas-
                        sionate youngest son.) (20a); (20b).
L31.   Youngest brother helps elder. (45).

b.   Unpromising hero (heroine) L112.2.

L112.2.   Very small hero. (32); (33); (34); (35); (40).

c.   Triumph of the weak L300.+. — L311.

L300.+.   Triumph of the oppressed. (L300. Triumph
                        of the weak.) (65).
L311.   Weak (small) hero overcomes large fighter.
                        (32); (33); (34); (35); (61).

d.   Pride brought low L430.

L430.   Arrogance repaid. (53).

M.   ORDAINING THE FUTURE

a.   Curses M411.1. — M416.

M411.1.   Curse by parent. (28).

M416. Curse given to negate good wish. (10); (11); (12).

N. CHANCE AND FATE

a. The ways of luck and fate N131.+.

N131.+. Good luck by breaking bird's egg. (N131. Acts performed for changing luck.) (31).

b. Unlucky accidents N360.

N360. Man unwittingly commits crime. (4).

c. Lucky accidents N440. — N681.0.1.+.

N440. Valuable secrets learned. (3); (4); (32); (65).

N440.+. Secret learned. (N440. Valuable secrets learned.) (27); (28); (34); (41); (45); (62).

N440.+. Secret revealed. (N440. Valuable secrets learned.) (36).

N450. Secrets overheard. (17).

N451. Secrets overheard from animal (demon) conversation. (31).

N452.1.+. Remedy for lack of water in certain place found by spying on birds. (N452.1. Remedy for lack of water in certain place overheard in conversation of animals [demons].) (22).

N455. Overheard (human) conversation. (38); (65).

N455.+. Overheard animal conversation. (N455. Overheard [human] conversation.) (51); (52).

N455.6.+. Husband learns of wife's infidelity through conversation overheard. (N455.6. Husband learns of wife's fidelity through conversation overheard.) (31).

N455.9.+.   Location of sought man learned from over-
                     heard conversation. (N455.9. Location of
                     sought object learned from overheard con-
                     versation.) (53).
N681.0.1.+.   Return home to witness one's own mourn-
                     ing rites. (N681.0.1. Return home to one's
                     own funeral.) (40).

d.   Accidental encounters N731.

N731.   Unexpected meeting of father and son.
                     (62).

e.   Helpers N800.+. — N845.

N800.+.   Stranger as helper. (N800. Helpers.) (18).
N818.1.   Sun as helper. (1); (3).
N820.   Human helpers. (34).
N827.   Child as helper. (24); (45); (53).
N828.   Wise woman as helper. (13); (14); (17).
N832.   Boy as helper. (62).
N838.   Hero (culture hero) as helper. (32); (33);
                     (35).
N845.   Magician as helper. (66).

P.   SOCIETY

a.   The family P211. — P291.

P211.   Wife chooses father's side in feud. Must
                     choose between husband and father. (23);
                     (55).
P214.+.   Wife eats flesh of slain husband. (P214.
                     Wife drinks blood of slain husband.) (19).
P231.   Mother and son. (20a); (20b); (24); (26).
P231.3.   Mother-love. (5); (26); (45).
P231.5.+.   Foster father reveals fact that son is off-
                     spring of supernatural father. (P231.5.

Q.   REWARDS AND PUNISHMENTS

Q72.	Loyalty rewarded. (54).
Q83.1.	Reward for wife's fidelity. (40).

b.   Deeds punished Q211. — Q395.

Q211.	Murder punished. (4).
Q215.	Cannibalism punished. (18).
Q241.	Adultery punished. (30); (36); (38); (48); (49); (57).
Q242.	Incest punished. (27); (28); (29); (30).
Q242.3.	Punishment for man who makes advances to sister-in-law. (30).
Q252.1.	Wife-stealing punished with death. (4); (30).
Q253.1.	Bestiality punished. (19).
Q261.2.	Treacherous wife punished. (41); (65).
Q276.	Stinginess punished. (22); (32); (37); (39); (41).
Q285.	Cruelty punished. (18); (24); (46); (54).
Q288.	Punishment for mockery. (23); (25); (30); (53); (54); (64).
Q330.	Overweening punished. (53).
Q395.	Disrespect punished. (55); (56).

c.   Kinds of punishment Q411. — Q595.

Q411.	Death as punishment. (18); (32); (53).
Q411.0.1.	Husband kills returning adulteress. (57).
Q411.0.1.2.	Man (fairy) kills wife's lover. (38).
Q411.0.2.	Husband kills wife and paramour. (36).
Q411.4.	Death as punishment for treachery. (65).
Q411.6.	Death as punishment for murder. (25); (35); (46); (47); (48); (49); (59); (60).
Q415.	Punishment: being eaten by animals. (30).
Q450.	Cruel punishments. (19).
Q451.	Mutilation as punishment. (57).
Q451.0.1.	Hands and feet cut off as punishment. (25).
Q451.10.1.	Punishment: castration. (27).
Q461.3.	Impaling as punishment for adultery. (36); (38); (48); (49).

Q467.	Punishment by drowning. (39).
Q467.5.	Marooning as punishment. (53).
Q470.	Humiliating punishments. (38).
Q551.2.1.+.	Magic adhesion to whale as punishment. (Q551.2.1. Magic adhesion to object as punishment [for opposition to holy person].) (54); (55).
Q551.3.	Punishment: transformation. (54); (55).
Q552.20.1.	Miraculous darkness as punishment. (56).
Q580.	Punishment fitted to crime. (24); (30).
Q581.1.	Unusual murder avenged in like manner. (46); (47).
Q584.2.	Transformation of man to animal as fitting punishment. (27); (29).
Q595.	Loss or destruction of property as punishment. (41).

R. CAPTIVES AND FUGITIVES

a. Captivity R9.1. — R11.

R9.1.	Sun captured. (1).
R11.	Abduction by monster (ogre). (33); (62).

b. Rescues R153.2. — R155.2.

R153.2.	Father rescues children. (31).
R153.3.	Father rescues son(s). (53).
R154.1.	Son rescues mother. (20a).
R155.1.	Youngest brother rescues his elder brothers. (45).

c. Escapes and pursuits R210. — R245.

R210.	Escapes. (23); (57).
R211.	Escape from prison. (47).
R220.	Flights. (57); (58a); (58b).

R227.	Wife flees from husband. (31).
R227.2.	Flight from hated husband. (41); (42).
R228.+.	Child leaves home because grandmother is stingy with food. (R228. Children leave
R236.4.	Fugitive has magic wind against him, pursuer with him (caused by goddess). (31).
R243.	Fugitives aided by helpful animal. (57).
R245.	Whale-boat. (40).

d. Refuges and recapture R315.

R315.	Cave as refuge. (19).

S. UNNATURAL CRUELTY

a. Cruel relatives S0. — S73.1.4.

S0.	Cruel relative. (30).
S20.2.+.	Grandfather hides food from starving grandsons. (S20.2. Child hides food from starving parents.) (39).
S21.	Cruel son. (20b).
S31.	Cruel stepmother. (18).
S41.	Cruel grandmother. (37).
S42.	Cruel grandfather. (39).
S50.+.	Cruel brothers-in-law. (S50. Cruel relatives-in-law.) (25).
S55.	Cruel sister-in-law. (45).
S70.+.	Cruel brothers. (S70. Other cruel relatives.) (19).
S71.	Cruel uncle. (24).
S73.1.	Fratricide. (63).
S73.1.2.+.	Brothers kill and eat animal brother-in-law. (S73.1.2. Brother kills and eats brother.) (19).
S73.1.4.	Fratricide motivated by love-jealousy. (30).

b. Revolting murders or mutilations S100. — S185.+.

S100.	Revolting murders or mutilations. (66).
S100.+.	Murder by biting off breast. (S100. Revolting murders or mutilations.) (33).
S112.+.	Murder by introducing hot stone into vagina. (S112. Burning to death.) (35).
S112.2.+.	Murder with hot stone. (S112.2. Murder with hot iron.) (35); (57).
S115.	Murder by stabbing. (25).
S116.	Murder by crushing. (53).
S116.4.	Murder by crushing head. (46); (47).
S131.	Murder by drowning. (45).
S139.2.1.	Slain sea lion brother-in-law dismembered. (S139.2. Slain person dismembered.) (19).
S139.2.2.	Other indignities to corpse. (18).
S145.	Abandonment on an island. (23); (53).
S183.	Frightful meal. (19); (24); (47); (54); (58a).
S185.+.	Cruelty to pregnant whale. (S185. Cruelty to pregnant woman.) (66).

c. Cruel sacrifices S260.1. — S263.4.+.

S260.1.	Human sacrifice. (60).
S263.4.+.	Sacrifice to water-spirit who has stopped boat in midstream. (S263.4. Sacrifice to river-god who has stopped boat in midstream.) (60).

d. Abandoned or murdered children S302.1. — S325.0.1.

S302.1.	All new-born male children slaughtered. (33).
S325.0.1.	Monstrous (deformed) child exposed. (33).

e. Cruel persecutions S400.

S400.	Cruel persecutions. (54).

T.   SEX

a.   Love T11.3.2. — T92.10.

b.   Marriage T117.11. — T148.

c.   Married life T210.1. — T292.

f.   Conception and birth T538. — T589.2.

    T538.   Unusual conception in old age. (45).
    T589.2.   Boy cut in two: each half becomes a boy. (18).

g.   Care of children T615. — T685.

    T615.   Supernatural growth. (27); (62).
    T615.1.   Precocious speech. (45).
    T675.1.+.   Child prefers foster father. (T675.1. Children prefer foster mother.) (62).
    T681.   Each likes his own children best. (62).
    T685.   Twins. (18).

U.   THE NATURE OF LIFE

a.   Nature of life—miscellaneous U243.

    U243.   Courage conquers all and impossible is made possible. (40).

W.   TRAITS OF CHARACTER

a.   Favorable traits of character W10. — W34.

    W10.   Kindness. (31).
    W11.   Generosity. (24); (38); (41).
    W11.+.   Generosity toward faithless wife. (W11. Generosity.) (31).
    W11.5.   Generosity toward enemy. (65).
    W26.   Patience. (43).

W27.   Gratitude. (13); (14).
W31.   Obedience. (57).
W34.   Loyalty. (53); (54).

b. Unfavorable traits of character W116. — W187.

W116.   Vanity. (56).
W117.   Boastfulness. (53).
W126.   Disobedience. (60).
W128.   Dissatisfaction. (41); (43).
W152.   Stinginess. (22); (32); (37); (39); (41); (46); (47).
W154.2.   Monster ungrateful for rescue. (33).
W155.   Hardness of heart. (32); (66).
W155.3.   Man unable to weep for hardness of heart. (20b).
W155.5.   Permission refused to drink from water tank. (22).
W155.5.+. Permission refused to drink from lagoon. (W155.5. Permission refused to drink from water tank.) (32).
W181.   Jealousy. (17); (45).
W182.   The crying child. (18).
W185.   Violence of temper. (6); (7).
W187.   Insolence. (55).

X. HUMOR

a. Humor of disability — physical X137.

X137.   Humor of ugliness. (23).

b. Humor of lies and exaggeration X1503.

X1503.   Schlaraffenland. (15).

Z.   MISCELLANEOUS GROUPS OF MOTIFS

   a.   Heroes Z221. — Z293.

        Z221.   Eldest brother as hero. (47).
        Z293.   Return of the hero. (40).

   b.   Unique exceptions Z311. — Z356.

        Z311.   Achilles heel. Invulnerability except in one
                           spot. (33).
        Z356.   Unique survivor. (59).

Alphabetical Motif Index

ABANDONED. — Marooned woman abandoned . . . B772.+. (51).

ABANDONMENT on an island S145. (23); (53).

ABDUCTION by monster (ogre) R11. (33); (62).

ABILITY. — Recognition by unique ability H31. (40).

ABSENT. — Why certain animals are absent from countries A2434.2. (52).

ABSURD wishes . . . J2079. (10); (11); (12); (15).

ACHILLES HEEL . . . Z311. (33).

ACQUISITION of tools A1446. (9); (12); (13); of weapons A1459.1. (9); (13).

ACTION. — Inappropriate action . . . J1820. (26).

ADHESION. — Magic adhesion . . . Q551.2.1.+. (54); (55).

ADULTERESS chooses loathly paramour T232.2. (62); gets rid of husband . . . K1514. (36); (38); makes excuse . . . K1514.18. (36); outwits husband K1510. (41); (42). — Husband kills returning adulteress Q411.0.1. (57); husband outwits adulteress . . . K1550. (38); husband spies on adulteress . . . K1551.+. (36).

ADULTEROUS. — Cuckold. Husband deceived by adulteress wife K1501. (30); (31); (36); (38).

ADULTERY T481. (31); (36); (38); (41); (42); (48); (49); punished Q241. (30); (36); (38); (48); (49); (57). — Deception connected with adultery K1500. (27); husband discovers wife's adultery K1550.1. (27); (30); (31); (36); (38); impaling as punishment for adultery Q461.3. (36); (38); (48); (49).

ADVANCES. — Punishment for man who makes advances . . . Q242.3. (30).

ADVICE from magician (fortune-teller, etc.) D1814.1. (66).

AGE. — Unusual conception in old age T538. (45).

AIDED. — Fugitives aided by . . . animal R243. (57).

ALBATROSS. — Marriage . . . to albatross B670.+. (31).

AMAZONS. — Women warriors F565.1. (1).

AMBUSH betrayed by movements of birds J53.+. (4).

AMBUSHED trickster killed . . . K1641. (25); (46); (47).

ANCESTORS. — Topographical features caused by . . . ancestors A901.+. (65).

ANCIENT. — Animal characteristics: change in ancient animal A2210. (22).

ANIMAL calls the dawn . . . B755. (56); characteristics as punishment A2230. (25); characteristics: change . . . A2210. (22); characteristics from battle A2257.+. (65); characteristics from duel A2257. (4); characteristics from transformation A2260. (65); characteristics: imitation . . . A2272. (30); characteristics: punishment for greed A2238. (24); characteristics: wings A2377. (41); . . . killed from within K952. (40); kills ogre G512.9. (34); paramour B610. (19); saves man from pursuer B523. (57); takes revenge on man B299.1. (6); (7); (23). — Animal's occupation: hunting A2452. (51); animal's occupation: stealing A2455. (3); brothers . . . eat animal brother-in-law S73.1.2.+. (19); culture hero . . . recovered from animal A535. (40); extraordinary growth of animal F983. (55); fugitives aided by . . . animal R243. (57); girl's animal lover slain . . . B610.1. (19); helpful animal brothers-in-law B314. (19); hero overcomes devastating animal G510.4. (34); human offspring from marriage to animal B631. (19); hunt for . . . animal F989.15. (40); magic animal proof . . . D1841.5.2. (40); magic storm produced by animal D2141.0.11. (6); (7); origin of animal characteristics: head A2320. (19); origin . . . of animal's tongue A2344. (27); overheard animal conversation N455.+. (51); (52); resuscitated eaten animal E32. (54); (55); secrets . . . from animal . . . conversation N451. (31); tabu: mocking animal C94.3. (23); transformation . . . to animal as fitting punishment Q584.2. (27); (29); transformation to animal by imitation D599.+. (30); wild animal . . . tamed B771. (53).

ANIMALS carry . . . burden F982. (51); provide food . . . B531. (51); serve as bridge . . . B555. (57); that inhabit water A2433.2.2. (65). — Ascent to stars. . . . animals . . . become stars A761. (1); (21); how animals received their names A2571. (21); (45); origin of body paint: imitation of designs on animals . . . A1595.+. (17); punishment: being eaten by animals Q415. (30); thirsty animals fight . . . B266.1.+. (32); transformation: women to animals D100.+. (65); why animals have tail A2378.1. (65); why certain animals are absent from countries A2434.2. (52); why there is enmity between certain animals and man A2585. (25).

ANNOUNCE. — Night-heron's call announces . . . B147.2.+. (53).

ANOTHER. — Dream about a marriage with another's wife T11.3.2. (50).

APPEAR. — Soul appears like the body it left . . . E722.1.+. (47).

APPROACH. — Victim . . . approaches trickster . . . K815. (25); (46); victim lured into approach . . . K839.2. (25).

ARGUE. — Culture hero argues . . . A525.1.+. (10); (11); (12); (15); (20a).

ARK. — Deluge: escape in boat (ark) A1021. (7).

ARROGANCE repaid L430. (53).

ARROWHEAD. — Origin of arrowhead A1459.1.+. (13).

ARTS. — Culture hero teaches arts . . . A541. (9); (10); (13); (14).

ASCEND. — Ascent to stars. People . . . ascend to sky . . . A761. (1); (21); culture hero ascends to heaven A566.2. (1); (3); (21).

ASCENT to stars. . . . A761. (1); (21).

ATTACK. — Hypocrite . . . attacks K2010. (19); (23); ogre attacks intruders G475. (34).

ATTEND. — Adulteress makes excuse to . . . attend to bodily needs . . . K1514.18. (36).

ATTENDANT. — Culture hero has faithful attendant A515.4. (3).

ATTENTION secured . . . K477. (40); (42); to warnings J1050. (65).

ATTRIBUTES. — Physical attributes of sun A738.1. (3).

AVENGE. — Brothers strive to avenge each other P251.3.1.(25); father avenges son P233.6.+. (54); son avenges father P233.6. (48); (49); woman avenges scorned love T71.2. (45).

AVENGED. — Unusual murder avenged . . . Q581.1. (46); (47).

AVOIDANCE of others' power J640. (41).

AVOIDING enemy's revenge J647. (65); the unfaithful wife T251.1.+. (31).

BACK. — Why cormorants always look back A2471.9.+. (22); why crustacean swims on its back A2444.+. (38); why parasites cling to whale's back A2310.+. (54).

BAFFLED. — Humiliated or baffled lovers K1210. (54).

BAG. — Wife carried . . . in bag . . . J2133.5.1. (30).

BALD. — Swallowed person becomes bald F921. (40).

BALDNESS . . . cured D2161.3.4. (40).

BALL GAME in lower world E494. (2).

BARE. — Why mountain tops are bare today . . . A900.+. (1); (6).

BATTLE rage F873.0.1. (65). — Animal characteristics from battle A2257.+. (65); defeat in battle P555. (65); furious battle F1084. (65).

BEAK. — Why woodpecker has strong beak A2343.3.2.+. (27).

BEAUTIFUL child . . . P264.+. (45). — Remarkably beautiful child F575.3. (45); remarkably beautiful woman F575.1. (3); (4); (17); (31); (48); (61).

BECOME. — Boy cut in two. Each half becomes a boy T589.2. (18).

BEGINNING of division of labor A1472. (65).

BEHAVIOR. — Extraordinary behavior of fire F964. (52); extraordinary behavior of sun F961.1. (1); (2); extraordinary behavior of wind F963. (45).

BEHIND. — Murder from behind K959.4. (39); (46).

BELLY. — Victims rescued from swallower's belly F913. (40).

BELOVED. — Man scorned by his beloved T75. (17); (54).

BENEVOLENT. — Sun as benevolent leader A738.2.+. (3).

BEST. — Each likes his own children best T681. (62).

BESTIALITY punished Q253.1. (19).

BETRAYED. — Ambush betrayed by movements of birds J53.+. (4).

BETTER things at home K1952.2. (41).

BIRD as culture hero A522.2. (32); (33); (34); (35); as sign of spring A2536.+. (6); of dawn B34. (56); sheds tears B736.1. (31). — Good luck by breaking bird's egg N131.+. (31); magic bird B172. (6); (7); (51); (52); marriage to bird . . . B652. (17); (18); (23); origin of color of bird A2411.2. (4); (17); (26); sensitive bird A2520.+. (6); (7); speaking bird B211.3. (23); (31); (51); (52); (55); transformation: man to bird D150. (26); (33); (36); (37); transformation: woman to bird D150.+. (51); why bird is monogamous A2497.+. (26); why people treat bird respectfully A2545.+. (6).

BIRDS have meeting . . . A235.+. (51); (52); with human traits B200.+. (51); (52). — Ambush betrayed by movements of birds J53.+. (4); cries of birds A2426.2. (24); markings on birds A2412.2. (65); marooned woman abandoned by birds B772.+. (51); omens from flight of birds D1812.5.0.2. (40); (55); origin of body paint: imitation of designs on . . . birds A1595.+. (17); remedy . . . found by spying on birds N452.1.+. (22); war between . . . birds B263.5. (22); why certain birds flock together A2492.+. (33).

BIRTH. — Culture hero establishes customs pertaining to childbirth A545.+. (18); origin of childbirth A1351.(18); wife of culture hero gives birth . . . A592.2.1.+. (18).

BITING. — Murder by biting off breast S100.+. (33).

BLIND. — Extraordinary perception of blind men F655. (62).

BLINDED. — Ogre blinded G511. (33); (34).

BLUFFING. — Deception through bluffing K1700. (37).

BOASTFULNESS W117. (53).

BOASTING. — Custom: boasting of sexual prowess P665. (31); tabu: boasting C450. (53).

BOASTS. — Foolish boasts get man into trouble J2353.1. (53).

BOAT. — Deluge: escape in boat (ark) A1021. (7); extraordinary boat (ship) F841. (23); sacrifice to water-spirit who has stopped boat . . . S263.4.+. (60); self-propelling (ship) boat D1523.2. (60); whale-boat R245. (40).

BOAT-BUILDING. — Origin of boat-building A1445.1. (43).

BODIES of water from tears A911. (37).

BODILY. — Adulteress makes excuse to . . . attend to bodily needs . . . K1514.18. (36); death or bodily injury . . . D2060. (54); vital bodily members E780. (54); (55).

BODY. — Disguise by painting body K1821.2. (44); (65); origin of body paint . . . A1595.+. (17); resuscitation from fragments of body E35. (33); sham cure by pretended extracting . . . from patient's body K1871.2. (33); shaman concealed in body . . . F1034.+. (54), (55); soul appears like the body it left . . . E722.1.+. (47); victim speaks from swallower's body F915. (40).

BOIL. — Ocean boils F932.7.+. (1).

BORN. — All new-born male children slaughtered S302.1. (33).

BOY as helper N832. (62); cut in two . . . T589.2. (18). — Clever boy J1113. (45); wife . . . gives birth to boy A592.2.1.+. (18).

BOYS. — Ogre seeks firewood to roast boys E257.+. (18).

BREAD. — Man to earn bread . . . A1346. (11); (15).

BREAKING. — Curse . . . for breaking tabu C987. (28); death by being swallowed for breaking tabu C929.5. (60); death of wife for breaking tabu C920.2. (30); good luck by breaking . . . egg N131.+. (31).

BREAST. — Murder by biting off breast S100.+. (33).

BRIDE purchased T52. (17). — Quest for bride H1381.3.1. (17).

BRIDGE. — Animals serve as bridge . . . B555. (57); extraordinary bridge F842. (59).

BROAD. — Why otter has broad tail A2378.9.+. (65).

BROTHER-sister incest T415. (28); (29); -sister marriage T415.5. (28). — Culture hero argues with his elder brother A525.1.+. (10); (11); (12); (15); (20a); eldest brother as hero Z221. (47); lecherous brother. . . . T415.1. (29); oldest brother alone succeeds . . . H1242.+. (25); rainbow is sun's brother A220.2.+. (4); treacherous younger brother K2211.0.2. (30); youngest brother helps elder L31. (45); youngest brother rescues . . . R155.1. (45).

BROTHER-IN-LAW seduces (seeks to seduce) sister-in-law T425. (30). — Brothers kill . . . brother-in-law S73.1.2.+. (19); sisters-in-law seduce brother-in-law T425.+. (45); slain . . . brother-in-law dismembered S139.2.+. (19); treacherous brother-in-law K2211.1. (19); (25); (46); (47).

BROTHERS . . . eat animal brother-in-law S73.1.2.+. (19); strive to avenge each other P251.3.1. (25). — Cruel brothers S70.+. (19); culture heroes brothers A515.1. (10); (11); (15); (20a); (20b); culture heroes two brothers and a sister A515.1.+. (9); (12); (13); (14); (17); culture heroes two brothers and several sisters A515.1.+. (21); hostile brothers P251.5.3. (30); (63); one sister and two brothers P253.0.2. (9); (12); (13); two brothers as contrasts P251.5.4. (9); (10); (11); (12); (15); (20a); (20b); woman's . . . brothers kill her husband . . . K959.2.1. (19); youngest brother rescues his elder brothers R155.1.(45).

BROTHERS-IN-LAW. — Cruel brothers-in-law S50.+. (25); helpful animal brothers-in-law B314. (19).

BROW. — Man to earn bread by sweat of his brow A1346. (11); (15).

BUILD. — Ghosts build canoe E599.+. (47).

BUNGLING fool J2650. (50).

BURDEN. — Animals carry extraordinary burden F982. (51).

BURN. — Snow magically caused to melt (burn) D2143.6.4. (6); (7).

BURNED. — Ogre burned to death G512.3. (33); victim burned in his own house . . . K812. (33).

BURST. — Monster bursts . . . G304.2.5.+. (33); stream unexpectedly bursts . . . A934.9. (32).

BUSHY. — Why fox has bushy tail A2378.6.1. (65).

CALAMITY. — New race . . . after world calamity A1006.1. (7); (8); preservation . . . during world calamity A1005. (7); (8).

CALL of Magellanic cormorant A2426.2.+. (22). — Animal calls the dawn . . . B755. (56); night-heron's call anounces . . . B147.2.+. (53); person hears call . . . D1827.2. (19).

CAMP. — Fast runners sent through enemy's camp . . . K2350.+. (65).

CANNIBAL ogre G312. (34); tribe G11.18. (58a); (58b). — Children flee from . . . cannibal G31.+. (18); unwitting marriage to cannibal G81. (18).

CANNIBALISM punished Q215. (18).

CANOE. — Ghosts build canoe E599.+. (47).

CAPTOR. — Escape from captor . . . K572. (41); (42).

CAPTURE by deception K700. (23); by decoy K750. (53); through . . . woman K778. (23).

CAPTURED. — Souls of dead captured E752.1.3.+. (47); sun captured R9.1. (1).

CARRIED. — Wife carried up tree . . . J2133.5.1. (30).

CARRY. — Animals carry . . . burden F982. (51); giants carry trees F531.3.10. (33); sea lion carries girl . . . B551.+. (19).

CAST. — Islands from stones cast by hero A955.6.+. (35).

CASTRATE. — Husband castrates paramour K1558.1. (27).

CASTRATION. — Punishment: castration Q451.10.1. (27).

CAUSE. — Formerly great heat . . . causes distress . . . A720.2. (1); (2); (6); moon-woman causes flood A1015.+. (8); object causes magic sleep D1364. (58a); (58b).

CAUSED. — Flood caused by melting of ice . . . A1016.3.(7); snow magically caused to melt (burn) D2143.6.4. (6); (7); topographical features caused by . . . ancestors A901.+. (65); topographical features caused by . . . hero A901. (35).

CAVE as refuge R315. (19).

CAVES. — Giants live in mountains or caves F531.6.2.1. (62).

CEREMONIAL continence T310.1. (17). — Origin of girls' initiation ceremonial A1530.+. (17).

CEREMONIALS. — Origin of social ceremonials A1530. (58b).

CEREMONY. — Magic results produced by religious ceremony D1766. (56).

CHANGE. — Animal characteristics: change . . . A2210.(22); person changes size at will D631.1. (27).

CHANNELS. — Origin of sea channels A920.2. (35).

CHARACTERISTICS. — Animal characteristics as punishment A2230. (25); animal characteristics: change . . . A2210. (22); animal characteristics from battle A2257.+. (65); animal characteristics from duel A2257. (4); animal characteristics from transformation A2260. (65); animal characteristics: imitation . . . A2272. (30); animal characteristics: punishment for greed A2238. (24); animal characteristics: wings A2377. (41); origin of animal characteristics: head A2320. (19).

CHEST. — Giant with face on chest F511.1.+. (62).

CHILD as helper N827. (24); (45); (53); leaves home . . . R228.+. (37); prefers foster father T675.1.+. (62). — Beautiful child . . . P264.+. (45); monstrous (deformed) child exposed S325.0.1. (33); remarkably beautiful child F575.3. (45); retort from underfed servant (child) J1341. (24); (37); (39); the crying child W182. (18).

CHILDBIRTH. — Culture hero establishes customs pertaining to childbirth A545.+. (18); origin of childbirth A1351. (18).

CHILDREN flee from stepmother . . . G31.+. (18); of the sun A736.5. (65). — All . . . children slaughtered S302.1. (33); each likes his own children best T681. (62); father rescues children R153.2.(31); magic power of children D1717. (24); undutiful children P236. (3); woman plans to eat her children G72.1. (18).

CHOOSE. — Adulteress chooses loathly paramour T232.2. (62); wife chooses father's side . . . P211. (23); (55).

CLANDESTINE. — Unknown (clandestine) paramour T475. (27).
CLEVER boy J1113. (45); girl J1111. (61). — Remarkably clever culture heroine A527.+. (9); (13); (14); twin culture heroes—one clever . . . A515.1.1.2. (15).
CLEVERNESS in dealing with the enemy J1681. (65).
CLING. — Why parasites cling to whale's back A2310.+. (54).
COLD. — Flood . . . after great spell of cold A1016.3. (7); magic control of cold . . . D2144. (6).
COLOR of mussel A2411.5.4. (39). — Origin of color of bird A2411.2. (4); (17); (26); origin of color of guanaco A2411.1.+. (44); origin of color of tree-creeper A2411.2.+. (37); person of unusual color F527. (45).
COMBATING. — Means of combating water-spirits . . . F405.+. (64).
COMING of culture hero . . . A513. (9); (13). — Night heron's call announces the coming of visitors B147.2.+. (53).
COMMAND. — Magic results produced by command D1765. (41).
COMMIT. — Man . . . commits crime N360. (4).
COMMON. — Uniting against a common enemy J624. (65).
COMPANIONS. — Extraordinary companions F601. (47).
COMPASSIONATE elder son L13.+. (20a); (20b).
CONCEALED. — Shaman concealed . . . F1034.+. (54); (55).
CONCEPTION. — Unusual conception in old age T538. (45).
CONFEDERATE. — Ghost as confederate . . . E379.4. (47).
CONFLICT. — Forethought in conflict . . . J610. (41).
CONQUER. — Courage conquers all . . . U243. (40); culture hero conquers sea monster A531.4. (34).
CONTEST between magicians D615.1.+. (63); in magic D1719.1. (63. — Decision made by contest H217. (63).
CONTESTS. — Dream contests K66. (63).
CONTINENCE. — Ceremonial continence T310.1. (17).
CONTINENT. — Islands originally form continent . . . A955.11. (35).
CONTINUOUS winter . . . A1040. (6).
CONTRASTS. — Two brothers as contrasts P251.5.4. (9); (10); (11); (12); (15); (20a); (20b).
CONTROL. — Magic control of cold . . . D2144. (6).
CONTROLLED. — Winds controlled . . . D2142. (31).
CONVERSATION. — Husband learns of wife's infidelity through conversation overheard N455.6.+. (31); location . . . learned from . . . conversation N455.9.+. (53); overheard animal conversation N455.+. (51); (52); overheard (human) conversation N455.(38); (65); secrets . . . from . . . conversation N451. (31).
CONVERSE. — Man converses with dead E545.13.(47).

COPULATE. — Why young female guanacos copulate . . . A2496.+. (44).

CORMORANT. — Call of Magellanic cormorant A2426.2.+. (22); why Magellanic cormorant nests on lower ground A2431.+. (22); why tufted cormorant nests . . . A2431.+. (22); why voice of tufted cormorant is hoarse A2423.1.+. (22).

CORMORANTS. — Thirsty cormorants fight . . . B266.1.+. (22); transformation: cormorants to stone D423.+. (35); why cormorants always look back A2471.9.+. (22).

CORPSE. — Other indignities to corpse S139.2.2. (18).

CORPSES. — Why fox . . . eats human corpses A2435.3.+. (18).

COUNTRIES. — Why certain animals are absent from countries A2434.2. (52).

COURAGE conquers all . . . U243. (40).

CRAFTS. — Culture hero teaches . . . crafts A541. (9); (10); (13); (14).

CRAFTSMEN. — Skillful craftsmen F660.+. (13).

CREATION of first man's (woman's) mate A1275. (16); of man A1200. (18).

CREATOR of rivers A930.1. (32); (35).

CRIES of birds A2426.2. (24).

CRIME. — Man . . . commits crime N360. (4); punishment fitted to crime Q580. (24); (30).

CRUEL brothers S70.+. (19); brothers-in-law S50.+. (25); grandfather S42. (39); grandmother S41. (37); persecutions S400. (54); punishments Q450. (19); relative S0. (30); sister-in-law S55. (45); son S21. (20b); stepmother S31. (18); uncle S71. (24).

CRUELTY punished Q285. (18); (24); (46); (54); to pregnant whale S185.+. (66).

CRUSHING. — Murder by crushing S116. (53); murder by crushing head S116.4. (46); (47).

CRUSTACEAN. — Transformation: man to crustacean D100.+. (38); why crustacean swims on its back A2444.+. (38).

CRYING. — The crying child W182. (18).

CUCKOLD. — Husband deceived by adulterous wife K1501. (30); (31); (36); (38).

CULTURE HERO argues . . . A525.1.+. (10); (11); (12); (15); (20a); as . . . hunter A526.2. (1); (11); (40); as magician A527.3. (11); ascends to heaven A566.2. (1); (3); (21); conquers sea monster A531.4. (34); establishes customs A545. (9); (11); (12); (15); establishes customs pertaining to childbirth A545.+. (18); establishes customs pertaining to menstruation A545.+. (17); establishes law and order A530.(9); has . . . attendant A515.4.(3); . . .

overcomes monsters A531. (33); performs . . . feats . . . A526.7. (32); (33); (35); precocious A527.1. (45); swallowed . . . A535. (40); teaches arts . . . A541. (9); (10); (13); (14). — Bird as culture hero A522.2. (32); (33); (34); (35); coming of culture hero . . . A513. (9); (13); culture hero's (demigod's) departure A560. (21); (33); extraordinary weapons of culture hero A524.2. (12); (14); (17); (34); (35); hero (culture hero) as helper N838. (32); (33); (35); miraculous growth of culture hero A511.4.1. (45); origin of fire— culture hero strikes rocks together A1414.3.+. (10); sun as father of culture hero A512.4. (1); wife of culture hero . . . A592.2.1.+. (18).

CULTURE HEROES brothers A515.1.(10); (11); (15); (20a); (20b); two brothers and a sister A515.1.+. (9); (12); (13); (14); (17); two brothers and several sisters A515.1.+. (21). — Father and son as culture heroes A515.2. (1); twin culture heroes . . . A515.1.1.2. (15).

CULTURE HEROINE as leader . . . A520.+. (13). — Remarkably clever culture heroine A527.+. (9); (13); (14).

CURE. — Magic cure of wound D2161.2. (57); sham cure . . . K1871.2. (33); strenuous cure for madness J1434. (47).

CURED. — Baldness magically cured D2161.3.4. (40); madness . . . cured F959.1.(47).

CURES. — Marvelous cures F950. (40).

CURSE by parent M411.1. (28); . . . for breaking tabu C987. (28); given to negate good wish M416. (10); (11); (12). — Transformation through curse D525. (28).

CUSTOM: boasting of sexual prowess P665. (31).

CUSTOMS. — Culture hero establishes customs A545. (9); (11); (12); (15); culture hero establishes customs pertaining to childbirth A545.+. (18); culture hero establishes customs pertaining to menstruation A545.+. (17); mourning customs P681. (4); (34); (37); (40); (41); (55); (57); origin of hunting . . . customs A1520. (9); (11); (12).

CUT. — Boy cut in two . . . T589.2. (18); genitals cut off . . . J1919.5. (50); hands and feet cut off . . . Q451.0.1. (25).

CUTTING. — Victim kills . . . by cutting F912.2. (40).

DANGER. — Escape from . . . danger by deception K500. (18); father feels that son is in danger D1813.0.3. (18).

DARKNESS. — Miraculous darkness as punishment Q552.20.1. (56).

DAUGHTER. — Father and daughter P234. (31); father-daughter incest T411. (33); (44); father . . . seduces daughter T411.1.2. (44); lecherous father. Unnatural father wants to marry his own daughter T411.1. (44); man marries widow and her daughter

T145.0.1.+. (35); mother and daughter P232. (35); treacherous daughter K2214.1. (65).

DAWN. — Animal calls the dawn . . . B755. (56); bird of dawn B34. (56); origin of dawn A1179.2. (56).

DAY produced . . . D2146.1.3. (56).

DAYS. — Great flood lasts two days A1010.2.+. (7).

DEAD mother's . . . return E323. (20b); relative's friendly return E320. (47). — Land of the dead E481.(2); limbs of dead . . . E31. (54); (55); man converses with dead E545.13. (47); return from the dead . . . E361. (20b); souls of dead . . . E752.1.3.+. (47); the dead speak E545. (47).

DEALING. — Cleverness in dealing with the enemy J1681. (65).

DEATH as punishment Q411. (18); (32); (53); as punishment for murder Q411.6. (25); (35); (46); (47); (48); (49); (59); (60); as punishment for treachery Q411.4. (65); by being swallowed for breaking tabu C929.5. (60); . . . by magic D2060. (54); from hearing of son's (sons') death F1041.1.2.2.4. (45); of wife for breaking tabu C920.2. (30). — Deception by feigned death . . . K1860. (4); dupe tricked into jumping to his death K891. (48); escape from death . . . by deception K500. (18); faithfulness . . . in death T211. (40); father feigning death . . . T411.1.2. (44); ogre burned to death G512.3. (33); origin of death A1335. (20a); (20b); seduction by feigned death K1325. (44); soul appears like the body it left at death E722.1.+. (47); wife-stealing punished with death Q252.1. (4); (30).

DEATH-GIVING glance D2061.2.1. (11).

DEATHLIKE sleep D1960.4. (20a).

DECEIVED. — Cuckold. Husband deceived . . . K1501. (30); (31); (36); (38).

DECEIVER falls into own trap K1600. (4).

DECEPTION by feigned death . . . K186.0. (4); by frightening K2320. (45); (65); by pretended lousing K874. (53); by pretending sleep K1868. (26); (31); connected with adultery K1500. (27); in order to meet lover T35.+. (19); into humiliating position K1200. (65); into self-injury K1000. (33); through bluffing K1700. (37). — Capture by deception K700. (23); escape . . . by deception K500. (18); fatal deception into trickster's power K810. (4); (25); killing . . . by deception K800. (19); subordination . . . by deception J421.+. (65).

DECISION made by contest H217. (63).

DECLARATION of love T57. (17).

DECOY. — Capture by decoy K750. (53).

DEFEAT in battle P555. (65).

DEFEATED. — Ogre defeated G500. (61).

DEITY. — Disguise as deity . . . K1828. (65).

DELUGE: escape in boat (ark) A1021. (7). — Escape from deluge on mountain A1022. (7); (8).

DEMONS. — Evil demons set world on fire A1031.3. (2).

DEPARTURE. — Culture hero's (demigod's) departure A560. (21); (33).

DESIGNS. — Origin of body paint: imitation of designs . . . A1595.+. (17).

DESTROY. — Continuous winter destroys the race A1040. (6).

DESTRUCTION. — Loss or destruction of property . . . Q595. (41).

DETECTION of hypocrisy K2060. (41); (65).

DETESTED. — Wife refuses to sleep with detested husband T288. (54).

DEVASTATING monster G346. (33); whale B16.2.+. (54); (55). — Hero overcomes devastating animal G510.4. (34).

DISAPPEARANCE. — Magic disappearance D2188. (24).

DISCOVER. — Husband discovers wife's adultery K1550.1. (27); (30); (31); (36); (38).

DISCUSS. — Birds . . . discuss their journeys B235.+. (51); (52).

DISGUISE as deity . . . K1828. (65); by painting body K1821.2. (44); (65); by veiling face K1821.3. (65). — Father . . . returns in disguise .. . T411.1.2. (44); seduction by disguise . . . K1310. (44).

DISINTEGRATION: man eats himself . . . F1035. (58b).

DISMEMBER. — Disintegration: man . . . dismembers himself F1035. (58b).

DISMEMBERED. — Slain sea lion brother-in-law dismembered S139.2.+. (19).

DISOBEDIENCE W126. (60).

DISOBEDIENT wife punished T254.6. (57).

DISRESPECT punished Q395. (55); (56). — Tabu: showing disrespect . . . C170.+. (55).

DISSATISFACTION W128. (41); (43).

DISTANCE. — Person hears call . . . from great distance D1827.2. (19).

DISTRESS. — Formerly great heat . . . causes distress . . . A720.2. (1); (2); (6).

DIVISION. — Beginning of division of labor A1472. (65).

DOG. — Enmity between dog and otter A2494.4.+. (25).

DOLPHIN. — Why dolphin has high dorsal fin A2350.+. (55).

DORSAL FIN. — Why dolphin has high dorsal fin A2350.+. (55).

DRAG. — Water-spirit drags women . . . F420.5.2.1.5.+. (42).

DREAM about a marriage . . . T11.3.2. (50); contests K66. (63). — Fight in dream . . . F1068.2.2. (63); wisdom . . . from dream J157. (66).

DRINK. — Lover refuses . . . drink T24.6. (44); permission refused to drink from lagoon W155.5.+. (32); permission refused to drink from water tank W155.5. (22).

DROWNING. — Murder by drowning K958. (39); murder by drowning S131. (45); punishment by drowning Q467. (39).

DRY. — Rivers . . . made dry D2151.2.3. (18); sun dries out earth . . . A733.5. (1).

DUCKS. — Haunts of ducks A2433.4.+. (40); transformation: women to ducks D161.3.+. (65).

DUEL — Animal characteristics from duel A2257. (4).

DUPE induced to look about . . . K832. (39); (46); tricked into jumping . . . K891. (48); tricked into killing himself K890. (49); (50).

DUTY. — Filial duty Q65.+. (4).

DYING. — Wise words of dying father J154. (44).

EARN — Man to earn bread . . . A1346. (11); (15).

EARTH restored . . . A1036.+. (2). — Escape by hiding in the earth K515.6. (33); inhabitant of upper world visits earth F30. (2); sun as man who left earth A711. (1); (3); (65); sun dries out earth . . . A733.5. (1).

EAT. — Brothers . . . eat animal brother-in-law S73.1.2.+. (19); disintegration: man eats himself . . . F1035. (58b); evil spirit . . . eats person F402.1.11.2. (60); revenants eat E541. (47); why fox . . . eats . . . A2435.3.+. (18); wife eats flesh . . . P214.+. (19); woman plans to eat her children G72.1. (18).

EATEN. — Excrements . . . eaten J1772.9. (47); punishment: being eaten . . . Q415. (30); relative's flesh eaten . . . G61. (19); resuscitated eaten animal E32. (54); (55).

EATING. — Man-eating fish B16.2.+. (57); transformation: man-eating sea lion to stone D429.2.2.1.+. (34).

EDGE. — Woman leads pursuers to edge . . . K893.1.+. (61).

EGG. — Good luck by breaking bird's egg N131.+. (31).

ELDER. — Compassionate elder son L13.+. (20a); (20b); culture hero argues with his elder brother A525.1.+. (10); (11); (12); (15); (20a); youngest brother helps elder L31. (45); youngest brother rescues his elder brothers R155.1. (45).

ELDEST brother as hero Z221. (47).

ENDOWED. — Sun endowed with wisdom . . . A738.2.2. (65).

ENEMY. — Avoiding enemy's revenge J647. (65); cleverness in dealing with the enemy J1681. (65); escaping before enemy can strike J641. (18); fast runners sent through enemy's camp . . . K2350.+. (65); generosity toward enemy W11.5. (65); prevention . . . by inspiring fear in enemy J623. (65); transformation to kill enemy D651.1. (30); uniting against a common enemy J624. (65).

ENIGMATIC statements H580. (65).

ENMITY between dog and otter A2494.4.+. (25). — Why there is enmity between certain animals and man A2585. (25).

ENTERTAIN. — Adulteress . . . entertains lover K1514. (36); (38).

ESCAPE . . . by deception K500. (18); by hiding K515. (54); (65); by hiding in the earth K515.6. (33); from captor . . . K572. (41); (42); from deluge on mountain A1022. (7); (8); from prison R211. (47). — Deluge: escape in boat (ark) A1021. (7).

ESCAPES R210. (23); (57); by magic D2165. (64).

ESCAPING before enemy can strike J641. (18).

ESTABLISH. — Culture hero establishes customs A545. (9); (11); (12); (15); culture hero establishes customs pertaining to childbirth A545.+. (18); culture hero establishes customs pertaining to menstruation A545.+. (17); culture hero establishes law and order A530. (9); survivors . . . establish homes A1029.6. (7).

EVIL demons set world on fire A1031.3. (2); spirit kills . . . F402.1.11.2. (60). — Hero kills . . . evil strong men G512.0.1. (33); sun as evil tyrant . . . A738.2.+. (1).

EXCELLENT. — Sun is excellent hunter A738.+. (65).

EXCESSIVE. — Wounding self because of excessive grief F1041.21.6.1. (5).

EXCREMENTS thought to be meat . . . J1772.9. (47).

EXCUSE. — Adulteress makes excuse . . . K1514.18. (36).

EXOGAMY T131.5. (41).

EXPERIENCES. — Topographical features caused by experiences of ancestors A901.+. (65); topographical features caused by experiences of . . . hero A901. (35).

EXPOSED. — Monstrous (deformed) child exposed S325.0.1. (33).

EXTRACTING. — Sham cure by pretended extracting . . . K1871.2. (33).

EXTRAORDINARY behavior of fire F964. (52); behavior of sun F961.1. (1); (2); behavior of wind F963. (45); boat (ship) F841. (23); bridge F842. (59); companions F601. (47); fire F882. (52); food F851. (24); (41); (43); growth . . . F983. (55); perception . . . F655. (62); sling F830.+. (4); thunder . . . F968. (58a); weapons of culture hero A524.2. (12); (14); (17); (34); (35). — Animals carry extraordinary burden F982. (51); hunt for extraordinary . . . animal F989.15. (40); recognition by extraordinary prowess H32. (40).

EYE. — Giant with one eye . . . F531.1.1.1. (62); magic eye D993. (20a).

EYES. — Stone man's eyes . . . like foreigner's G630.+. (33); why falcon has red eyes A2332.5.+. (31).

FACE. — Disguise by veiling face K1821.3. (65); giant with face on chest F511.1.+. (62).

FAITHFUL wife T210.1. (35). — Culture hero has faithful attendant A515.4. (3).

FAITHFULNESS to marriage . . . T211. (40).

FAITHLESS. — Generosity toward faithless wife W11.+. (31); the faithless widow T231. (19); (40).

FAITHLESSNESS in marriage T230. (4); (30); (31).

FALCON. — Marriage of falcon . . . B670.+. (31); transformation: man to falcon D152.4.+. (30); why falcon has red eyes A2332.5.+. (31).

FALL. — Deceiver falls into own trap K1600. (4); woman leads pursuers to edge of thin ice . . . ; they fall through K893.1.+. (61).

FALSE. — Victim lured . . . by false token K839.2. (25).

FAMILY. — The sun-god and his family A220.2. (1); (3).

FAMINE F969.7. (66).

FAST runners sent . . . K2350.+. (65).

FATAL deception into trickster's power K810. (4); (25); imitation J2401. (49); (50).

FATHER and daughter P234. (31); and son P233. (1); (4); (53); and son as culture heroes A515.2. (1); avenges son P233.6.+. (54); -daughter incest T411. (33); (44); feels that son is in danger D1813.0.3. (18); feigning death . . . T411.1.2. (44); rescues children R153.2. (31); rescues son(s) R153.3. (53). — Foster father reveals fact that son is offspring of supernatural father P231.5.+. (62); lecherous father . . . T411.1. (44); son avenges father P233.6. (48); (49); sun as father of culture hero A512.4. (1); sun-father A221. (3); unexpected meeting of father and son N731. (62); why . . . guanacos copulate with their father A2496.+. (44); wife chooses father's side . . . P211. (23); (55); wise words of dying father J154. (44); woman's father and brothers kill her husband . . . K959.2.1. (19).

FATHER-IN-LAW. — Son-in-law supports father-in-law P265.+. (43); tabu: showing disrespect for father-in-law C170.+. (55).

FEAR. — Prevention . . . by inspiring fear . . . J623. (65); wise fear of the weak . . . J613. (65).

FEATS. — Culture hero performs . . . feats . . . A526.7. (32); (33); (35); quest to recover one's honor through feats H1223.1. (23); (25).

FEATURES. — Ogres with monstrous features G360. (62); topographical features caused by . . . ancestors A901.+. (65); topographical features caused by . . . hero A901. (35).

FEEL. — Father feels that son is in danger D1813.0.3. (18).

FEET. — Hands and feet cut off . . . Q451.0.1. (25).

FEIGNED. — Deception by feigned death . . . K1860. (4); seduction by feigned death K1325. (44).

FEIGNING. — Father feigning death . . . T411.1.2. (44).

FEMALE. — Origin of female sex organs A1313.2. (16); why young female guanacos copulate . . . A2496.+. (44).

FEUD. — Wife chooses father's side in feud. . . . P211. (23); (55).

FIDELITY. — Oft-proved fidelity T320.1. (35); reward for wife's fidelity Q83.1. (40).

FIGHT in dream . . . F1068.2.2. (63). — Thirsty animals fight . . . B266.1.+. (32); thirsty cormorants fight . . . B266.1.+. (22).

FIGHTER. — Weak . . . hero overcomes . . . fighter L311. (32); (33); (34); (35); (61).

FILIAL duty Q65.+. (4).

FIN. — Why dolphin has high dorsal fin A2350.+. (55).

FIRE. — Earth restored after world-fire A1036.+. (2); evil demons set world on fire A1031.3. (2); extraordinary behavior of fire F964. (52); extraordinary fire F882. (52); men hide from world-fire A1038.+. (2); origin of fire—culture hero strikes rocks together A1414.3.+. (10); theft of fire A1415. (52); world-fire A1030. (1); (2).

FIREWOOD. — Ogre seeks firewood . . . E257.+. (18).

FIRST. — Creation of first man's (woman's) mate A1275. (16).

FISH. — Giant fish B874. (40); helpful fish B470. (57); Jonah. Fish . . . swallows a man F911.4. (40); man-eating fish B16.2.+. (57); markings on fish A2412.4. (65); transformation: man to fish D170. (19).

FISHERMAN. — Mighty fisherman F634. (37); (48).

FISHING. — Origin of . . . fishing customs A1520. (9); (11); (12).

FITTED. — Punishment fitted to crime Q580. (24); (30).

FITTING. — Transformation . . . as fitting punishment Q584.2. (27); (29).

FLAT. — Why gerfalcon's head is flat A2320.+. (35).

FLATTERY. — Escape . . . by means of flattery K572. (41); (42).

FLEE. — Children flee from stepmother . . . G31.+. (18); wife flees from husband R227. (31).

FLESH. — Relative's flesh eaten . . . G61. (19); wife eats flesh . . . P214.+. (19).

FLIGHT from hated husband R227.2. (41); (42). — Magic flight D670. (18); omens from flight of birds D1812.5.0.2. (40); (55); reversed obstacle flight. . . . D673. (31).

FLIGHTS R220. (57); (58a); (58b).

FLOCK. — Why certain birds flock together A2492.+. (33).

FLOOD as punishment A1018. (8); brought as revenge for injury A1018.3. (6); (7); (8); caused by melting of ice . . . A1016.3. (7). — Great flood . . . A1010.2.+. (7); indentations . . . from primeval flood A900.+. (7); moon-woman causes flood A1015.+. (8); survivors of flood . . . A1029.6. (7).

FLY. — Ghost flies E599.5.+. (47).

FOOD tabu during menses C140.+. (60). — Animals provide food . . . B531. (51); child leaves home because grandmother is stingy with food R228.+. (37); extraordinary food F851. (24); (41); (43); forethought in provision for food J710. (45); grandfather hides food . . . S20.2.+. (39); kindness unwise when it imperils one's food supply J715. (32); lover refuses food . . . T24.6. (44); women induce owners to give up food K330.+. (17).

FOOL. — Bungling fool J2650. (50).

FOOLISH boasts . . . J2353.1. (53). — Twin culture heroes—one foolish . . . A515.1.1.2. (15).

FOOT. — Recognition by foot H79.+. (45).

FOREHEAD. — Giant with one eye in middle of forehead F531.1.1.1. (62).

FOREIGNER. — Stone man's eyes . . . like foreigner's G630.+. (33).

FORETHOUGHT in conflict . . . J610. (41); in provision . . . J710. (45).

FORM. — Islands originally form continent . . . A955.11. (35); marriage to bird in human form B652. (17); (18); (23); marriage to fox in human form B651.1. (18).

FORMED. — Rivers formed . . . A934.2. (35).

FORMER intercourse by navel A1352.3. (16).

FORMERLY great heat of sun . . . A720.2. (1); (2); (6).

FOSTER FATHER reveals fact . . . P231.5.+. (62). — Child prefers foster father T675.1.+. (62).

FOUND. — Remedy . . . found by spying . . . N452.1.+. (22).

FOX. — Marriage to fox . . . B651.1. (18); why fox . . . eats human corpses A2435.3.+. (18); why fox has bushy tail A2378.6.1. (65).

FRAGMENTS. — Resuscitation from fragments . . . E35. (33).

FRATRICIDE S73.1. (63); motivated by love-jealousy S73.1.4. (30).

FRIENDLY. — Dead mother's friendly return E323. (20b); dead relative's friendly return E320. (47).

FRIENDSHIP. — Hypocrite pretends friendship . . . K2010. (19); (23).

FRIGHTENING. — Deception by frightening K2320. (45); (65).

FRIGHTFUL meal S183. (19); (24); (47); (54); (58a).

FUGITIVE has magic wind . . . R236.4. (31). — . . . Magic obstacles raised in front of fugitive D673. (31).

FUGITIVES aided by . . . animal R243. (57).

FURIOUS battle F1084. (65).

FUTURE revealed . . . D1812.4. (19).

GAME. — Ball game in lower world E494. (2).

GATHER. — Fast runners sent . . . to gather information K2350.+.
   (65).
GENEROSITY W11. (24); (38); (41); toward enemy W11.5. (65);
   toward faithless wife W11.+. (31).
GENITALS cut off . . . J1919.5. (50).
GERFALCON. — Why gerfalcon's head is flat A2320.+. (35).
GHOST as confederate . . . E379.4. (47); flies E599.5.+. (47);
   summoned . . . E381. (20b). — Walking ghost . . . E440.(20b).
GHOSTS build canoe E599.+. (47); go hunting E599.+. (47).
GIANT fish B874. (40); responsible . . . A977.1. (33); sea lion B871.2.+.
   (19); with face on chest F511.1.+. (62); with one eye . . . F531.1.1.1.
   (62). — One-armed giant F531.1.6.7. (62); one-legged giant
   F531.1.3.3.1. (62); trees pulled up by giant F621.2. (33).
GIANTS carry trees F531.3.10. (33); live in mountains . . . F531.6.2.1.
   (62). — Stone giants G371. (33).
GIGGLE. — Why guanaco giggles A2425.+. (44).
GIRL tricked into man's room . . . K1330. (29). — Clever girl J1111.
   (61); girl's animal lover slain . . . B610.1. (19); sea lion carries girl
   . . . B551.+. (19).
GIRLS. — Origin of girls' initiation ceremonial A1530.+. (17).
GIVE UP. — Women induce owners to give up food K330.+. (17).
GLACIERS. — Origin of glaciers A990.+. (6).
GLANCE. — Death-giving glance D2061.2.1. (11).
GOD. — The sun-god and his family A220.2. (1); (3).
GODDESS. — Moon-goddess A240.1. (8).
GODS teach people . . . A1404. (9). — Two sun-gods A227. (1).
GOING. — Tabu: going forth during menses C141. (17).
GOOD luck by breaking . . . egg N131.+. (31). — Curse . . . to negate
   good wish M416. (10); (11); (12).
GRADUAL transformation D681. (30).
GRANDFATHER P291. (53); hides food . . . S20.2.+. (39). — Cruel
   grandfather S42. (39).
GRANDMOTHER. — Child leaves home because grandmother is
   stingy . . . R228.+. (37); cruel grandmother S41. (37).
GRANDSONS. — Grandfather hides food from starving grandsons
   S20.2.+. (39).
GRATITUDE W27. (13); (14).
GREAT. — Humility of the great J910. (13).
GREED. — Animal characteristics: punishment for greed A2238. (24).
GRIEF. — Wounding self because of excessive grief F1041.21.6.1. (5).
GROUND. — Why Magellanic cormorant nests on lower ground
   A2431.+. (22); why tufted cormorant nests on high ground
   A2431.+. (22).

GROUPS. — Origin of groups of stones A977. (58a); (59); (65); war between groups of birds B263.5. (22).

GROWTH. — Extraordinary growth . . . F983. (55); miraculous growth of culture hero A511.4.1. (45); supernatural growth T615. (27); (62).

GUANACO. — Origin of color of guanaco A2411.1.+. (44); why guanaco giggles A2425.+. (44).

GUANACOS. — Why young female guanacos copulate . . . A2496.+. (44).

GUARDIAN. — Means of hoodwinking the guardian . . . K330. (41).

GULLIBLE husbands J2301. (41).

HALF. — Boy cut in two. Each half becomes a boy T589.2. (18).

HANDS and feet cut off . . . Q451.0.1. (25).

HANDSOME man F575.2. (3); (4); (5); (57).

HAPPINESS. — "Idleness begets woe; work brings happiness" J21.50. (10); (11); (12); (15).

HARDNESS of heart W155. (32); (66). — Man unable to weep for hardness of heart W155.3. (20b).

HARPOON. — Magic harpoon D1080.+. (12); self-returning harpoon D1602.6.+. (12).

HARPOONPOINT. — Origin of harpoonpoint A1459.1.+. (14).

HATED. — Fligt from hated husband R227.2. (41); (42); sun . . . hated by people A738.2.+. (1).

HAUNTS of ducks A2433.4.+. (40).

HEAD. — Murder by crushing head S116.4. (46); (47); origin of animal characteristics: head A2320. (19); why gerfalcon's head is flat A2320.+. (35); why woodpecker has red head A2412.2.+. (28); (29).

HEADLESS ogre G361.3. (62).

HEAR. — Person hears call . . . D1827.2. (19).

HEARING. — Death from hearing of son's (sons') death F1041.1.2.2.4. (45).

HEART. — Hardness of heart W155. (32); (66); man unable to weep for hardness of heart W155.3. (20b).

HEAT. — Formerly great heat of sun . . . A720.2. (1); (2); (6); magic control of . . . heat D2144. (6); monster bursts from heat G304.2.5.+. (33); sun dries out earth with its heat A733.5. (1).

HEAVEN. — Culture hero ascends to heaven A566.2. (1); (3); (21).

HEAVY. — Object magically becomes heavy D1687. (24).

HEEL. — Achilles heel. . . . Z311. (33).

HELD BACK. — Ship held back . . . D2072.0.3. (31).

HELP. — Person hears call for help . . . D1827.2. (19); youngest brother helps elder L31. (45).

HOT. — Murder by introducing hot stone . . . S112.+. (35); murder with hot stone S112.2.+. (35); (57); sun originally so hot . . . A727.1. (1).

HOUSE. — Victim burned in his own house . . . K812. (33); victim lured into house and killed K811. (53); (58a); victims lured into house and wounded K811.+. (61).

HUMAN helpers N820. (34); offspring . . . B631. (19); sacrifice S260.1. (60). — Birds with human traits B200.+. (51); (52); marriage to bird in human form B652. (17); (18); (23); marriage to fox in human form B651.1. (18); ogre keeps human prisoners G334. (33); overheard (human) conversation N455. (38); (65); sun as human being A736. (1); (3); why fox . . . eats human corpses A2435.3.+. (18).

HUMILIATED . . . lovers K1210. (54).

HUMILIATING punishments Q470. (38). — Deception into humiliating position K1200. (65).

HUMILITY of the great J910. (13).

HUMMINGBIRD. — Helpful hummingbird B450.+. (32); (33); (34); (35).

HUMOR of ugliness X137. (23).

HUNT for extraordinary . . . animal F989.15. (40). — Treacherous murder during hunt K917. (47).

HUNTER. — Culture hero as mighty hunter A526.2. (1); (11); (40); skillful hunter F679.5. (17); (24); (38); (40); (45); (65); sun is excellent hunter A738.+. (65).

HUNTING. — Animal's occupation: hunting A2452. (51); ghosts go hunting E599.+. (47); origin of hunting . . . customs A1520. (9); (11); (12).

HUSBAND castrates paramour K1558.1. (27); discovers wife's adultery K1550.1. (27); (30); (31); (36); (38); kills returning adulteress Q411.0.1. (57); kills surprised paramour K1569.9. (38); kills wife and paramour Q411.0.2. (36); learns of wife's infidelity . . . N455.6.+. (31); outwits adulteress . . . K1550. (38); spies on adulteress . . . K1551.+. (36); surprises wife . . . K1569.2. (36). — Adulteress gets rid of husband . . . K1514. (36); (38); adulteress outwits husband K1510. (41); (42); cuckold. Husband deceived . . . K1501. (30); (31); (36); (38); flight from hated husband R227.2. (41); (42); jealous wife or husband T257. (30); (64); paramour . . . hidden from husband K1521. (27); (38); wife carried . . . in bag in husband's teeth J2133.5.1. (30); wife chooses father's side . . . Must choose between husband and father P211. (23); (55); wife eats flesh of . . . husband P214.+. (19); wife flees from husband R227. (31);

wife refuses to sleep with . . . husband T288. (54); wife sold . . .
by husband T292. (17); woman's . . . brothers kill her husband
. . . K959.2.1. (19).

HUSBANDS. — Gullible husbands J2301. (41).

HYPOCRISY. — Detection of hypocrisy K2060. (41); (65).

HYPOCRITE pretends friendship . . . K2010. (19); (23).

HYPOCRITICAL. — The hypocritical wife T263. (41).

ICE produced . . . D2144.5.1. (6); (7). — Flood caused by melting of
ice . . . A1016.3. (7); woman leads pursuers to edge of thin ice . . .
K893.1. +. (61).

IDENTIFICATION by tokens . . . H88. (54).

IDENTITY. — Tabu: revealing identity of certain person C422. (65).

"IDLENESS begets woe . . ." J21.50. (10); (11); (12); (15).

IGNORANCE. — Genitals cut off through ignorance J1919.5. (50).

IMITATION. — Animal characteristics: imitation . . . A2272. (30);
fatal imitation J2401. (49); (50); origin of body paint: imitation . . .
A1595. +. (17); transformation to animal by imitation D599. +.
(30).

IMMODERATELY. — Beautiful child immoderately loved . . .
P264. +. (45).

IMPALING as punishment . . . Q461.3. (36); (38); (48); (49).

IMPERIL. — Kindness unwise when it imperils one's food supply J715.
(32).

IMPOSSIBLE. — Courage conquers all and impossible is made possible
U243. (40).

IMPOUNDED water A1111. (32).

INAPPROPRIATE action from misunderstanding J1820. (26).

INATTENTION to warnings J652. (28); (30); (31).

INCEST punished Q242. (27); (28); (29); (30). — Brother-sister incest
T415. (28); (29); father-daughter incest T411. (33); (44); mother-
son incest T412. (26); (27); tabu: incest C114. (17); (26); (27); (28);
(29); (30).

INDELIBLE mark D1654.3.1. (7).

INDENTATIONS on mountain top . . . A900. +. (7).

INDIGNITIES. — Other indignities to corpse S139.2.2. (18).

INDUCE. — Women induce owners . . . K330. +. (17).

INDUCED. — Dupe induced to look about . . . K832. (39); (46); magic
sleep induced by shaman D1964.4. +. (58a); (58b).

INFIDELITY. — Husband learns of wife's infidelity . . . N455.6. +.
(31).

INFORMATION. — Fast runners sent . . . to gather information
K2350. +. (65).

INHABIT. — Animals that inhabit water A2433.2.2. (65).

INHABITANT of upper world . . . F30. (2).

INITIATION. — Origin of girls' initiation ceremonial A1530.+. (17).

INJURY. — Death or bodily injury . . . D2060. (54); deception into self-injury K1000. (33); flood brought as revenge for injury A1018.3. (6); (7); (8).

INSOLENCE W187. (55).

INSPIRING. — Prevention . . . by inspiring fear . . . J623. (65).

INTENDED. — Ambushed trickster killed by intended victim K1641. (25); (46); (47).

INTERCOURSE. — Former intercourse by navel A1352.3. (16); origin of sexual intercourse A1352. (16); transformation by sexual intercourse D565.5.1. (26).

INTRODUCING. — Murder by introducing hot stone . . . S112.+. (35).

INTRUDERS. — Ogre attacks intruders G475. (34).

INVULNERABILITY. — Achilles heel. Invulnerability . . . Z311. (33); magic invulnerability of ogres D1840.3. (33).

ISLAND. — Abandonment on an island S145. (23); (53).

ISLANDS from stones . . . A955.6.+. (35); originally form continent . . . A955.11. (35).

JEALOUS wife or husband T257. (30); (64).

JEALOUSY W181. (17); (45). — Fratricide motivated by love-jealousy S73.1.4. (30).

JONAH. Fish . . . swallows a man F911.4. (40).

JOURNEY. — Magic journey D2121. (24); sun's night journey. . . . A722.+. (3).

JOURNEYS. — Birds . . . discuss their journeys B235.+. (51); (52).

JUMPING. — Dupe tricked into jumping . . . K891. (48).

KILL. — Animal kills ogre G512.9. (34); brothers kill . . . brother-in-law S73.1.2.+. (19); evil spirit kills . . . F402.1.11.2. (60); hero kills . . . strong men G512.0.1. (33); husband kills returning adulteress Q411.0.1. (57); husband kills surprised paramour K1569.9. (38); husband kills wife and paramour Q411.0.2. (36); man . . . kills wife's lover Q411.0.1.2. (38); ogre kills men . . . G477. (33); transformation to kill enemy D651.1. (30); victim kills swallower . . . F912.2. (40); woman's . . . brothers kill her husband . . . K959.2.1. (19).

KILLED. — Ambushed trickster killed . . . K1641. (25); (46); (47); animal (monster) killed from within K952. (40); dupe . . . seized and killed K832. (39); (46); men lured into trap . . . and killed K912.2.+. (25); (46); (47); rival in love killed T92.10 (48); (49);

(50); victim . . . approaches trickser and is killed K815. (25); (46); victim lured into house and killed K811. (53); (58a).

KILLING . . . by deception K800. (19). — Dupe tricked into killing himself K890. (49); (50).

KIND and unkind Q2. (20a); (20b). — Victim lured by kind words . . . K815. (25); (46).

KINDNESS W10. (31); unwise . . . J715. (32).

KNOW. — Gods teach people all they know A1404. (9).

KNOWLEDGE. — Future revealed by presentiment: "knowledge within" D1812.4. (19); magic knowledge of magician D1810.0.2. (66); wisdom (knowledge) from dream J157. (66).

LABOR. — Beginning of division of labor A1472. (65).

LACK. — Remedy for lack of water . . . N452.1.+. (22).

LAGOON. — Permission refused to drink from lagoon W155.5.+. (32).

LAID. — Walking ghost "laid" E440. (20b).

LAKES. — Magic stone makes rivers and lakes D1486.1. (35).

LAND of plenty F701. (24); of the dead E481. (2).

LARGE. — Weak . . . hero overcomes large fighter L311. (32); (33); (34); (35); (61).

LARGER. — Penis becomes larger D489.+. (17).

LAST. — Great flood lasts . . . A1010.2.+. (7).

LAW. — Culture hero establishes law and order A530. (9).

LEAD. — Woman leads pursuers . . . K893.1.+. (61).

LEADER. — Culture heroine as leader . . . A520.+. (13); sun as benevolent leader A738.2.+. (3).

LEARN. — Husband learns of wife's infidelity . . . N455.6.+. (31).

LEARNED. — Location of sought man learned . . . N455.9.+. (53); secret learned N440.+. (27); (28); (34); (41); (45); (62); valuable secrets learned N440. (3); (4); (32); (65).

LEAVE. — Child leaves home . . . R228.+. (37); ogres leave signs . . . G310.+. (62).

LECHEROUS brother. . . . T415.1. (29); father. Unnatural father wants to marry his own daughter T411.1. (44); son T410.+. (26).

LEFT. — Identification by tokens left as trail H88. (54); soul appears like the body it left . . . E722.1.+. (47); sun as man who left earth A711. (1); (3); (65).

LEGS. — Why otter has short legs A2371.+. (25).

LEVELING. — Magic leveling . . . D2152.1. (24).

LIFE. — Person comes to life E1. (20a); (20b); preservation of life . . . A1005. (7); (8); sun . . . threatens all life A727.1. (1); transformation: statue comes to life D435.1.1. (33).

LIGHTNING. — Extraordinary . . . lightning F968. (58a).

LIKE. — Each likes his own children best T681. (62); unusual murder avenged in like manner Q581.1. (46); (47).

LIMBS of dead . . . E31. (54); (55).

LIVE. — Giants live in mountains . . . F531.6.2.1. (62); why tribe lives in certain place A1620.+. (65).

LOATHLY. — Adulteress chooses loathly paramour T232.2. (62).

LOCATION of sought man . . . N455.9.+. (53).

LONG penis F547.3.1. (17); (27). — Recognition by long penis H79.+. (27).

LOOK. — Dupe induced to look about . . . K832. (39); (46); why cormorants always look back A2471.9.+. (22).

LOSS of magic sight D1822. (20a); . . . of property . . . Q595. (41).

LOST. Magic powers lost D1741. (11); quest for lost persons H1385. (37).

LOUDEST mourners not greatest sorrowers J261. (47).

LOUSING. — Deception by pretended lousing K874. (53).

LOVE-sickness T24.1 (44). — Declaration of love T57. (17); fratricide motivated by love-jealousy S73.1.4. (30); madness from love T24.3. (45); mother-love P231.3. (5); (26); (45); rival in love killed T92.10. (48); (49); (50); rivals in love T92. (17); (45); woman avenges scorned love T71.2. (45).

LOVED. — Beautiful child . . . loved . . . P264.+. (45).

LOVER refuses food . . . T24.6. (44). — Adulteress . . . entertains lover K1514. (36); (38); adulteress . . . meets lover K1514.18. (36); deception in order to meet lover T35.+. (19); girl's animal lover slain . . . B610.1. (19); husband spies on . . . lover K1551.+. (36); man . . . kills wife's lover Q411.0.1.2. (38); the scorned lover T70. (35); (61).

LOVERS. — Humiliated or baffled lovers K1210. (54); lovers' rendezvous T35. (28); (36); (38); lovers' signal T41.3. (19).

LOWER. — Ball game in lower world E494. (2); why Magellanic cormorant nests on lower ground A2431.+. (22).

LOYALTY W34. (53); (54); rewarded Q72. (54).

LUCK. — Good luck by breaking . . . egg N131.+. (31).

LURE. — Water-spirits lure mortal . . . F420.5.2.1. (59).

LURED. — Men lured into trap . . . K912.2.+. (25); (46); (47); victim lured by kind words . . . K815. (25); (46); victim lured into approach . . . K839.2. (25); victim lured into house and killed K811. (53); (58a); victims lured into house and wounded K811.+. (61).

MADNESS from love T24.3. (45); miraculously cured F959.1. (47). — Strenuous cure for madness J1434. (47).

MAGELLANIC CORMORANT. — Call of Magellanic cormorant A2426.2.+. (22); why Magellanic cormorant nests on lower ground A2431.+. (22).

MAGIC adhesion . . . Q551.2.1.+. (54); (55); animal proof . . . D1841.5.2. (40); bird B172. (6); (7); (51); (52); control of cold . . . D2144. (6); cure of wound D2161.2. (57); disappearance D2188. (24); eye D993. (20a); flight D670. (18); harpoon D1080.+. (12); invulnerability of ogres D1840.3. (33); journey D2121. (24); knowledge of magician D1810.0.2. (66); leveling . . . D2152.1. (24); mountain D932. (24); mud . . . D1486.1.+. (32); multiplication . . . D2106. (55); murder D2061. (55); power of children D1717. (24); powers lost D1741. (11); results produced by command D1765. (41); results produced by religious ceremony D1766. (56); singing D2173. (56); sleep induced . . . D1964.4.+. (58a); (58b); sling D1087. (34); (35); stone makes rivers . . . D1486.1. (35); storm produced . . . D2141.0.11. (6); (7); strength D1830. (24); suspension of weight D1691. (24); whale B175.+. (54); (55). — Contest in magic D1719.1. (63); day produced by magic D2146.1.3. (56); death . . . by magic D2060. (54); escapes by magic D2165. (64); fugitive has magic wind . . . R236.4. (31); hunt for extraordinary (magic) animal F989.15. (40); ice produced by magic D2144.5.1. (6); (7); loss of magic sight D1822. (20a); night produced by magic D2146.2.1. (56); object causes magic sleep D1364. (58a); (58b); resuscitation by magic E50. (20a); reversed obstacle flight. Magic obstacles raised . . . D673. (31); ship held back by magic D2072.0.3. (31); snow produced by magic D2143.6.3. (6); (7); sympathetic magic D1782. (45); winds controlled . . . D2142. (31).

MAGICALLY. — Baldness magically cured D2161.3.4. (40); object magically becomes heavy D1687. (24); rivers magically made dry D2151.2.3. (18); snow magically caused to melt (burn) D2143.6.4. (6); (7); thunderbolt magically produced D2149.1. (58a); winter magically produced D2145.1. (6); (7).

MAGICIAN D1711. (66); as helper N845. (66). — Advice from magician (fortune-teller, etc.) D1814.1. (66); culture hero as magician A527.3. (11); magic knowledge of magician D1810.0.2. (66); rainbow as magician D1711.+. (4).

MAGICIANS. — Contest between magicians D615.1.+. (63).

MAIMING. — Killing or maiming by deception K800. (19).

MALE. — All new-born male children slaughtered S302.1. (33).

MALEVOLENT water-spirits F420.5.2. (59).

MAN . . . commits crime N360. (4); converses with dead E545.13. (47); . . . kills wife's lover Q411.0.1.2. (38); marries widow . . . T145.0.1.+. (35); scorned by his beloved T75. (17); (54); to earn bread . . . A1346. (11); (15); unable to weep . . . W155.3. (20b). — A man undertakes to do his wife's work J2431. (36); animal saves man from pursuer B523. (57); animal takes revenge on man B299.1. (6); (7); (23); creation of first man's (woman's) mate A1275. (16); creation of man A1200. (18); disintegration: man eats himself . . . F1035. (58b); foolish boasts get man into trouble J2353.1. (53); ghost as confederate of man E379.4. (47); girl tricked into man's room . . . K1330. (29); handsome man F575.2. (3); (4); (5); (57); Jonah. Fish . . . swallows a man F911.4. (40); location of sought man . . . N455.9.+. (53); marooned man reaches home . . . K1616. (23); (53); punishment for man who makes advances . . . Q242.3. (30); stone man's eyes . . . like foreigner's G630.+. (33); sun and moon as man and woman A736.1. (65); sun as man who left earth A711. (1); (3); (65); transformation: man to bird D150. (26); (33); (36); (37); transformation: man to crustacean D100.+. (38); transformation: man to falcon D152.4.+. (30); transformation: man to fish D170. (19); transformation: man to owl D153.2. (24); transformation: man to star D293. (5); (21); (65); transformation: man to woodpecker D153.1. (27); (29); transformation of man . . . as fitting punishment Q584.2. (27); (29); transformation: sun-man to star D293.+. (1); why there is enmity between certain animals and man A2585. (25); woman . . . tempted by man T331.+. (57).

MAN-EATING fish B16.2.+. (57). — Transformation: man-eating sea lion to stone D429.2.2.1.+. (34).

MANKIND. — Formerly great heat of sun causes distress to mankind A720.2. (1); (2); (6).

MARK. — Indelible mark D1654.3.1. (7).

MARKINGS of seal A2412.1.+. (65); of whale A2412.1.+. (65); on birds A2412.2. (65); on fish A2412.4. (65).

MARKSMAN. — Skillful marksman F661. (32); (34); (35); (50).

MAROONED man reaches home . . . K1616. (23); (53); woman abandoned . . . B772.+. (51).

MAROONER. — Marooned man . . . outwits marooner K1616. (23); (53).

MAROONING as punishment Q467.5. (53).

MARRIAGE of falcon . . . B670.+. (31); of woman to sea lion B600.+. (19); to a statue T117.11. (16); to bird . . . B652. (17);

(18); (23); to fox . . . B651.1. (18). — Brother-sister marriage
T415.5. (28); dream about a marriage . . . T11.3.2. (50); faith-
fulness to marriage . . . T211. (40); faithlessness in marriage
. . . T230. (4); (30); (31); human offspring from marriage . . .
B631. (19); unwitting marriage . . . G81. (18).

MARRIED. — Moon and rainbow married A753.+. (65); woman's . . .
brothers kill her husband . . . for having married . . . K959.2.1.
(19).

MARRY. — Lecherous brother. Wants to seduce (marry) his sister
T415.1. (29); lecherous father. Unnatural father wants to marry his
own daughter T411.1. (44); man marries widow . . . T145.0.1.+.
(35).

MARVELOUS cures F950. (40); runner F681. (65).

MATE. — Creation of first man's (woman's) mate A1275. (16).

MATRIARCHY T148. (3); (65).

MEAL. — Frightful meal S183. (19); (24); (47); (54); (58a).

MEAT. — Excrements thought to be meat . . . J1772.9. (47).

MEDICINE. — Urine used in medicine D1500.1.37. (47).

MEET. — Adulteress . . . meets lover K1514.18. (36); deception in
order to meet lover T35.+. (19).

MEETING. — Birds have meeting . . . B235.+. (51); (52); unexpected
meeting . . . N731. (62).

MELT. — Snow magically caused to melt (burn) D2143.6.4. (6); (7).

MELTING. — Flood caused by melting of ice . . . A1016.3. (7).

MEMBERS. — Vital bodily members E780. (54); (55).

MEN hide from world-fire A1038.+. (2); lured into trap . . .
K912.2.+. (25); (46); (47). — Animals provide food for men
B531. (51); extraordinary perception of blind men F655. (62); hero
kills . . . strong men G512.0.1. (33); ogre kills men . . . G477. (33);
why women are subservient to men A1372.9. (3); (7); (65).

MENSES. — Food tabu during menses C140.+. (60); tabu connected
with menses C140. (17); tabu: going forth during menses C141. (17).

MENSTRUATION. — Culture hero establishes customs pertaining to
menstruation A545.+. (17); origin of menstruation A1355. (17).

MENTIONING. — Tabu: mentioning secret water spring C429.1. (22);
(32).

MIDDLE. — Giant with one eye in middle of forehead F531.1.1.1. (62).

MIDSTREAM. — Sacrifice to water-spirit who has stopped boat in
midstream S263.4.+. (60).

MIGHTY fisherman F634. (37); (48); wrestler F617. (4). — Culture
hero as mighty hunter A526.2. (1); (11); (40).

MIRACULOUS darkness as punishment Q552.20.1. (56); growth of
culture hero A511.4.1. (45).

MIRACULOUSLY. — Madness miraculously cured F959.1. (47); wild animal miraculously tamed B771. (53).

MISUNDERSTANDING. — Inappropriate action from misunderstanding J1820. (26).

MOCKERY. — Punishment for mockery Q288. (23); (25); (30); (53); (54); (64).

MOCKING. — Tabu: mocking animal C94.3. (23).

MONOGAMOUS. — Why bird is monogamous A2497.+. (26); why woodpecker is monogamous A2497.+. (28).

MONSTER bursts . . . G304.2.5.+. (33); ungrateful for rescue W154.2. (33). — Abduction by monster R11. (33); (62); culture hero conquers sea monster A531.4. (34); devastating monster G346. (33); sucking monster G332. (33).

MONSTERS. — Culture hero (demigod) overcomes monsters A531. (33).

MONSTROUS (deformed) child exposed S325.0.1. (33). — Ogres with monstrous features G360. (62).

MOON and rainbow married A753.+. (65); has son A745.+. (5); spots are scarifications A751.5.5.+. (5). — Sun and moon as man and woman A736.1. (65); why moon is red A750.+. (5); woman in the moon A751.8. (5); (65).

MOON-GODDESS A240.1. (8).

MOON-WOMAN causes flood A1015.+. (8).

MORTAL. — Water-spirits lure mortal . . . F420.5.2.1. (59).

MOTHER and daughter P232. (35); and son P231. (20a); (20b); (24); (26); -love P231.3. (5); (26); (45); -son incest T412. (26); (27). — Dead mother's friendly return E323. (20b); son rescues mother R154.1. (20a).

MOTIVATED. — Fratricide motivated by love-jealousy S73.1.4. (30).

MOUNTAIN. — Escape from deluge on mountain A1022. (7); (8); indentations on mountain . . . A900.+. (7); magic leveling of mountain D2152.1. (24); magic mountain D932. (24); stream . . . from side of mountain A934.9. (32); why mountain tops are bare today . . . A900.+. (1); (6).

MOUNTAINS. — Giants live in mountains . . . F531.6.2.1. (62).

MOURNERS. — Loudest mourners not greatest sorrowers J261. (47).

MOURNFUL. — Origin of mournful sound . . . A925.5. (65).

MOURNING customs P681. (4); (34); (37); (40); (41); (55); (57). — Return home to witness one's own mourning rites N681.0.1.+. (40).

MOVED. — Ship moved by sacrifice D2136.8. (60).

MOVEMENTS. — Ambush betrayed by movements of birds J53.+. (4).

MUD. — Magic mud . . . D1486.1.+. (32).

MULTIPLICATION. — Magic multiplication . . . D2106. (55).

MURDER by biting off breast S100.+. (33); by crushing S116. (53); by crushing head S116.4. (46); (47); by drowning K958. (39); by drowning S131. (45); by introducing hot stone . . . S112.+. (35); by stabbing S115. (25); by strategy K910. (40); (53); (58a); from behind K959.4. (39); (46); in one's sleep K959.2. (54); (55); punished Q211. (4); with hot stone S112.2.+. (35); (57). — Death as punishment for murder Q411.6. (25); (35); (46); (47); (48); (49); (59); (60); magic murder D2061. (55); treacherous murder during hunt K917. (47); unusual murder avenged . . . Q581.1. (46); (47).

MURDERS. — Revolting murders . . . S100. (66).

MUSSEL. — Color of mussel A2411.5.4. (39).

MUTILATION as punihsment Q451. (57).

MUTILATIONS. — Revolting . . . mutilations S100. (66).

NAGGING. — The nagging wife T253. (64).

NAMES. — All things receive names A1191. (21); how animals received their names A2571. (21); (45).

NATURE. — Origin and nature of animal's tongue A2344. (27).

NAVEL. — Former intercourse by navel A1352.3. (16).

NECESSITY of work J702. (10); (11); (12); (15).

NEEDS. — Adulteress makes excuse to . . . attend to bodily needs . . . K1514.18. (36).

NEGATE. — Curse given to negate good wish M416. (10); (11); (12).

NEPHEW. — Treacherous nephew K2210.+. (47).

NEST. — Why Magellanic cormorant nests . . . A2431.+. (22); why tufted cormorant nests . . . A2431.+. (22).

NEW race . . . after world calamity A1006.1. (7); (8).

NEW-BORN. — All new-born male children slaughtered S302.1. (33).

NIGHT produced . . . D2146.2.1. (56). — Sun's night journey. . . . A722.+. (3).

NIGHT-HERON. — Night-heron's call announces . . . B147.2.+. (53).

OBEDIENCE W31. (57). Test of wife's obedience H473. (57).

OBSTACLE. — Reversed obstacle flight. . . . D673. (31).

OCCUPATION. — Animal's occupation: hunting A2452. (51); animal's occupation: stealing A2455. (3).

OCEAN boils F932.7.+. (1).

OFFENDING. — Tabu: offending water-spirit C41. (41); (42).

OFFSPRING. — Foster father reveals fact that son is offspring of supernatural father P231.5.+. (62); human offspring . . . B631. (19).

OFT-PROVED fidelity T320.1. (35).

OGRE attacks intruders G475. (34); blinded G511. (33); (34); burned to

death G512.3. (33); defeated G500. (61); keeps human prisoners
G334. (33); kills men . . . G477. (33); seeks firewood to roast boys
E257.+. (18). — Abduction by monster (ogre) R11. (33); (62);
animal kills ogre G512.9. (34); cannibal ogre G312. (34); headless
ogre G361.3. (62); rescue from ogre G550. (54); sea lion as ogre
G352.+. (34).
OGRES leave signs . . . G310.+. (62); with monstrous features G360.
(62). — Magic invulnerability of ogres D1840.3. (33).
OLD. — Unusual conception in old age T538. (45).
OLDEST brother alone succeeds . . . H1242.+. (25).
OMENS from flight of birds D1812.5.0.2. (40); (55).
ONE sister and two brothers P253.0.2. (9); (12); (13). — Achilles heel.
Invulnerability except in one spot Z311. (33); giant with one eye
. . . F531.1.1.1. (62); men lured into trap one by one
K912.2.+. (25); (46); (47).
ONE-ARMED giant F531.1.6.7. (62).
ONE-LEGGED giant F531.1.3.3.1. (62).
OPPRESSED. — Triumph of the oppressed L300.+. (65).
ORDER. — Culture hero establishes law and order A530. (9).
ORGANS. — Origin of female sex organs A1313.2. (16); remarkable
sexual organs F547. (30).
ORIGIN of animal characteristics: head A2320. (19); . . . of animal's
tongue A2344. (27); of arrowhead A1459.1.+. (13); of boat-
building A1445.1. (43); of body paint . . . A1595.+. (17); of
childbirth A1351. (18); of color of bird A2411.2. (4); (17); (26); of
color of guanaco A2411.1.+. (44); of color of tree-creeper
A2411.2.+. (37); of dawn A1179.2. (56); of death A1335. (20a);
(20b); of female sex organs A1313.2. (16); of fire—culture hero
strikes rocks together A1414.3.+. (10); of girls' initiation ceremonial A1530.+. (17); of glaciers A990.+. (6); of harpoonpoint
A1459.1.+. (14); of hunting and fishing customs A1520. (9); (11);
(12); of menstruation A1355. (17); of particular rock A977.5. (34);
(35); of particular stones . . . A977. (58a); (59); (65); of plains
A990.+. (65); of sea channels A920.2. (35); of secret society
A1530.+. (65); of sexual intercourse A1352. (16); of shape of
vagina A1313.2.+. (17); of the sinker A1457.1.+. (37); of social
ceremonials A1530. (58b); of . . . sound of sea A925.5. (65); of
the rainbow A791. (4); (65); of . . . waves A925.1. (65).
ORIGINALLY. — Islands originally form continent . . . A955.11. (35);
sun originally so hot . . . A727.1. (1).
OTHERWORLD. — Sun's night journey. Goes to otherworld A722.+.
(3).
OTTER. — Enmity between dog and otter A2494.4.+. (25); why otter

has broad tail A2378.9.+. (65); why otter has short legs A2371.+. (25); why otter keeps hidden in holes underground A2433.3.+. (25).

OUTWIT. — Adulteress outwits husband K1510. (41); (42); husband outwits adulteress . . . K1550. (38); marooned man . . . outwits marooner K1616. (23); (53).

OVERCOME. — Culture hero (demigod) overcomes monsters A531. (33); hero overcomes . . . animal G510.4. (34); weak . . . hero overcomes large fighter L311. (32); (33); (34); (35); (61).

OVERHEARD animal conversation N455.+. (51); (52); (human) conversation N455. (38); (65). — Husband learns . . . through conversation overheard N455.6.+. (31); location . . . learned from overheard conversation N455.9.+. (53); secrets overheard N450. (17); secrets overheard from . . . conversation N451. (31).

OVERTHROWN. — Parliament of women overthrown F565.3.+. (3); (7); (8); (65).

OVERWEENING punished Q330. (53).

OWL. — Transformation: man to owl D153.2. (24).

OWN. — Each likes his own children best T681. (62).

OWNER. — Means of hoodwinking the . . . owner K330. (41).

OWNERS. — Women induce owners . . . K330.+. (17).

PAINT. — Origin of body paint . . . A1595.+. (17).

PAINTING. — Disguise by painting body K1821.2. (44); (65); means of combating water-spirits: painting them white F405.+. (64).

PAIR. — New race from single pair . . . A1006.1. (7); (8).

PALMS. — Stone man's eyes, palms . . . like foreigner's G630.+. (33).

PARAMOUR . . . hidden . . . K1521. (27); (38). — Adulteress chooses loathly paramour T232.2. (62); animal paramour B610. (19); husband castrates paramour K1558.1. (27); husband kills surprised paramour K1569.9. (38); husband kills wife and paramour Q411.0.2. (36); husband outwits . . . paramour K1550. (38); husband surprises wife and paramour K1569.2. (36); unknown . . . paramour T475. (27).

PARASITES. — Why parasites cling to whale's back A2310.+. (54).

PARENT. — Curse by parent M411.1. (28).

PARLIAMENT of women F565.3. (1); (4); (13); (65); . . . overthrown F565.3.+. (3); (7); (8); (65).

PASSION. — Sun endowed with . . . passion A738.2.2. (65).

PATIENCE W26. (43). — Tests of patience H1553. (43).

PATIENT. — Sham cure by pretended extracting . . . from patient's body K1871.2. (33).

PECULIARITIES. — Recognition through personal peculiarities H30. (40).

PENIS becomes larger D489.+. (17). — Long penis F547.3.1. (17); (27); recognition by long penis H79.+. (27); red penis F547.3.+. (17).

PEOPLE. — Ascent to stars. People . . . become stars A761. (1); (21); culture heroine as leader of people A520.+. (13); gods teach people . . . A1404. (9); sun . . . hated by people A738.2.+. (1); why people treat bird respectfully A2545.+. (6).

PERCEPTION. — Extraordinary perception . . . F655. (62).

PERFORM. — Culture hero performs . . . feats . . . A526.7. (32); (33); (35).

PERMISSION refused to drink from lagoon W155.5.+. (32); refused to drink from water tank W155.5. (22).

PERSECUTIONS. — Cruel persecutions S400. (54).

PERSON changes size at will D631.1. (27); comes to life E1. (20a); (20b); hears call . . . D1827.2. (19); of unusual color F527. (45). — Evil spirit . . . eats person F402.1.11.2. (60); resuscitation by supernatural person E121. (20a); swallowed person becomes bald F921. (40); tabu: revealing identity of certain person C422. (65); transformation: stone to person D432.1. (33).

PERSONAL. — Recognition through personal peculiarities H30. (40).

PERSONS. — Quest for lost persons H1385. (37).

PHYSICAL attributes of sun A738.1. (3).

PLACE. — Remedy for lack of water in certain place . . . N452.1.+. (22); why tribe lives in certain place A1620.+. (65).

PLACED. — Rivers formed where certain stones are placed A934.2. (35).

PLAINS. — Origin of plains A990.+. (65).

PLAN. — Woman plans to eat her children G72.1. (18).

PLENTY. — Land of plenty F701. (24).

POLYANDRY T146. (17).

POLYGYNY T145.0.1. (40).

POSITION. — Deception into humiliating position K1200. (65).

POSSIBLE. — Courage conquers all and impossible is made possible U243. (40).

POWER. — Avoidance of others' power J640. (41); fatal deception into trickster's power K810. (4); (25); girl tricked into man's room (or power) K1330. (29); magic power of children D1717. (24).

POWERS. — Magic powers lost D1741. (11).

PRECOCIOUS speech T615.1. (45). — Culture hero precocious A527.1. (45); hero's precocious strength. . . . F611.3.2. (24).

PREFER. — Child prefers foster father T675.1.+. (62).

PREGNANT. — Cruelty to pregnant whale S185.+. (66).

PRESENTIMENT. — Future revealed by presentiment . . . D1812.4. (19).

PRESERVATION of life . . . A1005. (7); (8).

PRETEND. — Hypocrite pretends friendship . . . K2010. (19); (23).

PRETENDED virtue K2050. (38). — Deception by pretended lousing K874. (53); sham cure by pretended extracting . . . K1871.2. (33).

PRETENDING. — Deception by pretending sleep K1868. (26); (31).

PREVENTION of hostility . . . J623. (65).

PRIMEVAL. — Indentations . . . from primeval flood A900.+. (7).

PRIMITIVE. — Topographical features caused by . . . primitive hero A901. (35).

PRISON. — Escape from prison R211. (47).

PRISONERS. — Ogre keeps human prisoners G334. (33).

PRODIGAL son returns P233.8. (54).

PRODUCED. — Day produced . . . D2146.1.3. (56); ice produced . . . D2144.5.1. (6); (7); magic results produced by . . . ceremony D1766. (56); magic results produced by command D1765. (41); magic storm produced . . . D2141.0.11. (6); (7); night produced . . . D2146.2.1. (56); snow produced . . . D2143.6.3. (6); (7); thunderbolt magically produced D2149.1. (58a); winter . . . produced D2145.1. (6); (7).

PROOF. — Magic animal proof . . . D1841.5.2. (40).

PROPELLING. — Self-propelling (ship) boat D1523.2. (60).

PROPERTY. — Loss . . . of property . . . Q595. (41).

PROVED. — Oft-proved fidelity T320.1. (35).

PROVIDE. — Animals provide food for men B531. (51).

PROVISION. — Forethought in provision . . . J710. (45).

PROWESS. — Custom: boasting of sexual prowess P665. (31); recognition by extraordinary prowess H32. (40).

PULLED UP. — Trees pulled up . . . F621.2. (33).

PUNISHED. — Adultery punished Q241. (30); (36); (38); (48); (49); (57); bestiality punished Q253.1. (19); cannibalism punished Q215. (18); cruelty punished Q285. (18); (24); (46); (54); disobedient wife punished T254.6. (57); disrespect punished Q395. (55); (56); incest punished Q242. (27); (28); (29); (30); murder punished Q211. (4); overweening punished Q330. (53); stinginess punished Q276. (22); (32); (37); (39); (41); treacherous wife punished Q261.2. (41); (65); wife-stealing punished with death Q252.1. (4); (30).

PUNISHMENT: being eaten by animals Q415. (30); by drowning Q467. (39); castration Q451.10.1. (27); fitted to crime Q580. (24); (30); for man who makes advances . . . Q242.3. (30); for mockery Q288. (23); (25); (30); (53); (54); (64); transformation Q551.3. (54); (55). — Animal characteristics as punishment A2230. (25); animal characteristics: punishment for greed A2238. (24); curse as

RED penis F547.3.+. (17). — Why falcon has red eyes A2332.5.+. (31); why moon is red A750.+. (5); why woodpecker has red head A2412.2.+. (28); (29).

REFUGE. — Cave as refuge R315. (19).

REFUSE. — Lover refuses food . . . T24.6. (44); wife refuses to sleep . . . T288. (54).

REFUSED. — Permission refused to drink from lagoon W155.5.+. (32); permission refused to drink from water tank W155.5. (22).

REFUSING. — Tabu: refusing a request . . . C871.+. (23).

REJECTED suitors' revenge T75.2.1. (17); (35); (54); (61).

RELATIVE. — Cruel relative S0. (30); dead relative's . . . return E320. (47); relative's flesh eaten . . . G61. (19).

RELATIVES. — Girl's animal lover slain by . . . relatives B610.1. (19); tabu: refusing a request from wife's relatives C871.+. (23).

RELATIVES-IN-LAW. — Treacherous relatives-in-law K2218. (53).

RELIGIOUS. — Magic results produced by religious ceremony D1766. (56).

REMARKABLE sexual organs F547. (30); skill F660. (34); (35); (40); voice F556. (47). — Culture hero performs remarkable feats . . . A526.7. (32); (33); (35).

REMARKABLY beautiful child F575.3. (45); beautiful woman F575.1. (3); (4); (17); (31); (48); (61); clever culture heroine A527.+. (9); (13); (14).

REMEDY for lack of water . . . N452.1.+. (22).

RENDEZVOUS. — Lovers' rendezvous T35. (28); (36); (38).

REPAID. — Arrogance repaid L430. (53).

REPENTANCE. — Reward for repentance Q36. (56).

REQUEST. — Tabu: refusing a request . . . C871.+. (23).

RESCUE from ogre G550. (54). — Father rescues children R153.2. (31); father rescues son(s) R153.3. (53); monster ungrateful for rescue W154.2. (33); son rescues mother R154.1. (20a); youngest brother rescues . . . R155.1. (45).

RESCUED. — Victims rescued . . . F913. (40).

RESPECTFULLY. — Why people treat bird respectfully A2545.+. (6).

RESPONSIBLE. — Giant responsible . . . A977.1. (33).

RESTORED. — Earth restored . . . A1036.+. (2).

RESULT. — Animal calls the dawn. The sun rises as result . . . B755. (56); fight . . . with real result F1068.2.2. (63).

RESULTS. — Magic results produced by . . . ceremony D1766. (56); magic results produced by command D1765. (41).

RESUSCITATED eaten animal E32. (54); (55).

RESUSCITATION by magic E50. (20a); by supernatural person E121. (20a); by weeping (tears) E58. (20b); from fragments . . . E35. (33).

RETORT from . . . (child) J1341. (24); (37); (39).

RETURN from the dead . . . E361. (20b); home . . . N681.0.1.+. (40); of the hero Z293. (40). — Dead mother's . . . return E323. (20b); dead relative's friendly return E320. (47); father . . . returns . . . T411.1.2. (44); prodigal son returns P233.8. (54).

RETURNING. — Husband kills returning adulteress Q411.0.1. (57); self-returning harpoon D1602.6.+. (12).

REVEAL. — Foster father reveals fact . . . P231.5.+. (62).

REVEALED. — Future revealed . . . D1812.4. (19); secret revealed N440.+. (36).

REVEALING. — Tabu: revealing identity . . . C422. (65).

REVENANTS eat E541. (47).

REVENGE. — Animal takes revenge on man B299.1. (6); (7); (23); avoiding enemy's revenge J647. (65); flood brought as revenge . . . A1018.3. (6); (7); (8); rejected suitors' revenge T75.2.1. (17); (35); (54); (61).

REVERSED obstacle flight. . . . D673. (31).

REVIVE. — Limbs of dead . . . revive E31. (54); (55).

REVOLTING murders . . . S100. (66).

REWARD for repentance Q36. (56); for wife's fidelity Q83.1. (40).

REWARDED. — Loyalty rewarded Q72. (54).

RID. — Adulteress gets rid of husband . . . K1514. (36); (38).

RISE. — Animal calls the dawn. The sun rises . . . B755. (56).

RITES. — Return home to witness one's own mourning rites N681.0.1.+. (40).

RIVAL in love killed T92.10. (48); (49); (50).

RIVALS in love T92. (17); (45).

RIVERS formed . . . A934.2. (35); . . . made dry D2151.2.3. (18). — Creator of rivers A930.1. (32); (35); magic mud makes rivers D1486.1.+. (32); magic stone makes rivers . . . D1486.1. (35).

ROAST. — Ogre seeks firewood to roast boys E257.+. (18).

ROCK. — Origin of particular rock A977.5. (34); (35).

ROCKS. — Origin of fire—culture hero strikes rocks together A1414.3.+. (10).

ROOM. — Girl tricked into man's room . . . K1330. (29).

RUNNER. — Marvelous runner F681. (65).

RUNNERS. — Fast runners sent . . . K2350.+. (65).

SACRIFICE to water-spirit . . . S263.4.+. (60). — Human sacrifice S260.1. (60); ship moved by sacrifice D2136.8. (60).

SAVE. — Animal saves man from pursuer B523. (57).

SCARIFICATIONS. — Moon spots are scarifications A751.5.5.+. (5).

SCHLARAFFENLAND X1503. (15).

SCORCHED. — Why mountain tops are bare today: scorched by sun A900.+. (1); (6).

SCORNED. — Man scorned by his beloved T75. (17); (54); the scorned lover T70. (35); (61); woman avenges scorned love T71.2. (45).

SEA. — Culture hero conquers sea monster A531.4. (34); origin of high sea waves A925.1. (65); origin of sea channels A920.2. (35); origin of . . . sound of sea A925.5. (65).

SEAL. — Markings of seal A2412.1.+. (65).

SEA LION as ogre G352.+. (34); as suitor B621.+. (19); carries girl . . . B551.+. (19). — Giant sea lion B871.2.+. (19); marriage of woman to sea lion B600.+. (19); slain sea lion . . . dismembered S139.2.+. (19); speaking sea lion B211.2.7.+. (19); transformation: man-eating sea lion to stone D429.2.2.1.+. (34).

SECRET learned N440.+. (27); (28); (34); (41); (45); (62); revealed N440.+. (36). — Origin of secret society A1530.+. (65); tabu: mentioning secret water spring C429.1. (22); (32).

SECRETS . . . from . . . conversation N451. (31); overheard N450. (17). — Tabu: uttering secrets C420. (65); valuable secrets learned N440. (3); (4); (32); (65).

SEDUCE. — 'Brother-in-law seduces (seeks to seduce) sister-in-law T425. (30); father . . . seduces daughter T411.1.2. (44); lecherous brother. Wants to seduce . . . sister T415.1. (29); sisters-in-law seduce brother-in-law T425.+. (45).

SEDUCTION by disguise . . . K1310. (44); by feigned death K1325. (44).

SEEK. — Ogre seeks firewood . . . E257.+. (18).

SEIZED. — Dupe . . . seized and killed K832. (39); (46).

SELF-INJURY. — Deception into self-injury K1000. (33).

SELF-PROPELLING (ship) boat D1523.2. (60).

SELF-RETURNING harpoon D1602.6.+. (12).

SENSITIVE bird A2520.+. (6); (7).

SENT. — Fast runners sent . . . K2350.+. (65).

SEPARATED. — Islands . . . form continent, later separated A955.11. (35).

SERVE. — Animals serve as bridge . . . B555. (57).

SEVERAL. — Culture heroes two brothers and several sisters A515.1.+. (21); new race from single pair (or several) . . . A1006.1. (7); (8).

SEX. — Origin of female sex organs A1313.2. (16).

SEXUAL. — Custom: boasting of sexual prowess P665. (31); origin of sexual intercourse A1352. (16); remarkable sexual organs F547. (30); transformation by sexual intercourse D565.5.1. (26).

SHAM cure . . . K1871.2. (33).

SHAMAN concealed in body . . . F1034.+. (54); (55); summons water-spirits . . . F404.+. (64). — Magic sleep induced by shaman D1964.4.+. (58a); (58b).

SHAPE. — Origin of shape of vagina A1313.2.+. (17).

SHED. — Bird sheds tears B736.1. (31).

SHIP held back . . . D2072.0.3. (31); moved by sacrifice D2136.8. (60). — Extraordinary boat (ship) F841. (23); self-propelling (ship) boat D1523.2. (60); water-spirit holds ship back F420.5.2.7.4. (64); water-spirit wrecks ship F420.5.2.7.3. (59).

SHORT. — Why otter has short legs A2371.+. (25).

SHOWING. — Tabu: showing disrespect . . . C170.+. (55).

SICKNESS. — Love-sickness T24.1. (44).

SIDE. — Stream . . . from side of mountain A934.9. (32); wife chooses father's side . . . P211. (23); (55).

SIGHT. — Loss of magic sight D1822. (20a).

SIGN. — Bird as sign of spring A2536.+. (6).

SIGNAL. — Lovers' signal T41.3. (19).

SIGNS. — Ogres leave signs . . . G310.+. (62).

SINGING. — Magic singing D2173. (56).

SINGLE. — New race from single pair . . . A1006.1. (7); (8).

SINKER. — Origin of the sinker A1457.1.+. (37).

SISTER. — Brother-sister incest T415. (28); (29); brother-sister marriage T415.5. (28); culture heroes two brothers and a sister A515.1.+. (9); (12); (13); (14); (17); lecherous brother. Wants to seduce . . . sister T415.1. (29); one sister and two brothers P253.0.2. (9); (12); (13); treacherous sister K2212. (19).

SISTER-IN-LAW. — Brother-in-law seduces (seeks to seduce) sister-in-law T425. (30); cruel sister-in-law S55. (45); punishment for . . . advances to sister-in-law Q242.3. (30); treacherous sister-in-law K2212.2. (19).

SISTERS. — Culture heroes two brothers and several sisters A515.1.+. (21).

SISTERS-IN-LAW seduce brother-in-law T425.+. (45). — Beautiful child . . . loved by sisters-in-law P264.+. (45).

SIZE. — Person changes size at will D631.1. (27).

SKILL. — Culture hero performs . . . feats of . . . skill A526.7. (32); (33); (35); remarkable skill F660. (34); (35); (40).

SKILLFUL craftsmen F660.+. (13); hunter F679.5. (17); (24); (38); (40);

(45); (65); marksman F661. (32); (34); (35); (50); tracker F677. (53).

SKY. — Ascent to stars. People . . . ascend to sky . . . A761. (1); (21);
wife carried . . . to sky . . . J2133.5.1. (30).

SLAIN sea lion . . . dismembered S139.2.+. (19). — Girl's animal
lover slain . . . B610.1. (19); wife eats flesh of slain husband
P214.+. (19).

SLAUGHTERED. — All . . . children slaughtered S302.1. (33).

SLEEP. — Deathlike sleep D1960.4. (20a); deception by pretending
sleep K1860. (26); (31); magic sleep induced . . . D1964.4.+. (58a);
(58b); murder in one's sleep K959.2. (54); (55); object causes magic
sleep D1364. (58a); (58b); shaman summons water-spirits in sleep
F404.+. (64); wife refuses to sleep . . . T288. (54); woman's . . .
brothers kill her husband in sleep . . . K959.2.1. (19).

SLING. — Extraordinary sling F830.+. (4); magic sling D1087. (34);
(35).

SMALL. — Very small hero L112.2. (32); (33); (34); (35); (40); weak
(small) hero overcomes large fighter L311. (32); (33); (34); (35);
(61).

SNOW magically caused to melt (burn) D2143.6.4. (6); (7); produced
. . . D2143.6.3. (6); (7).

SOCIAL. — Origin of social ceremonials A1530. (58b).

SOCIETY. — Origin of secret society A1530.+. (65).

SOLD. — Wife sold . . . T292. (17).

SOLES. — Stone man's . . . soles like foreigner's G630.+. (33).

SON avenges father P233.6. (48); (49); of the sun A225. (1); (3);
rescues mother R154.1. (20a). — Compassionate elder son L13.+.
(20a); (20b); cruel son S21. (20b); death from hearing of son's
(sons') death F1041.1.2.2.4. (45); father and son P233. (1); (4);
(53); father and son as culture heroes A515.2. (1); father avenges
son P233.6.+. (54); father feels that son is in danger D1813.0.3.
(18); father rescues son(s) R153.3. (53); foster father reveals fact
that son is offspring of supernatural father P231.5.+. (62);
lecherous son T410.+. (26); moon has son A745.+. (5); mother
and son P231. (20a); (20b); (24); (26); mother-son incest T412.
(26); (27); prodigal son returns P233.8. (54); unexpected meeting
of father and son N731. (62); victorious youngest son L10. (46).

SONG. — Sparrow's song A2426.2.+. (56).

SON-IN-LAW supports father-in-law P265.+. (43).

SORROWERS. — Loudest mourners not greatest sorrowers J261. (47).

SOUGHT. — Location of sought man . . . N455.9.+. (53).

SOUL appears like the body it left . . . E722.1.+. (47).

SOULS of dead . . . E752.1.3.+. (47).

SOUND. — Origin of . . . sound of sea A925.5. (65).

SPARROW. — Sparrow's song A2426.2.+. (56).

SPEAK. — The dead speak E545. (47); victim speaks . . . F915. (40).

SPEAKING bird B211.3. (23); (31); (51); (52); (55); sea lion B211.2.7.+. (19).

SPEECH. — Precocious speech T615.1. (45).

SPELL. — Flood . . . after great spell of cold A1016.3. (7).

SPIRIT. — Disguise as deity (or spirit) K1828. (65); evil spirit kills . . . F402.1.11.2. (60); quest for spirit H1370.+. (65); sacrifice to water-spirit . . . S263.4.+. (60); tabu: offending water-spirit C41. (41); (42); transformation: water-spirit to stone D231.+. (59); water-spirit drags women . . . F420.5.2.1.5.+. (42); water-spirit holds ship back F420.5.2.7.4. (64); water-spirit wrecks ship F420.5.2.7.3. (59).

SPIRITS. — Home of water-spirits F420.2. (41); (59); malevolent water-spirits F420.5.2. (59); means of combating water-spirits . . . F405.+. (64); shaman summons water-spirits . . . F404.+. (64); water-spirits lure mortal . . . F420.5.2.1. (59).

SPOT. — Achilles heel. Invulnerability except in one spot Z311. (33).

SPOTS. — Moon spots are scarifications A751.5.5.+. (5).

SPRING. — Bird as sign of spring A2536.+. (6); tabu: mentioning secret water spring C429.1. (22); (32).

SPY. — Husband spies on adulteress . . . K1551.+. (36).

SPYING. — Girl's animal lover slain by spying relatives B610.1. (19); remedy . . . found by spying . . . N452.1.+. (22).

STABBING. — Murder by stabbing S115. (25).

STAKE. — Transformation: wooden stake to stone D471.6.+. (7).

STAR. — Transformation: man to star D293. (5); (21); (65); transformation: sun-man to star D293.+. (1).

STARS. — Ascent to stars. . . . A761. (1); (21).

STARVING. — Grandfather hides food from starving grandsons S20.2.+. (39).

STATEMENTS. — Enigmatic statements H580. (65).

STATUE. — Marriage to a statue T117.11. (16); transformation: statue comes to life D435.1.1. (33).

STEALING. — Animal's occupation: stealing A2455. (3); wife-stealing punished with death Q252.1. (4); (30).

STEPMOTHER. — Children flee from stepmother . . . G31.+. (18); cruel stepmother S31. (18).

STINGINESS W152. (22); (32); (37); (39); (41); (46); (47); punished Q276. (22); (32); (37); (39); (41).

STINGY. — Child leaves home because grandmother is stingy with food R228.+. (37).

STONE giants G371. (33); man's eyes . . . like foreigner's G630.+.

(33). — Magic stone makes rivers . . . D1486.1. (35); murder by introducing hot stone . . . S112.+. (35); murder with hot stone S112.2.+. (35); (57); transformation: cormorants to stone D423.+. (35); transformation: man-eating sea lion to stone D429.2.2.1.+. (34); transformation: object to stone D471. (58a); transformation: stone to person D432.1. (33); transformation: water-spirit to stone D231.+. (59); transformation: wooden stake to stone D471.6.+. (7).

STONES. — Giant responsible for certain stones A977.1. (33); islands from stones . . . A955.6.+. (35); origin of particular stones . . . A977. (58a); (59); (65); rivers formed where certain stones are placed A934.2. (35).

STOP. — Return . . . to stop weeping E361. (20b).

STOPPED. — Sacrifice to water-spirit who has stopped boat . . . S263.4.+. (60).

STORM. — Magic storm . . . D2141.0.11. (6); (7).

STRANGER as helper N800.+. (18).

STRATEGY. — Murder by strategy K910. (40); (53); (58a).

STREAM unexpectedly bursts . . . A934.9. (32). — Animals serve as bridge across stream B555. (57).

STRENGTH. — Culture hero performs . . . feats of strength A526.7. (32); (33); (35); hero's precocious strength. . . . F611.3.2. (24); magic strength D1830. (24).

STRENUOUS cure for madness J1434. (47).

STRIKE. — Escaping before enemy can strike J641. (18); origin of fire—culture hero strikes rocks together A1414.3.+. (10).

STRIVE. — Brothers strive to avenge each other P251.3.1. (25).

STRONG. — Hero kills . . . strong men G512.0.1. (33); subordination of strong . . . J421.+. (65); subordination . . . to strong J421. (65); why woodpecker has strong beak A2343.3.2.+. (27); wise fear . . . for the strong J613. (65).

SUBORDINATION of strong to weak . . . J421.+. (65); of weak to strong J421. (65).

SUBSERVIENT. — Why women are subservient to men A1372.9. (3); (7); (65).

SUBSTITUTION. — Seduction by . . . substitution K1310. (44).

SUCCEED. — Oldest brother alone succeeds . . . H1242.+. (25).

SUCKING monster G332. (33).

SUITOR. — Sea lion as suitor B621.+. (19).

SUITORS. — Rejected suitors' revenge T75.2.1. (17); (35); (54); (61).

SUMMON. — Shaman summons water-spirits . . . F404.+. (64).

SUMMONED. — Ghost summoned . . . E381. (20b).

SUN and moon as man and woman A736.1. (65); as benevolent leader A738.2.+. (3); as evil tyrant . . . A738.2.+. (1); as father of culture hero A512.4. (1); as helper N818.1. (1); (3); as human being A736. (1); (3); as man who left earth A711. (1); (3); (65); captured R9.1. (1); dries out earth . . . A733.5. (1); endowed with wisdom . . . A738.2.2. (65); is excellent hunter A738.+. (65); originally so hot . . . A727.1. (1). — Animal calls the dawn. The sun rises . . . B755. (56); children of the sun A736.5. (65); extraordinary behavior of sun F961.1. (1); (2); formerly great heat of sun . . . A720.2. (1); (2); (6); physical attributes of sun A738.1. (3); rainbow is sun's brother A220.2.+. (4); raising the sun A727. (1); son of the sun A225. (1); (3); sun's night journey. . . . A722.+. (3); war with the sun A739.2. (1); why mountain tops are bare today: scorched by sun A900.+. (1); (6).

SUN-FATHER A221. (3).

SUN-GOD. — The sun-god and his family A220.2. (1); (3).

SUN-GODS. — Two sun-gods A227. (1).

SUN-MAN. — Transformation: sun-man to star D293.+. (1).

SUPERNATURAL growth T615. (27); (62). — Foster father reveals fact that son is offspring of supernatural father P231.5.+. (62); resuscitation by supernatural person E121. (20a).

SUPPLY. — Kindness unwise when it imperils one's food supply J715. (32).

SUPPORT. — Son-in-law supports father-in-law P265.+. (43).

SURPRISE. — Husband surprises wife . . . K1569.2. (36).

SURPRISED. — Husband kills surprised paramour K1569.9. (38).

SURVIVOR. — Unique survivor Z356. (59).

SURVIVORS of flood . . . A1029.6. (7).

SUSPENSION. — Magic suspension of weight D1691. (24).

SWALLOW. — Jonah. Fish . . . swallows a man F911.4. (40).

SWALLOWED person becomes bald F921. (40). — Culture hero swallowed . . . A535. (40); death by being swallowed for breaking tabu C929.5. (60).

SWALLOWER. — Victim kills swallower . . . F912.2. (40); victim speaks from swallower's body F915. (40); victims rescued from swallower's belly F913. (40).

SWEAT. — Man to earn bread by sweat . . . A1346. (11); (15).

SWERVE. — Woman . . . swerves suddenly . . . K893.1.+. (61).

SWIM. — Why crustacean swims on its back A2444.+. (38).

SYMPATHETIC magic D1782. (45).

TABU: boasting C450. (53); connected with menses C140. (17); going forth during menses C141. (17); incest C114. (17); (26); (27); (28);

(29); (30); mentioning secret water spring C429.1. (22); (32); mocking animal C94.3. (23); offending water-spirit C41. (41); (42); refusing a request . . . C871.+. (23); revealing identity . . . C422. (65); showing disrespect . . . C170.+. (55); uttering secrets C420. (65). — Curse . . . for breaking tabu C987. (28); death by being swallowed for breaking tabu C929.5. (60); death of wife for breaking tabu C920.2. (30); food tabu during menses C140.+. (60).

TAIL. — Why animals have tail A2378.1. (65); why fox has bushy tail A2378.6.1. (65); why otter has broad tail A2378.9.+. (65).

TAMED. — Wild animal . . . tamed B771. (53).

TANK. — Permission refused to drink from water tank W155.5. (22).

TEACH. — Culture hero teaches arts . . . A541. (9); (10); (13); (14); gods teach people . . . A1404. (9).

TEARS. — Bird sheds tears B736.1. (31); bodies of water from tears A911. (37); resuscitation by weeping (tears) E58. (20b).

TEETH. — Wife carried . . . in bag in husband's teeth J2133.5.1. (30).

TEMPER. — Violence of temper W185. (6); (7).

TEMPTED. — Woman . . . tempted by man T331.+. (57).

TEST of . . . obedience H473. (57).

TESTS of patience H1553. (43).

THEFT of fire A1415. (52).

THIN. — Woman leads pursuers to edge of thin ice . . . K893.1.+. (61).

THIRSTY animals fight . . . B266.1.+. (32); cormorants fight . . . B266.1.+. (22).

THREATEN. — Sun . . . threatens all life A727.1. (1).

THUNDER. — Extraordinary thunder . . . F968. (58a).

THUNDERBOLT . . . produced D2149.1. (58a).

TOKEN. — Victim lured . . . by false token K839.2. (25).

TOKENS. — Identification by tokens . . . H88. (54).

TONGUE. — Origin . . . of animal's tongue A2344. (27).

TOOLS. — Acquisition of tools A1446. (9); (12); (13).

TOP. — Indentations on mountain top . . . A900.+. (7).

TOPS. — Why mountain tops are bare today . . . A900.+. (1); (6).

TOPOGRAPHICAL features caused by . . . ancestors A901.+. (65); features caused by . . . hero A901. (35).

TRACKER. — Skillful tracker F677. (53).

TRAIL. — Identification by tokens left as trail H88. (54).

TRAITS. — Birds with human traits B200.+. (51); (52).

TRANSFORMATION . . . as fitting punishment Q584.2. (27); (29); by sexual intercourse D565.5.1. (26); by urine D562.2. (47); cormorants to stone D423.+. (35); man to bird D150. (26); (33);

(36); (37); man to crustacean D100.+. (38); man to falcon D152.4.+. (30); man to fish D170. (19); man to owl D153.2. (24); man to star D293. (5); (21); (65); man to woodpecker D153.1. (27); (29); man-eating sea lion to stone D429.2.2.1.+. (34); object to stone D471. (58a); statue comes to life D435.1.1. (33); stone to person D432.1. (33); sun-man to star D293.+. (1); through curse D525. (28); to animal by imitation D599.+. (30); to kill enemy D651.1. (30); water-spirit to stone D231.+. (59); woman to bird D150.+. (51); women to animals D100.+. (65); women to ducks D161.3.+. (65); wooden stake to stone D471.6.+. (7). — Animal characteristics from transformation A2260. (65); gradual transformation D681. (30); punishment: transformation Q551.3. (54); (55).

TRAP. — Deceiver falls into own trap K1600. (4); men lured into trap . . . K912.2.+. (25); (46); (47).

TREACHEROUS brother-in-law K2211.1. (19); (25); (46); (47); daughter K2214.1. (65); murder during hunt K917. (47); nephew K2210.+. (47); relatives-in-law K2218. (53); sister K2212. (19); sister-in-law K2212.2. (19); wife K2213. (23); (41); (42); (48); (49); (53); (54); (62); (65); wife punished Q261.2. (41); (65); younger brother K2211.0.2. (30).

TREACHERY. — Death as punishment for treachery Q411.4. (65).

TREAT. — Why people treat bird respectfully A2545.+. (6).

TREE. — Wife carried up tree . . . J2133.5.1. (30).

TREE-CREEPER. — Origin of color of tree-creeper A2411.2.+. (37).

TREES pulled up . . . F621.2. (33). — Giants carry trees F531.3.10. (33); ogres leave signs on trees G310.+. (62).

TRIBE. — Cannibal tribe G11.18. (58a); (58b); why tribe lives in certain place A1620.+. (65).

TRIBES. — Wandering of tribes A1630. (65).

TRICKED. — Dupe tricked into jumping . . . K891. (48); dupe tricked into killing himself K890. (49); (50); girl tricked into man's room . . . K1330. (29).

TRICKERY. — Attention secured by trickery K477. (40); (42).

TRICKSTER. — Ambushed trickster killed . . . K1641. (25); (46); (47); fatal deception into trickster's power K810. (4); (25); victim . . . approaches trickster . . . K815. (25); (46).

TRIUMPH of the oppressed L300.+. (65).

TROUBLE. — Foolish boasts get man into trouble J2353.1. (53).

TROUBLE-MAKING. — Hero kills trouble-making . . . men G512.0.1. (33).

TUFTED CORMORANT. — Why tufted cormorant nests on high ground A2431.+. (22); why voice of tufted cormorant is hoarse A2423.1.+. (22).

UTTERING. — Tabu: uttering secrets C420. (65).

VAGINA. — Murder by introducing hot stone into vagina S112.+. (35); origin of shape of vagina A1313.2.+. (17).

VALUABLE secrets learned N440. (3); (4); (32); (65).

VANITY W116. (56).

VEILING. — Disguise by veiling face K1821.3. (65).

VICTIM burned in his own house . . . K812. (33); kills swallower . . . F912.2. (40); lured by kind words . . . K815. (25); (46); lured into approach . . . K839.2. (25); lured into house and killed K811. (53); (58a); pushed into water K926. (39); speaks . . . F915. (40). — Ambushed trickster killed by intended victim K1641. (25); (46); (47).

VICTIMS lured into house and wounded K811.+. (61); rescued . . . F913. (40).

VICTORIOUS youngest son L10. (46).

VIOLENCE of temper W185. (6); (7).

VIRTUE. — Pretended virtue K2050. (38).

VISIT. — Inhabitant of upper world visits earth F30. (2).

VISITORS. — Night-heron's call announces . . . visitors B147.2.+. (53).

VITAL bodily members E780. (54); (55).

VOICE. — Recognition by voice H79.3. (44); (53); remarkable voice F556. (47); why voice of tufted cormorant is hoarse A2423.1.+. (22).

VOLUNTARILY. — Limbs of dead voluntarily reassemble . . . E31. (54); (55).

WALKING ghost "laid" E440. (20b).

WANDERING of tribes A1630. (65).

WAR between . . . birds B263.5. (22); with the sun A739.2. (1).

WARNINGS. — Attention to warnings J1050. (65); inattention to warnings J652. (28); (30); (31).

WARRIORS. — Amazons. Women warriors F565.1. (1).

WATER. — Animals that inhabit water A2433.2.2. (65); bodies of water from tears A911. (37); impounded water A1111. (32); remedy for lack of water . . . N452.1.+. (22); sea lion carries girl across water B551.+. (19); victim pushed into water K926. (39); water-spirit drags women into water F420.5.2.1.5.+. (42); water-spirits lure mortal into water F420.5.2.1. (59).

WATER-SPIRIT drags women . . . F420.5.2.1.5.+. (42); holds ship back F420.5.2.7.4. (64); wrecks ship F420.5.2.7.3. (59). — Sacrifice to water-spirit . . . S263.4.+. (60); tabu: offending water-spirit

C41. (41); (42); transformation: water-spirit to stone D231.+. (59).

WATER-SPIRITS lure mortal . . . F420.5.2.1. (59). — Home of water-spirits F420.2. (41); (59); malevolent water-spirits F420.5.2. (59); means of combating water-spirits . . . F405.+. (64); shaman summons water-spirits . . . F404.+. (64).

WATER SPRING. — Tabu: mentioning secret water spring C429.1. (22); (32).

WATER TANK. — Permission refused to drink from water tank W155.5. (22).

WAVES. — Origin of high sea waves A925.1. (65).

WEAK (small) hero overcomes large fighter L311. (32); (33); (34); (35); (61). — Subordination of weak . . . J421. (65); subordination . . . to weak . . . J421.+. (65); wise fear of the weak . . . J613. (65).

WEAPONS. — Acquisition of weapons A1459.1. (9); (13); extraordinary weapons of culture hero A524.2. (12); (14); (17); (34); (35); magic animal proof against weapons D1841.5.2. (40).

WEEP. — Man unable to weep . . . W155.3. (20b).

WEEPING. — Ghost summoned by weeping E381. (20b); resuscitation by weeping (tears) E58. (20b); return . . . to stop weeping E361. (20b).

WEIGHT. — Magic suspension of weight D1691. (24).

WELL. — Thirsty animals fight over well B266.1.+. (32); thirsty cormorants fight over well B266.1.+. (22).

WHALE. — Cruelty to pregnant whale S185.+. (66); devastating whale B16.2.+. (54); (55); magic adhesion to whale . . . Q551.2.1.+. (54); (55); magic whale B175.+. (54); (55); markings of whale A2412.1.+. (65); shaman concealed in . . . whale F1034.+. (54); (55); why parasites cling to whale's back A2310.+. (54).

WHALE-BOAT R245. (40).

WHITE. — Means of combating water-spirits: painting them white F405.+. (64).

WIDOW. — Man marries widow . . . T145.0.1.+. (35); the faithless widow T231. (19); (40).

WIFE carried up tree . . . J2133.5.1. (30); chooses father's side . . . P211. (23); (55); eats flesh . . . P214.+. (19); flees from husband R227. (31); of culture hero . . . A592.2.1.+. (18); refuses to sleep . . . T288. (54); sold . . . T292. (17). — A man undertakes to do his wife's work J2431. (36); avoiding the unfaithful wife T251.1.+. (31); cuckold. Husband deceived by adulterous wife K1501. (30);

(31); (36); (38); death of wife for breaking tabu C920.2. (30); disobedient wife punished T254.6. (57); dream about a marriage with another's wife T11.3.2. (50); faithful wife T210.1. (35); generosity toward faithless wife W11.+. (31); husband discovers wife's adultery K1550.1. (27); (30); (31); (36); (38); husband kills wife and paramour Q411.0.2. (36); husband learns of wife's infidelity . . . N455.6.+. (31); husband surprises wife . . . K1569.2. (36); jealous wife or husband T257. (30); (64); man . . . kills wife's lover Q411.0.1.2. (38); reward for wife's fidelity Q83.1. (40); tabu: refusing a request from wife's relatives C871.+. (23); test of wife's obedience H473. (57); the hypocritical wife T263. (41); the nagging wife T253. (64); the ungrateful wife T261. (36); treacherous wife K2213. (23); (41); (42); (48); (49); (53); (54); (62); (65); treacherous wife punished Q261.2. (41); (65).

WIFE-STEALING punished with death Q252.1. (4); (30).

WILD animal . . . tamed B771. (53).

WILES. — Capture through the wiles of a woman K778. (23).

WILL. — Person changes size at will D631.1. (27).

WIND. — Extraordinary behavior of wind F963. (45); fugitive has magic wind . . . R236.4. (31).

WINDS controlled . . . D2142. (31).

WINGS. — Animal characteristics: wings A2377. (41).

WINTER . . . produced D2145.1. (6); (7). — Continuous winter . . . A1040. (6).

WISDOM . . . from dream J157. (66). — Sun endowed with wisdom . . . A738.2.2. (65).

WISE fear of the weak . . . J613. (65); woman as helper N828. (13); (14); (17); words of dying father J154. (44).

WISH. — Curse . . . to negate good wish M416. (10); (11); (12).

WISHES. — Absurd wishes . . . J2079. (10); (11); (12); (15); woman's . . . brothers kill her husband . . . for having married against their wishes K959.2.1. (19).

WITNESS. — Return home to witness . . . rites N681.0.1.+. (40).

WOE. — "Idleness begets woe . . ." J21.50. (10); (11); (12); (15).

WOMAN avenges scorned love T71.2. (45); in the moon A751.8. (5); (65); leads pursuers . . . K893.1.+. (61); plans to eat her children G72.1. (18); . . . tempted by man T331.+. (57). — Capture through . . . woman K778. (23); creation of first man's (woman's) mate A1275. (16); marooned woman abandoned . . . B772.+. (51); marriage of woman to sea lion B600.+. (19); remarkably beautiful woman F575.1. (3); (4); (17); (31); (48); (61); sun and moon as man and woman A736.1. (65); transformation: woman to bird D150.+. (51); wise woman as helper N828. (13); (14); (17); woman's father and brothers kill her husband . . . K959.2.1. (19).

WOMEN induce owners . . . K330.+. (17). — Amazons. Women warriors F565.1. (1); ogre . . . rapes women G477. (33); parliament of women F565.3. (1); (4); (13); (65); parliament of women overthrown F565.3.+. (3); (7); (8); (65); transformation: women to animals D100.+. (65); transformation: women to ducks D161.3.+. (65); water-spirit drags women . . . F420.5.2.1.5.+. (42); why women are subservient to men A1372.9. (3); (7); (65).

WOODEN. — Transformation: wooden stake to stone D471.6.+. (7).

WOODPECKER. — Transformation: man to woodpecker D153.1. (27); (29); why woodpecker has red head A2412.2.+. (28); (29); why woodpecker has strong beak A2343.3.2.+. (27); why woodpecker is monogamous A2497.+. (28).

WORDS. — Victim lured by kind words . . . K815. (25); (46); wise words of dying father J154. (44).

WORK. — A man undertakes to do his wife's work J2431. (36); "idleness begets woe; work brings happiness" J21.50 (10); (11); (12); (15); necessity of work J702. (10); (11); (12); (15).

WORLD. — Ball game in lower world E494. (2); evil demons set world on fire A1031.3. (2); inhabitant of upper world . . . F30. (2); new race . . . after world calamity A1006.1. (7); (8); preservation of life during world calamity A1005. (7); (8).

WORLD-FIRE A1030. (1); (2). — Earth restored after world-fire A1036.+. (2); men hide from world-fire A1038.+. (2).

WOUND. — Magic cure of wound D2161.2. (57).

WOUNDED. — Victims lured into house and wounded K811.+. (61).

WOUNDING self . . . F1041.21.6.1. (5).

WRECK. — Water-spirit wrecks ship F420.5.2.7.3. (59).

WRESTLER. — Mighty wrestler F617. (4).

YOUNG. — Hero's precocious strength. Has full strength when very young F611.3.2. (24); why young female guanacos copulate . . . A2496.+. (44).

YOUNGER. — Treacherous younger brother K2211.0.2. (30).

YOUNGEST brother helps elder L31. (45); brother rescues . . . R155.1. (45). — Victorious youngest son L10. (46).

Motif Distribution by Motif Group

In the Yamana stories the MYTHOLOGICAL motifs make up the largest single motif group (244 motifs), accounting for 21 percent of the total number. There is a marked reduction in frequency after this, to motifs about DECEPTIONS, which make up 13 percent (147 motifs) of the total. Then follows a cluster of motif groups in the 7-8 percent range: motifs about MAGIC and MARVELS constitute 8 percent each, with 101 and 99 motifs, respectively, and motifs about SEX and REWARDS AND PUNISHMENTS 7 percent (81 motifs) each. Of the remaining motif groups none comes to more than 4 percent of the total.

No one motif subgroup stands out numerically above the rest. The largest subgroups are *marvelous creatures* with 65 motifs, *demigods and culture heroes* with 64 motifs, and *animal characteristics* with 59, each making up 5 percent. The subgroup *magic powers and manifestations* has 51 motifs (4 percent), and *kinds of punishment* 39 (3 percent), after which there is a slow, gradual reduction in frequency.

Motif group	Motif subgroup	Number of motifs
MYTHOLOGICAL MOTIFS	Gods	8
	Demigods and culture heroes	64
	Cosmogony and cosmology	29
	Topographical features of the earth	23
	World calamities	21
	Establishment of natural order	3
	Creation and ordering of human life	37
	Animal characteristics	59
	Subtotal motifs	244

Motif group	Motif subgroup	Number of motifs
DECEPTIONS	Contests won by deception	1
	Thefts and cheats	4
	Escape by deception	6
	Capture by deception	33
	Fatal deception	32
	Deception into self-injury	1
	Deception into humiliating position	2
	Seduction or deceptive marriage	3
	Deceptions connected with adultery	22
	Deceiver falls into own trap	6
	Deception through shams	15
	Villains and traitors	19
	Other deceptions	3
	Subtotal motifs	147
MAGIC	Transformation	35
	Magic objects	15
	Magic powers and manifestations	51
	Subtotal motifs	101
MARVELS	Otherworld journeys	1
	Marvelous creatures	65
	Extraordinary places and things	9
	Extraordinary occurrences	24
	Subtotal motifs	99
SEX	Love	25
	Marriage	7
	Married life	17
	Chastity and celibacy	3
	Illicit sexual relations	21
	Conception and birth	2
	Care of children	6
	Subtotal motifs	81

Motif group	Motif subgroup	Number of motifs
REWARDS AND PUNISHMENTS	Deeds rewarded	6
	Deeds punished	36
	Kinds of punishment	39
	Subtotal motifs	81
ANIMALS	Mythical animals	4
	Magic animals	7
	Animals with human traits	16
	Friendly animals	10
	Marriage of person to animal	10
	Fanciful traits of animals	4
	Miscellaneous animal motifs	2
	Subtotal motifs	53
THE WISE AND THE FOOLISH	Acquisition and possession of wisdom (knowledge)	7
	Wise and unwise conduct	20
	Cleverness	7
	Fools (and other unwise persons)	14
	Subtotal motifs	48
SOCIETY	The family	37
	Government	1
	Customs	8
	Subtotal motifs	46
UNNATURAL CRUELTY	Cruel relatives	14
	Revolting murders or mutilations	20
	Cruel sacrifices	2
	Abandoned or murdered children	2
	Cruel persecutions	1
	Subtotal motifs	39

Motif group	Motif subgroup	Number of motifs
CHANCE AND FATE	The ways of luck and fate	1
	Unlucky accidents	1
	Lucky accidents	21
	Accidental encounters	1
	Helpers	15
	Subtotal motifs	39
TRAITS OF CHARACTER	Favorable traits of character	12
	Unfavorable traits of character	24
	Subtotal motifs	36
THE DEAD	Resuscitation	10
	Ghosts and other revenants	15
	The Soul	4
	Subtotal motifs	29
OGRES	Kinds of ogres	16
	Falling into ogre's power	2
	Ogre defeated	8
	Other ogre motifs	1
	Subtotal motifs	27
TABU	Tabu connected with supernatural beings	3
	Sex tabu	10
	Speaking tabu	5
	Miscellaneous tabus	1
	Punishment for breaking tabu	3
	Subtotal motifs	22
CAPTIVES AND FUGITIVES	Captivity	3
	Rescues	4
	Escapes and pursuits	13
	Refuges and recapture	1
	Subtotal motifs	21

Motif group	Motif subgroup	Number of motifs
TESTS	Identity tests: recognition	8
	Tests of truth	1
	Marriage tests	1
	Tests of cleverness	1
	Tests of prowess: quests	7
	Other tests	1
	Subtotal motifs	19
REVERSAL OF FORTUNE	Victorious youngest child	4
	Unpromising hero (heroine)	5
	Triumph of the weak	6
	Pride brought low	1
	Subtotal motifs	16
MISCELLANEOUS GROUPS OF MOTIFS	Heroes	2
	Unique exceptions	2
	Subtotal motifs	4
ORDAINING THE FUTURE	Curses	4
	Subtotal motifs	4
HUMOR	Humor of disability—physical	1
	Humor of lies and exaggeration	1
	Subtotal motifs	2
THE NATURE OF LIFE	Nature of life—miscellaneous	1
	Subtotal motifs	1
22 MOTIF GROUPS	96 SUBGROUPS	
	TOTAL NUMBER OF MOTIFS	1,129

Glossary

Aiakélum (Aiakélem). — Daughter of the bottle-nosed whale or springer, *Orca magellanica*. She was married to Lefkóiya, the small wood owl, but left him for Húruf, the powerful storm bird.

Áiapux. — The big otter, *Lutra felina*.

Akáinix. — The rainbow, handsome brother of Lem, the younger sun-man, and married to Hánuxa, the moon-woman. He was an able shaman.

Akámuš. — Long stick used in making bird snares.

Ákel. — Red earth used for painting the body.

Alaánama. — The sea leopard, *Lobodon carcinophagus*, rare in the Cape Horn region. His five uncles returned from the dead to live with him.

Álem (álum). — Brother-in-law.

Amáim. — Berries.

Améra. — The male of the species *Lama huanachus* (guanaco). Lived in incestuous relationship with his own daughters.

Aporpánuwa. — In the eastern dialect this means the water sow bug, a small, very common type of isopod.

Ášim. — A type of mushroom, *Cyttaria harioti*.

Ašóula (Ašóulaxipa). — The grampus, *Pseudorca crassidens*.

Auáčix. — A type of mushroom, *Cyttaria darwinii*.

Auwéra. — The patella, a common mussel.

Bandurria. — See Léxuwa.

Big Hut. — Ceremonial hut where the *kína* took place.

Čámux. — The large wren, *Zonotrichia canicapilla*. Son of Lefkóiya, the little wood owl, and Aiakélum, the young bottle-nosed whale.

Čiéxaus. — Puberty ritual for Yamana boys and girls.

Čilawáia (Čilawáiakipa). — The big fox of Tierra del Fuego, *Canis seu Cerdocyon magellanicus*. Čilawáiakipa, the vixen, was the

---

EDITOR'S NOTE. Throughout the text and the glossary, I followed the original rendering of technical terms.

daughter of Lem, the younger sun-man, and second wife of the younger Yoálox.

Čokóa. — Bird (species not known). One of Hulušénuwa's wives.

Dášalux. — The big albatross, *Diomedea melanophrys*, father of Lúškipa.

Detehúrux. — *Dendrocopus lignarius*, the smaller of the two types of woodpecker living in the Cape Horn region.

Éetex (Éetexkípa). — The Magellanic cormorant, *Phalacrocorax magellanicus*.

Epáiači. — The bottle-nosed whale or springer, *Orca magellanica*.

Ésef. — Mushroom, *Cyttaria darwinii*.

Guanaco. — *Lama huanachus*.

Haféim. — A trunkfish, about as long as a hand, with short spines all over its body.

Hánnuš. — Giant ogres living in the woods.

Hánuxa. — The moon-woman, beautiful wife of Akáinix, the rainbow.

Hašamáif. — Branch from the beech tree, with a protruding growth as caused by the *Cyttaria* fungus. It was used as a club.

Hášaxuwa. — The male of the southern elephant seal, *Macrorhinus leoninus*.

Héšpul. — The small sparrow, *Taeniptera pyrope*, from the family of the Tyrannidae. He was a great shaman, with power to make the sun appear and disappear at will.

Hílix. — Ceremonial face masks.

Hulušénuwa. — The smaller of the two Fuegian types of wren, *Troglodytes hornensis*.

Húruf. — The powerful storm bird, *Macronectes gigantea*. He became the lover of Aiakélum, the young bottle-nosed whale.

Íla. — Bone wedge.

Ílax. — Pieces of bark lying lengthwise on the bottom of the canoe.

Ími. — Red earth used for painting the body.

Kálaka. — A game of ball.

Kalampáša. — Evil *kína*-spirit, greatly feared.

Kenós. — Demigod and servant of Temáukel, the Highest Being, who in the beginning of time sent him to earth to create the first people and order their life and customs.

Kéšpix. — The soul.

Ketéla. — The big gerfalcon, *Polyborus tharus*, known in Chile and Argentina as "traro" or "carancho."

Kéti. — Sausage made from sea lion or guanaco blood, generally considered a delicacy.

Kíli. — Sandals made of guanaco or sea lion skin.

Kímoa. — The Magellanic goose, *Chloëphaga picta.* Daughter of Lem, the younger sun-man.

Kína. — Secret ceremony of the Yamana men to which boys were introduced upon reaching puberty.

Kiwágu. — The very common large seagull, *Larus dominicanus.* Daughter of Lem, the younger sun-man.

Kíxinteka. — The gray gerfalcon, *Circus cinereus.* Originally he was a man who gradually transformed himself into a bird by imitating the behavior of birds.

Klóketen. — 1. Secret ceremony of the Selknam men to which boys were introduced upon reaching puberty. 2. A boy participating in this ceremony for the first time.

Kuhúrux. — The big eagle owl, *Bubo magellanicus.* Close relative of Omóra, the small hummingbird hero.

Lakúma. — Water-spirit.

Lána. — The large woodpecker of the Tierra del Fuego region, *Ipocrantor magellanicus.* It has coal black feathers, and the male has a bright scarlet tuft. It is strictly monogamous.

Lášix (Lášixkipa). — The black martin, *Iridoprocne (Tachycineta) meyeni.* Small hero.

Lefkóiya. — The small wood owl, *Glaucidium nanum.* Married to Aiakélum, the young bottle-nosed whale. Čámux, the large wren, was their son.

Lékakuta. — Bird (species not known). One of Hulušénuwa's wives.

Lem. — The younger sun-man, son of Táruwalem, and a handsome, kindly man. He helped free the men from female domination. Akáinix, the rainbow, was his brother.

Léxuwa (Léxuwakipa). — The sturdy, rusty brown spectacled ibis, *Theristicus melanopis.* Known as "bandurria" in southern South America.

Lóima-yékamuš. — A shamans' school.

Lúka. — Pieces of bark, bent to a half-circle, in the middle of a canoe.

Lúrux. — Bird (species not known).

Luš. — Red.

Lúškipa. — Faithless wife of Ketéla, the big gerfalcon.

Lušwuléwa. — Exceedingly handsome boy and a great hunter, who gave all animals their present-day names. He was seduced by his sisters-in-law and subsequently killed by them.

Máku. — The red flower of the *Embothrium coccineum,* a shrub common to Tierra del Fuego. The flower was a symbol of beauty among the Yamana.

Mákuxipa. — Beautiful wife of Hulušénuwa, whom she left for the two

Yoálox brothers. Through her, menstruation and childbirth began.

Malépa. — Bird (species not known). One of Hulušénuwa's wives.

Martúwux-yélluwa. — A person who thinks he knows everything.

Marutuwérelakípa. — The female of a certain sea bird of average size (species not known).

Mašakána. — Loincloth.

Omóra. — The hummingbird, *Sephanoides sephaniodes*. Small hero who on several occasions liberated the people from the tyranny of ogres. Very skilled in the use of the sling. With stones from his sling he opened the many channels and waterways which are found today in Tierra del Fuego. He was related to Kuhúrux, the eagle owl.

Púxel.   In the eastern dialect this means the big brass beetle, *Carabus auratus*. In the west it is called "uškúlempi."

Sínuluwatauinéiwa. — Giant stone man.

Sírsa. — A crab fork with four prongs.

Síta. — The brightly colored horn owl, *Nyctalops accipitrinus*.

Súna. — A type of thornfish. Before its transformation it was a boy, the son of a sister of the two Yoálox brothers and her sea lion husband.

Súna-yáka. — *Kína*-spirit.

Šáfina. — Sling.

Šalalakína. — Timid, nimble bird with chocolate-colored feathers and a beautiful voice. Fast runner. It lives in swampy regions.

Šamanáuye. — The two sons of Mákuxipa and the younger Yoálox. They were "the first real people," that is, the first people brought into the world by the actual process of birth.

Šamaxáni. — Distant land formerly inhabited by souls of the dead.

Šanamáim. — Usually the small, light-red berries of the *Pernettya pumila*, but sometimes also the larger berries of the *Pernettya mucronata*.

Šáneš. — Bird (species not known.) One of Hulušénuwa's wives.

Šégetex. — The kingfisher, *Ceryle torquata var. stellata*.

Šékuš. — The large, heavy wild goose, *Chloëphaga hybrida*.

Šewáli. — Stone for making fire.

Tákaša (Tákašakipa). — Seagull, *Larus belcheri*. Daughter of Lem, the younger sun-man.

Tánuwa. — 1. The highest being, thought to live in the sky. 2. Evil spirit, present at the *kína*-ceremony.

Táruwalem. — The older sun-man, hated by all people when he lived on earth in primeval times.

Tečikášina. — See Tulératéčix.

Tepérakipa. — The female of the ursine seal, *Arctocephalus australis*.

Téši. — Round black stones used as sinkers for fishing tackle. Believed to be fragments of dead stone monster.

Téšurkipa. — The female of a type of sparrow with yellow feathers, seldom seen in Tierra del Fuego.

Touwíšiwa. — The iridescent cormorant, *Phalacrocorax olivaceus*.

Túku. — Bucket.

Tulératéčix (Tečikášina). — The nimble tree creeper, *Aphrastura spinicauda*.

Túri (túrikipa). — A girl menstruating for the first time.

Túrikipa tátu. — Festive meal celebrating a girl's first menstruation.

Tútu. — Probably the *Myiotheretes rufiventris*, a small bird with black feathers and a white spot on the head.

Tuwín. — The so-called "jilgero," a small field bird with yellowish green feathers. These birds live in flocks. They used to be the many wives of a stone monster tyrant.

Túwux (Túwuxkipa). — In the western dialect this is the dark-grey night heron, *Nycticorax obscurus*. Same as "wekatána" in the eastern dialect.

Úfka. — String used in making bird snares.

Úkeša. — Long leather strap.

Úri. — Fibers found immediately under the bark on the stem of the *Nothophagus antarctica*. Used for sewing together pieces of bark.

Ušamína. — *Kína*-spirit.

Uškúlempi. — In the western dialect this is the big brass beetle, *Carabus auratus*.

Uškútta. — The winter pepper tree, *Drimus winteri*.

Wasénim. — The tufted cormorant, *Phalacrocorax gaimardi*.

Wasénim-yáka. — *Kína*-spirit.

Watauineiwábei. — "The two old men": two tufted cormorants, killed by Omóra for commiting murder. They subsequently turned into stone.

Watewémuwa. — In the western dialect this means the water sow bug, a small, very common type of isopod. It is called *aporpánuwa* in the east.

Wekatána (Wekatánaxipa). — In the eastern dialect this means the dark-gray night heron, *Nycticorax obscurus*. Same as "tuwux" in the western dialect.

Wémarkipa. — Seagull, *Larus glaucodes*. Daughter of Lem, the younger sun-man.

Wéoina. — The big roundheaded dolphin, *Globicephala melas.*

Wesána. — The rat. Daughter of Lem, the younger sun-man.

Wétawa. — Sling, or stone thrown by a sling.

Wetawémuwa. — A man skilled in the use of the sling.

Wípatux. — The duck, *Querquedula cyanoptera.* Daughter of Lem, the younger sun-man.

Wíyen. — The wild sea duck, *Anas cristata.* Daughter of Lem, the younger sun-man. This bird lives in flocks near the coast.

Wuléwa. — Boy.

Yái. — Son of Akáinix, the rainbow. He is the second, pale rainbow that sometimes accompanies the main one.

Yáiyi. — Small bag, made of a piece of gut and used for keeping *ákel* (red soil for painting the body).

Yamalašcmóina. — Mourning ceremony in which all the people took part.

Yékamuš. — Shaman.

Yékeslef. — The squid, *Loligo subulata.*

Yékuš. — Arrowhead.

Yéxalem. — Son of Lem, the younger sun-man.

Yoálox. — Culture hero family of two brothers and three sisters. They introduced fire, tools, and weapons among the first people, and gave the Yamana their customs and patterns of social interaction. The Yoálox also introduced death among men and the necessity to work hard for a living. Eventually they turned into stars.

Yoálox-tárnuxipa. — Clever sister of the two Yoálox brothers. Like them she turned into a star.

Yookalía. — The sparrow hawk, *Milvago chimango.* Like his father he was a shaman.

Bibliography

Bridges, E. Lucas
1948   *Uttermost Part of the Earth.* London.
Bridges, Thomas
1884   "Moeurs et coutumes des Fuégiens." *Bulletin de la Société d'Anthropologie de Paris* (Paris), ser.3, vol.7. Translated by Hyades from a MS prepared in 1866.
1933   *Yamana-English: A Dictionary of the Speech of Tierra del Fuego.* F. Hestermann and M. Gusinde, eds. Missionsdruckerei St. Gabriel, Mödling.
Cojazzi, Antonio
1914   "Los indios del Archipiélago Fueguino." *Revista Chilena de Historia y Geografía* (Santiago), 9:288-352; 10:5-51.
Cooper, John M.
1917   *Analytical and Critical Bibliography of the Tribes of Tierra del Fuego and Adjacent Territory.* Smithsonian Institution. Bureau of American Ethnology, Bulletin 63. Washington.
1946   "The Yahgan." *Handbook of South American Indians,* Julian H. Steward, ed. Smithsonian Institution. Bureau of American Ethnology, Bulletin 143, 1:81-106. Washington.
Coriat, Isador H.
1915   "Psychoneuroses among Primitive Tribes." *Journal of Abnormal Psychology,* 10,3:201-208.
Dabenne, Roberto
1911   "Los indígenas de la Tierra del Fuego." *Boletín del Instituto Geográfico Argentino* (Buenos Aires), 25,5-6: 163-226; 7-8:247-300.
Gusinde, Martin
1926   "Das Lautsystem der feuerländischen Sprachen." *Anthropos,* 21:1000-1024.
1931   *Die Feuerland-Indianer: Ergebnisse meiner vier Forschungsreisen in den Jahren 1918 bis 1924, unternommen im Auftrage des Ministerio de Instrucción Pública de*

> *Chile*. Vol. I, *Die Selknam: Vom Leben und Denken eines Jägervolkes auf der grossen Feüerlandinsel*. Mödling.

1937 *Die Feuerland-Indianer: Ergebnisse meiner vier Forschungsreisen in den Jahren 1918 bis 1924, unternommen im Auftrage des Ministerio de Instrucción Pública de Chile*. Vol. II, *Die Yamana: Vom Leben und Denken der Wassernomaden am Kap Horn*. Mödling.

1939 *Die Feuerland-Indianer: Ergebnisse meiner vier Forschungsreisen in den Jahren 1918 bis 1924, unternommen im Auftrage des Ministerio de Instrucción Pública de Chile*. Vol. III/2, *Anthropologie der Feuerland-Indianer*.

1961 *The Yamana: The Life and Thought of the Water Nomads of Cape Horn*. Trans. Frieda Schütze. Human Relations Area Files, 5 vols. New Haven.

1970 Review of Mireille Guyot, "Les mythes chez les Selk'nam et les Yamana de la Terre de Feu." (*Travaux et Memoires de l'Institut d'Ethnologie* [Paris 1968], 75:221.) *Anthropos*, 65:335-336.

1974 *Die Feuerland-Indianer: Ergebnisse meiner vier Forschungsreisen in den Jahren 1918 bis 1924, unternommen im Auftrage des Ministerio de Instrucción Pública de Chile*. Vol. III/1, *Die Halakwulup: Vom Leben und Denken der Wassernomaden in Westpatagonien*. Mödling.

Koppers, Wilhelm

1924 *Unter Feuerland-Indianern*. Stuttgart.

1968 "Mythologie und Weltanschauung der Yagan." *21st International Congress of Americanists*, Part II (Göteborg), 1924. Kraus Reprint. Nendel, Lichtenstein, 1968.

Lehmann-Nitsche, Roberto

1938 "Ein Mythenthema aus Feuerland und Nordamerika." *Anthropos*, 33:267-273.

Lothrop, Samuel K.

1928 "The Indians of Tierra del Fuego." *Contributions from the Museum of the American Indian, Heye Foundation*, Vol. 10. New York.

Lowie, Robert H.

1938 Review of Martin Gusinde, "Die Feuerland-Indianer." *American Anthropologist*, 40:395-503.

Martial, Louis Ferdinand

1888 *Mission scientifique du cap Horn 1882-83*, Vol. I, *Histoire du voyage*. Paris.

Schmidt, Wilhelm
1907   "Die Sprachlaute und ihre Darstellung." *Anthropos*,
            2:282-339; 508-587; 822-897; 1058-1105.
Thompson, Stith
1955-1958 *Motif-Index of Folk-Literature.* 6 vols. Bloomington,
            Indiana University Press.
Valory, Dale
1967   "Folklore of the Fuego-Patagonian Peoples: Annotated
            Bibliography." *Behavior Science Notes* (New Haven), 2,
            3:175-202.
Wilbert, Johannes
1963   *Indios de la región Orinoco-Ventuari.* Fundación La Salle
            de Ciencias Naturales, Monografía no. 8. Caracas.
1970   *Folk Literature of the Warao Indians: Narrative Material
            and Motif Content.* Latin American Studies, Vol. 15.
            UCLA Latin American Center Publications, University of
            California, Los Angeles.
1974   *Yupa Folktales.* Latin American Studies, Vol. 24. UCLA
            Latin American Center Publications, University of Cali-
            fornia, Los Angeles.
1975   *Folk Literature of the Selknam Indians: Martin Gusinde's
            Collection of Selknam Narratives.* Latin American
            Studies, Vol. 32. UCLA Latin American Center Publica-
            tions, University of California, Los Angeles.